WRITE A NOVEL IN 100 DAYS

WRITE A NOVEL IN 100 DAYS

The Busy Writer's Guide to Finishing Your Book Fast

Kim Purcell

TEN SPEED PRESS
California | New York

TEN SPEED PRESS
An imprint of the Crown Publishing Group
A division of Penguin Random House LLC
1745 Broadway
New York, NY 10019
tenspeed.com
penguinrandomhouse.com

A Ten Speed Press Trade Paperback Original

Typefaces: Adobe's Minion Pro, ITC's Avant Garde Gothic, NicolassFonts' Olyford
Typewriter art: Shutterstock.com/RUHUL DESIGN 1

Library of Congress Cataloging-in-Publication Data
Names: Purcell, Kim author
Title: Write a novel in 100 days : the busy writer's guide to
finishing your book fast / by Kim Purcell
LC record available at https://lccn.loc.gov/2026005739
LC ebook record available at https://lccn.loc.gov/2026005740

ISBN 978-0-593-83742-9
Ebook ISBN 978-0-593-83743-6

Acquiring editor: Kim Keller | Project editor: Thea Diklich-Newell
Production editors: Isabella Franco and Terry Deal
Designer: Andrea Lau | Cover designer: Karl Spurzem
Production designer: Mari Gill
Production: Dan Myers
Copy editor: Amy Brosey | Proofreaders: Michael Fedison, Tracy Rothschild Lynch
Marketer: Emily Hotaling | Publicist: Soren Eversoll

Manufactured in the United States of America

1st Printing

First Paperback Edition

The authorized representative in the EU for product safety and compliance is Penguin Random House Ireland, Morrison Chambers, 32 Nassau Street, Dublin D02 YH68, Ireland, https://eu-contact.penguin.ie.

This is dedicated to my daughters,
Madeline and Harper.
I love you both with all my heart.
Thank you for cheering on my dreams.
May you achieve your dreams too.

Thank you to all my students who tested these daily writing experiments and encouraged me to write this simple, straightforward guide. You brought such enthusiasm and creativity to our classes, and so much joy to my life.

Your Writing Road Map

ACT TWO

ACT THREE

ACT FOUR

Foreword

You have to start somewhere.

That's true of anything. We start things every day. We—most of us, anyway—don't overthink eating breakfast. We don't overthink beginning our drive to work. We don't overthink saying something now that we'll deeply regret later, although we probably should.

Why is it, then, that starting a novel is, for so many writers, a paralyzing undertaking? Why for some is it a Himalayan peak to climb? Why is the process a battle? Why is writing sometimes described as being akin to bleeding? Why is the simplest revision task—tightening—termed "kill your darlings"?

Given the difficulty of starting, the bloody injuries sustained in the execution, and the homicidal requirements of revision, why would anyone write a novel in the first place? I have to agree. When the process is so painful and destructive, be kind to yourself. Choose something else to do. There are better ways to die.

However, perhaps the difficulty of writing a novel has actually been a bit mythologized? Perhaps writers exaggerate in order to sound heroic, suffering artists sacrificing themselves in service of story? Maybe there is some preemptive protection to it? If the novel in question is unfinished, abandoned, or doesn't "work," then, hey, who would be surprised? There's no guilt attached. After all, writing a novel is *hard*.

More practically, writing a novel can feel difficult because it actually *is* difficult. There are many moving parts, more than a few balls in the air, hundreds of tools to master, and that is to say nothing of cranky, disobedient characters, or plots that necessarily come with holes. Lack any element and the task can feel overwhelming.

Whatever the factors or fears, writing a novel is fraught with difficulties and unknowns. The challenge doesn't get easier just because one is already a writer either. And if you're a busy writer already, is a novel worth the investment? The risk?

Here's my advice: Cut it down to size. There are ways to get it done. In fact, a decent working draft can come together in a matter of months. All you need is a method to help you through: knowledge of the nuts and bolts and a comfortable ease with the artistic aspects of it.

For that, you've come to the right place.

But what is this about 100 days? Surely that's impossible? It isn't. Here, Kim Purcell shows you how to scale the aforementioned Himalayan peak—it takes just fifteen *minutes* a day! Seriously?

Yes. However, there is method to her madness. Kim's fifteen minutes are not some free-writing, artists'-way, hope-filled joyride. Hers are fifteen focused minutes, focused in ways practical and productive. When you are grounded in what goes into a novel, that knowledge makes you efficient. And Kim is grounded.

What I like about the no-BS craft book you are about to read is that it isn't all rah-rah cheerleading, nor is it solely a list of butt-in-the-chair-type habits to follow. It is partially those things, naturally, but it's much more. Kim points you to the elements that make fiction effective, so that each writing session has a purpose.

The "magic" fifteen minutes Kim guides you through aren't really magic. They're guided directives to *the tools:* the tools of events, voice, authenticity, observation, emotion, improvisation, underlying motivation, and more. She knows that what "happens" (the plot) is only part of what makes a story come alive.

When you focus on other things too—the artful things—then the resulting draft is richer. You can face the revision process with confidence because you have already incorporated so much of what other writers attempt to hammer in as afterthought. Kim encourages you to plan, but not in the limited and rigid way of a plot outline set in cement. Follow her method and you will plan, not just plot, and write with skill, range, and power.

From story "stew" to *what if* to point of view to worldbuilding to character depth to arc to scene to sensory detail to villains to dialogue to dramatic rise to ending . . . Kim has you covered all the way and makes sure you will not be writing with a hand tied behind your back.

Many writers craft their stories with blinkers, biases, rules, avoidance, and all the other things that make a manuscript weak. Kim doesn't give you that option. Her method is not only built for speed, it's designed for quality. That's what I really love about *Write a Novel in 100 Days: The Busy Writer's Guide to Finishing Your Book Fast.* Follow Kim's advice and you'll write efficiently, but you'll also write well.

You have to start somewhere, and this is the place.

—Donald Maass,
author of *Writing the Breakout Novel* and
The Emotional Craft of Fiction

Dear Busy Writer,

If you picked up this guide, you have a dream: You want to write a novel, or possibly a memoir. It might be your first book or your tenth, but you need some help.

Most books on writing give you a ton of useful information and inspiration, but no progressive steps to help you actually sit down and write a novel from the beginning to the end. You close the book, and you're fired up, but you still don't know where to start.

This guide breaks down planning and writing your book into small, daily steps that will get you to the finish line.

Since I developed this system, I've helped thousands of people of all ages and skill levels write and finish their novels, and I can help you too.

How will you complete this creative marathon?

It's simple: Take it one step at a time, following the guide, and write for at least fifteen minutes a day.

I designed this program while teaching a group of busy working parents who were overwhelmed with jobs and kids but still wanted to pursue their dream of writing a novel. I was in the same boat, trying to write my next book while raising two daughters, running a growing teaching business, moving our family across the country multiple times, and completing my MFA. In the midst of all that craziness, I wrote and published two acclaimed novels. The hardest part was activating my creativity and diving into my imagination for short stints, despite stress and tight schedules. To do that, I needed a plan, and so did the busy people I was teaching.

This guide lays out a daily plan for making your dream a reality.

I firmly believe that anyone can write a book. Author Flannery O'Connor once said, "Anybody who has survived his childhood has enough information about life to last him the rest of his days."[1]

You don't need to be a literary genius or have an MFA or even a high school diploma. If you can tell a good story about your uptight boss and make your family laugh, or if your friend leans toward you in horror while you tell her about the crazy dude who smelled your hair in the cheese aisle, you're going to have no problem writing this book.

Often, the challenge is believing in yourself.

As a kid, I had a big imagination, but I never imagined myself as a writer. I wandered the woods, dreaming up stories, and sometimes I even wrote them down, but I never thought anyone would want to read them. I spent hours reading in the public library, but I never thought that *my* books could sit on those shelves. (Now they do.)

It took me a while to go for this dream, and maybe you're the same. Or maybe you've already published a book but now you're overwhelmed with life, and you need a system to get the next one down. This guide is also for you. I've been there, and I understand.

I wrote the guide I needed to exist in the world . . .

so now you can write the novel *you* need to exist in the world.

After ten years of writing every day while teaching and raising our kids, I got my first New York literary agent. Our daughters were one and four. Four years later, my first novel landed on bookstore shelves.

Becoming a published novelist has been a dream come true, but the best part has had nothing to do with publishing. Seeing my books on best-of lists, getting starred trade reviews, and hearing from readers have, of course, brought me a lot of joy. However, the simple, consistent act of writing has made me a happier human. It's allowed me to embrace my own weird imagination and connect with the humanity in others. We are all such wonderful, unique, creative souls.

Writing has also cleared away stress and trauma. Storytelling is therapy, and it's a heck of a lot cheaper than actual therapy, so if anyone complains when you write, just tell them: *You're welcome.*

One of my favorite parts of teaching novel writing is seeing the change that comes over people as they transport themselves into a story. After writing, their shoulders drop, their eyes soften, they sag into their chairs, and they smile. Quite simply, storytelling feels good.

This creative marathon will transform you.

Writing a book *is* hard work, but it's the very best kind of hard work, like chopping wood for a cozy fire or cooking a delicious dinner.

If you're still not quite sure if you can do this, that's normal. Maybe you're thinking you can't possibly write a novel when you have looming deadlines at work and a million unread emails. Or you're a parent, and they grow up only once, right?

Instead of thinking of your job or your kids as a reason *not* to write, make them your reason *to* write. Writing will make you a better co-worker, friend, and parent.

Our daughters have been a huge motivator for me. When they were young, I took them to coffee shops with me; they wrote their stories while I wrote mine. When they painted at the kitchen table, I painted or sketched settings and characters, showing them that I could pursue my dreams while supporting theirs. Then I sold my first book. At readings, seeing their proud faces in the audience was everything.

Let the people you love be your reason for pursuing your dreams.

This guide will show you how.

You can do this. (You really can.)

Happy writing,
Kim

WRITE A NOVEL IN 100 DAYS

The Busy Writer System: How It Works

Before You Start . . .

Read this section and the tips for writing your book before you jump into Day 1. Give yourself time to organize and schedule your writing so you're ready to embark on your dream.

Days 1–12: Plan your book.

The first twelve days will help you plan your story. Do not skip this. It will save you *years* of writing multiple drafts. Figure out your characters, world, and plot first. You'll need about an hour a day to read the guide and do the planning, but you can start small. The most important thing is to establish a writing habit in the beginning. Just fifteen minutes.

Days 13–100: Write your book.

I recommend scheduling an hour each day in which you plan to write (these don't need to be consecutive): fifteen minutes to read the guide, and then forty-five minutes to write. If you write for only fifteen minutes, that's fine, but if that's *all* you write every day, you'll have a shorter draft. No big deal. Short books might even be better in our busy world.

No time or mental energy to write? **Do 15 Magic Minutes.**

What Is 15 Magic Minutes?

15 Magic Minutes is your game changer.

In the middle of a busy life, on some days, you'll feel too exhausted or stressed to write your draft. On those days, you'll simply spend fifteen minutes writing *about* your story, characters, and world. You can brainstorm details for a scene or journal from a character's perspective.

This is your unfiltered time with your characters and story. Nobody will ever see those pages. It's for your eyes only and it will keep your imagination going.

I call it 15 *Magic* Minutes because this burst of creativity every day will feel magical in how it transforms your life and your ability to tell this story. It will help you hold on to your dream, even during a busy life. Your characters will start hanging out with you at the grocery store, the doctor's office, the marketing meeting—and trust me, they will have *opinions,* which will make those busy tasks a lot more fun.

15 Magic Minutes is intentionally not a serious writerly term. Please don't worry about being a "serious" writer in your first or second draft. Focus on entertaining yourself. Allow yourself to be playful, terrified, weird, brave, raw, and wild throughout this whole draft. Please be *un*-serious, except in how you show up for yourself.

Writing Prompts for 15 Magic Minutes

Here are fifteen ideas for what to work on during your 15 Magic Minutes when you don't feel ready to write your next scene. You'll find more inspiration throughout the guide as well.

1. **The 5 W's.** Write about: *where* it happens, *when* it happens, *why* it happens, *who* it happens to, and *what* exactly happens.
2. **Strong opinions.** Write your character's thoughts about others, food, TV, music, pet peeves, behaviors, morals, the news, themselves.
3. **5 senses: Imagine being in their body.** Write what they see, smell, hear, touch, and taste.
4. **Interesting objects.** Draw or list interesting objects in the scene or write about their significance.
5. **Character chart.** At the top of the page, write: GOAL, FLAW, LOVE, FEAR, MISBELIEF, PROBLEM, YEARNING. Down the side: Write your characters' names. Fill in your chart.
6. **Specific lists.** Write specific people, objects, plants, and animals that will appear in the next scene. Don't write "dog," write "Doberman." Don't write "plant," write "cactus."
7. **Metaphor exercise.** Write a list of your characters' emotions down one side of the page. Write a list of random nouns down the other side. Pair the emotion and the adjacent noun in a metaphor. For example, Anger + Toaster: His anger is burned toast.
8. **Weirdness.** Weirdness is the juice of good fiction. For your next scene, list out-of-place objects or characters (a poisonous berry

on a desk or a duck in the church), or weird occurrences (random dirt piles with ten worms show up—always *ten* worms).

9. **Dictionary words.** Open the dictionary, point at a random spot, and have your protagonist riff on that word.
10. **Three objects.** Ask someone to give you three random objects. For example: chewed-up gum, a broken guitar, and a crow feather. Then use them in a scene.
11. **An angry letter.** Your protagonist writes you an angry letter, telling you what you're getting wrong and how you're messing up their story.
12. **Money, love, and power.** How much money does each character have in their bank account and how does their money situation affect their life? Who do they love, and are they loved in return? Who has the power, who wants it, and what will they do to get it?
13. **Mentor book sentence.** A mentor book is one of your favorite novels, ideally from the same genre, published in the last thirty years. It serves as a reference while you write. Find a favorite sentence in your mentor book. Now write a sentence in your character's perspective, using their words, but with a similar rhythm, sentence structure, or literary device to the sentence in your mentor book.
14. **World.** Write about your characters' world. Focus on one world-building element: politics, geography, architecture, transportation, social rules, clothing, holidays, industry, technology, beliefs, laws, or conflicts between the new and old.
15. **Draw.** Yes, drawing counts as your 15 Magic Minutes, and it doesn't have to be good. Draw your next setting or a character.

Ten Top Tips to Finish Your Book

#1: Write every day for 15 Magic Minutes.

Write for small periods every day rather than "when inspiration strikes." Long writing sessions are great, but the reality is that with school, work, and family, sometimes all you can manage is a short writing sprint. This will keep your imagination in the game.

You could do it first thing in the morning, like Julia Cameron suggests in *The Artist's Way* for what she terms Morning Pages, essentially a brain dump. 15 Magic Minutes takes that idea and focuses it on your novel. But you don't have to do it in the morning. It could be at any time in the day: morning, noon, or late at night. Do it whenever it works for your schedule.

If you have to skip a day, don't beat yourself up. This is a no-guilt guide. Even *thinking* about your book every day will help. Have a little conversation in your head with your protagonist . . . "Hey, buddy, how you doin'?" And maybe your wild bounty hunter protagonist will give you some much-needed advice about whatever's going on in your life. They're your invisible friend from this point on; they'll be hanging out with you everywhere you go. The next day, you'll be buzzing with inspiration, and you'll dump your story onto the page in all its imperfect glory.

#2: Focus on a single skill every day.

One easy skill. That's it. Each day has a skill focus, and each skill builds on the last. The skills are grouped into four-day categories. These skill focuses work for anyone, from bestselling novelists to writers working on their first book. No matter how many books you've written, each book is a new problem to solve.

Do not read through all the skills at once. Take them day by day.

Focusing on everything all at once doesn't work . . . for anything.

Imagine if an instructor said the following to a group of kids at their first swimming lesson: "Hi, kids! I know you can't swim, but let me tell you everything about floating, gliding, front crawl, and butterfly. Now jump in the deep end!" What do you think would happen? They'd drown, just like the many writers who have drowned in the confusion of a bunch of skills they try to apply at once. Even when I was a competitive swimmer, I focused on a single skill in every practice—this is how I improved. If you play the piano, you do the same.

What do I mean by a single skill for fiction? Take the sense of smell. I imagine myself into the scene. A woman is ironing her abusive husband's shirt, breathing in the steam mixed with the scent of laundry detergent and a little of his body odor that didn't wash off, thinking about how she'd like to bash him in the head with the iron. And now I'm off!

If I tried to think ahead to the next three skills I was *also* going to try to implement here, my brain would be scrambled. By focusing on just the sense of smell, the scene comes to life.

#3: Plan first. Then write.

Does this mean you have to *plot*? In short, no.

I've developed a fast and fun method to *plan* your book with both freedom for writers who like to let the story unfold and a detailed plot structure for plotters. Planning simply means thinking about your characters, world, and story architecture a bit before writing. This guide works for plotters, pantsers (the type of writer who flies by the seat of their pants), and anyone in between.

You don't need a detailed outline, but if you don't plan at all, you may end up rewriting from scratch. Planning saves time.

When I first started writing, I planned nothing. I wrote fast and finished drafts, but editing didn't improve them. You know that expression about putting lipstick on a pig? Eventually, I rewrote from scratch, after planning my characters, world, and structure. That was when I sold my first book.

If you have a messy draft and don't know how to make it better, try rewriting it from scratch, following the guide. It'll go so much faster (100 days or less!), and you'll have a foundational draft you love.

One warning: Perfectionist pantsers often don't finish. If nothing is planned, and every word must be perfect, it's harder to write. If you're going to be a perfectionist in your writing, be a perfectionist in your planning as well. And remember, your first draft will never be perfect. Give yourself a break. Fix it in the next round.

#4: Write forward. Don't go backward.

Avoid revising while writing your first draft. Instead, write steadily forward for at least fifteen minutes a day. Don't reread. Don't backspace.

Writing a book *while* editing it is like driving halfway to the beach, realizing you forgot sunscreen, and driving home. Everyone piles out and now they're less enthusiastic to go. You might get them back into the car, but if you forget anything else, that's it.

You may be tempted to change one word, but I'm begging you: Don't do it. Fixing one word becomes a paragraph, then a chapter, and soon you'll decide that the entire beginning needs to be rewritten. Some people get stuck in the beginning, which is a giant waste of time because you'll spend days polishing a chapter that you end up cutting.

Don't edit until you finish the first draft. Save your perfectionism for later.

If you can't stop yourself from rereading your beginning, start each chapter in a fresh document and leave some notes for what comes next. Writing apps like Scrivener can also help.

#5: Build your creative confidence.

This is an early draft. It's your time to play.

In *Creative Confidence,* Tom Kelley and David Kelley explain that creative success comes from rapid prototyping (a fast first draft) and a trial-and-error mindset, which means you allow yourself to experiment.

Once you build your creative confidence, you'll take risks and be braver on the page.

When the editor brain takes over, creative confidence drops. I call it the green gremlin. It whispers, "*Oh, no,* you can't write *that.*" Everyone has this internal critic who loves to tear down our confidence. The trick is not *believing* it.

Choose the creator over the editor. Be kind to yourself.

Every book you love went through several drafts. Your first draft will not look like a finished draft when it pours onto the page. The first draft of the book you love didn't either; it was probably a big mess.

You can always fix your draft later. For now, be willing to experiment and have fun.

#6: Don't show anyone (or even talk about) your first draft.

Your creativity is a pressure cooker—let it vent out onto the page, but not into Aunt Margaret's ear while she's kneading dough for her famous quiche and can't *wait* to tell you why it's just the worst idea in the world. She's not even a writer. She doesn't know jack.

Avoid letting anyone read your book before you finish it. How can you develop a trial-and-error mindset or be brave on the page when you know that someone in your writing group is going to read and judge it? That's impossible. Sharing too early can slow progress and erode creative confidence.

If you really *must* show this first draft to someone before you've finished it, I encourage you to request positive-only feedback. Let this be a private time with your story. Creativity flourishes in an environment of safety.

Protect your beautiful, creative heart and nurture your dream.

#7. Say goodbye to "writer's block."

After helping thousands of writers finish novels and memoirs, I'm convinced that the biggest block isn't time, talent, skills, or so-called writer's block.

Let's call writer's block what it is: fear.

Over the years, writers have shared some of their common fears:

"What if I publish my book and everyone laughs?"

"What if I pour my heart and soul into this book and it's a giant waste of time?"

"What if I get bad reviews and everyone finds out I'm *actually* a bad writer?"

Nobody is immune to these fears. Not even bestselling novelists. If you have impostor syndrome or you worry you're not good enough, join the club.

You probably wish you could just confidently hammer out pages and say "*Tada!*" But here's a secret: Most writers struggle with insecurity, and that's good juice for your writing. Also, the "tada" writers? They never improve. Insecurity may even be an essential part of the process. We are, after all, writing about characters with flaws, insecurities, and limiting beliefs, so if you've got that inside you, do a little celebration: *Thank you, pain.*

Sometimes extreme writer's block is executive function paralysis, triggered by stress or overwhelm. It's common in people with ADHD due to a drop in dopamine, but it can happen to *any* busy, overwhelmed person.[1] Writing a novel can feel too big.

Fortunately, researchers have found some good solutions to help you overcome executive function paralysis. One option is to shrink a task down into small steps. (This is what I do for you in this guide.) You can also move your body, change your environment, or ask someone to write with you. They don't even have to write . . . just hang out with you while doing their own work. This is called body doubling. Another proven technique is to add novelty to the task. Write to a movie soundtrack. Do 15 Magic Minutes in multicolored markers. Dance wildly before writing. Add a weird object to the scene, like a banana peel or a plastic hand. Do a fifteen-minute writing sprint. Basically, add play to the writing and have fun.

#8: Nurture your creativity.

At the end of each four-day section, I've given you a self-care tool called Nurture Your Creativity. These tools decrease stress and help you stay on track.

Take a deep breath into your belly right now. Hold it. And release.

That's your first Nurture Your Creativity experiment. You've already done it. That's how simple it can be.

Writers often abandon stories because of anxiety and burnout. Before my first novel came out, I became a certified yoga and meditation teacher to get better at dealing with my own stress and help others do the same. The tools in this guide are fast and simple. A one-minute reset can be enough.

The writing itself can also help with trauma and stress. Author Charlie Jane Anders wrote in *Never Say You Can't Survive: How to Get Through Hard Times by Making Up Stories* that writing a story "grants you control over a whole world inside your mind even when the outside world feels like a constant torrent of awfulness."[2] Diving into your imagination and writing a book can be as transformative as meditation, yoga, traveling, running a marathon, or hiking the Appalachian Trail (and, bonus, no ticks). But I recognize that sometimes you've got to find a way to get yourself in the chair—the Nurture Your Creativity suggestions will help.

#9: Make yourself less "busy."

Look at what fills your day and decide what to cut, delegate, or simplify. Everyone has their responsibilities, so evaluate what takes you a lot of time, both at home and at work.

Here are a few ideas to save yourself at least fifteen minutes a day for writing . . . Batch your errands and do them in one day. Share household work. Don't fold your laundry. Batch-cook meals. Order meal prep kits delivered to your door. Preorder your groceries so that someone else shops for you. Auto-ship the boring stuff. Hire a cleaning person or a babysitter. Decrease volunteering. Don't take on extra projects at work, or bake extra cupcakes for the fundraiser. No more being "nice" at the risk of your own dreams. After the book is done, feel free to resume these activities.

Chores can be a good time to think about your book. Dog walks become plot walks. When cooking dinner, have a phone or a notebook nearby to jot down ideas for your next scene.

Most of all, protect your mental space and your inner joy. Avoid people, habits, and media that bring you down. Put the drama in your book instead. Don't doomscroll the news or look on Instagram at the high school friend who's in the Bahamas, sipping a piña colada. Instead, let your character sip that piña colada.

If you love social media, allow yourself this treat only after you've written for the day. Make sure it encourages you to go for your dreams. Follow me on YouTube, TikTok, or Instagram at authorkimpurcell. I'll cheer you on. You can do it.

Do this now: Pick one change and try it today.

#10: Create a writing habit.

We're about to jump into the actual work of writing your book, so it's time to plan *when* you'll write and for *how long*. Consistency is more important than the amount of time, especially in the beginning. Start small: Five minutes of writing is better than nothing.

When should you write? The conventional wisdom is to write first thing in the morning. But is morning *always* the most creative time to write? Night owls will be happy to know that it isn't. In researching this guide, I was surprised to learn that a bit of grogginess can actually help creativity. Dr. Sahar Yousef, a cognitive neuroscientist and lecturer at UC Berkeley, suggests scheduling "creative time and brainstorming in the late morning (if you're a super early bird) or afternoon, when most people physiologically have an afternoon dip."[3]

My most creative writing sessions have happened in a jet-lagged or sleep-deprived state, a kind of fever dream. Think about how goofy kids get when they're overtired. Writers are the same. We let go of perfectionism, become less inhibited, and are more likely to get in a flow state, entering the imaginative dream.

How long and how frequently should you write? I recommend planning four longer writing days per week and doing 15 Magic Minutes on any busier day. Schedule at least an hour on each of the long days to read the guide, plan your scene, and write. If that's all you do, you will finish the 100 Days with a solid, if short, draft.

Ease into the writing habit if this is new for you. You can start off with shorter sessions. The first three weeks are for planning. This is intentional, since it takes about three weeks to establish a habit.

Whatever time you choose, consistency matters more than how long you write. If you write at the same time each day, your imagination will activate around that time, and the muse will stroll along for a visit.

How Can You Establish a Writing Habit?

1. **Create a plan.** Habit researchers call this an *implementation intention.* In *Atomic Habits,* James Clear says planning time and location will help. It's not enough to say you will write, you need to say when and where. Clear suggests finding a new place because new "habits can be easier to change in a new environment."[4]
2. **Start small.** Keep new habits short. In *Tiny Habits,* Stanford professor BJ Fogg says that small commitments lead to greater long-term success because "you change best by *feeling good*—not by *feeling bad.*"[5]
3. **Stack habits.** Fogg also suggests attaching a new habit to an existing one. Link writing to something you already do: your morning coffee, a workout, or dropping kids at school.
4. **Create a habit train.** Habits follow other habits, like cars in a train. Look at what you need to do before your writing time. If you stay up watching a movie until 1:00 a.m., it's probably going to be impossible to leave the "station" at 6:00 a.m. to write.
5. **Create a visual cue.** Write a reminder on your fridge. Keep your notebook visible. Put up a sticky-note plot wall.
6. **Set alarms on your phone.** Habit research suggests it takes about three weeks to establish a new habit. Alarms help ensure that you don't forget.
7. **Create a comfortable writing space.** Add a writing blanket, a plant, or a candle. Cluttered spaces increase distractibility, so keep it simple.
8. **Push a reset button.** If you miss a day, no big deal. Reset. Try a new time or attach writing to a different habit. Reset the alarms and begin again.

Right now: Schedule your writing time and place. Put up a sign. Set alarms.

Nurture Your Creativity

A Tea Meditation

Welcome to your journey into creative joy. Here's your first stress-reduction tool, and also a possible writing ritual to activate your creativity. Make yourself some tea—any flavor you like. Hold the tea up and breathe in the steam as it steeps. Take in long, luxurious breaths, preparing to write, creating a separation between your regular busy life and your creative writing journey. Allow any anxiety you're holding to float up into the air with the steam.

Breathe in. Breathe out. You've got this.

Tim Wynne-Jones ***(The Emperor of Any Place)***

On Writing Your Unique Story

"Write the book you need to write. We all learn to write from emulation, but at some point, there is a story only you can tell. Write that."[6]

Busy Writer Road Map Days 1–4: Your Story Idea

You're about to start Day 1 of your dream. Congratulations! In the first four days, you'll develop a gripping story idea you can't wait to write. Try to do the days in order, but it's also okay to jump around or do two days at once. There's no right or wrong way to follow this guide—do whatever works best for you.

Warning: There are spoilers throughout this guide. We'll be looking at a wide range of novels and memoirs, all acclaimed and bestselling books. If you plan to read one of them, watch out for the title so you can jump to the next example and avoid the spoiler.

Day 1: Your Story Stew

Your story stew is uniquely yours, seasoned by your life experiences, values, interests, and imagination. Story ideas can sprout from anything: a mysterious death in a small teahouse you visited in Morocco, an old photo you found in the attic, a news story about a local kidnapping, or the dragon obsession you've had since you were a kid.

Plan Your Book: Create a story stew.

I'm going to encourage you to do some free association first to build a story idea. Pull out your story notebook and draw a stew pot (yes, really) and fill it with anything you'd like to include in your story. If you don't like drawing, you don't need to draw the pot (although drawing can stimulate your imagination in surprising ways). Instead, fill the page. Allow it to be messy.

Write good and bad ideas. Write sideways and upside down. Write raw and unfiltered. Be wild. Think of locations, characters, dangers, news events, interests, anything that makes you mad, any closely held beliefs, and traumatic experiences you want to process.

Here are some words from a recent story stew for my WIP: sculptor, big hands, John Coltrane, menopause, river, fishing with bread, chicken noodle soup, head injury, slam him in the head with a frying pan, poke him in the eyeballs, fridge magnets.

Random words or images may come into your brain, unbidden and surprising. Put them in your story stew: You're emptying the fridge here. Later, you'll decide what to keep.

Day 2: Narrative Heat

Do you have ideas bubbling up from your story stew? Maybe you have multiple ideas. Now, let's develop those ideas so you can choose the one with the most heat. Whatever scares you. Whatever you *must* write. That's heat.

What If?

Start by thinking about "what if" questions. Maybe you've wondered *what* would have happened *if* you'd chosen that girl or gone to that college or called that crying friend back in time. Maybe you want to write about your own neurodivergence or a physical disability, a news story that shocked you, or a fascination you've always had with Medusa.

In her craft guide, *The Magic Words,* editor Cheryl Klein suggests writing twenty "what if" ideas. "Having to come up with so many ideas will force you to push past obvious answers and dig down to something truly creative, so it's a useful technique to try whenever you feel stuck."[1] Writing "what if" adds a sense of delight to the storytelling journey. Before long, your muse struts across your desk, saying, "You called?"

"What If" Statements as Book Plots

***Fourth Wing* by Rebecca Yarros:** What if a girl with a connective tissue disorder (Yarros's real, lived experience[2]) tried to ride a dragon?

***The Midnight Library* by Matt Haig:** What if you could live your road not taken?

***Gone Girl* by Gillian Flynn:** What if a wife faked her own disappearance?

***Frankenstein* by Mary Shelley:** What if a scientist created a monster who turned on him?

***1984* by George Orwell:** What if a totalitarian government could control our lives?

***Trafficked* (my first novel):** I was teaching English as a Second Language when I read a news story about two trafficked women, and I thought—what if this happened to one of my students? Then I built from there: What if a boy next door suspected his neighbor had been trafficked? What if the traffickers threatened her family back home?

Why?

Now it's time to explore your reasons for writing this story. This is what will power you through many rewrites. For *Trafficked,* my *why* was easy: If this novel helps save one girl from human trafficking, it will be worth it. Why does *your* book matter to you?

Every writer's "why" is different. A. S. King said: "what inspires my books is what I'm angry about."[3] What makes *you* angry? What do you want to change?

When writers quit, it's often because their initial idea had no personal heat. They wrote it because they thought it was a good idea. Forget the "good" idea! There are a million good ideas. What matters is the passion you have for the story.

In the end, a novel is a question you're asking yourself. What question do you need to answer? That question is your personal fire to power you through to the end.

Who?

Who is your ideal reader? Picture a specific person, someone you know who will read this story. What age are they? What challenges are they facing in their life right now?

Writing for a specific reader will help you provide meaningful details, as well as shape the tone of the story. It'll help you to write clearly, in a gripping way, so that your reader leans in, eager to hear what happens next.

Can this reader be you? Sure . . . You're always your first reader. But imagining someone else can help you tell the story in a compelling way.

Plan Your Book: Journal on your *what if, why,* and *who.*

Step 1: Make a list of twenty what-if ideas. Then circle your favorites.

Step 2: Journal on your "why"—your personal heat behind these favorites. If you have no *why,* eliminate that option.

Step 3: Write about your ideal reader. Then write yourself a thank-you letter from this ideal reader for writing this book.

Day 3: Main Character, Perspective, POV

Main Character

Today, let's start by choosing a main character. You might be thinking: *I don't really have a main character; my story is about a bunch of charac-*

ters. I've heard this before, and it rarely ends well. I urge you to reconsider. Most stories have many characters, but powerful storytelling relies on a hero or heroine who is most affected by the central problem of the story. We cheer for their success, and we ache when they fail. Think of any book you love—does it have a hero? My guess is that it does.

Perspective

Most novels share the perspective of the main character. We see through their eyes, ears, and nose—this is *perspective.*

You may want to share multiple perspectives, alternating chapters. If this is your first book, I'm begging you: Please don't do it! This is an advanced skill and a recipe for disaster. Voices end up sounding the same and the plot gets messy. Two perspectives can work, but not more.

You're far more likely to finish your book if you stick with a singular perspective because you'll connect to this character in a deeper way . . . and so will the reader.

However, if you're determined, write one perspective at a time. Study novels that do multiple perspectives well, such as *How It Went Down* by Kekla Magoon, *Six of Crows* by Leigh Bardugo, and *A Game of Thrones* by George R. R. Martin.

POV (Point of View)

Point of view shapes the tone and psychic distance—how close or connected we feel to the main character's inner world. For a first novel, use first person or third person limited. These dominate the bestseller lists because they bring the reader closer.

1. **First person POV:** (I) The narrator is the main character, sharing only their thoughts. This POV is intimate and full of voice.
   ***Invisible Man* by Ralph Ellison:** I am invisible.[4]

2. **Third person limited POV:** (She/He/They) Similar to first person POV in that you show one character's internal world, but you have more distance.

   ***Trafficked* by Kim Purcell:** Hannah took two small steps forward in the immigration line entering America at LAX.[5]

3. **Second person POV:** (You) The main character is "you." It's not a letter; you aren't addressing readers.

   ***Damage* by A. M. Jenkins:** It's all yours. Your hands rise, fingers spread, ready to feel the firm scrape of the football, ready to pull it to you, ready to tuck it safely in.[6]

4. **Third person omniscient:** The narrator moves across multiple characters' minds, jumping space and time.

   ***The Covenant of Water* by Abraham Verghese:** She is twelve years old and will be married in the morning.[7]

5. **First person omniscient:** A narrator character uses "I" and often addresses the reader, which is called breaking the fourth wall. Then, like third person omniscient, you jump into the perspective and thoughts of different characters.

   ***The Book Thief* by Markus Zusak:** Death narrates this World War II story. White is without a question a color, and personally, I don't think you want to argue with me.[8]

Plan Your Book: Journal in your protagonist's voice.

Step 1: Choose your protagonist. If you're still torn, have each write you a half-page letter explaining why their story matters. Then choose one.

Step 2: Experiment with POV and verb tense. Write a half page about your protagonist's life before the inciting incident—four times. Do not look at the earlier versions as you write each one.

- Write in first person present tense.
- Write in third person present tense.

- Write in first person past tense.
- Write in third person past tense.

New details will come out in each. Which one do you like best?

Day 4: Your Elevator Pitch

An elevator pitch is a concise story idea that you could deliver in the time it takes to ride an elevator. The concept comes from Hollywood, but before you stick your thumbs in your leather belt and declare, "I'm writing a literary novel," please know that it's useful for any story. Think of this pitch as your book's premise, the copy you'd find on the book cover.

If you eventually want people to read your book or buy it, you'll need to be able to explain it clearly. More important, if you can't explain it, a key element may be missing. No matter how literary or highbrow your book is, you need to know what it's *about.*

At the core of any strong story pitch is the inciting incident, the before-and-after moment that sets everything into motion, and the high-stakes goal that the protagonist chases as a result. No goal, no story.

Inciting Incidents and Goals

1. ***Gone Girl* by Gillian Flynn**
   Inciting incident: His wife goes missing.
   Goal: Find her.
2. ***Hatchet* by Gary Paulsen**
   Inciting incident: The airplane crashes.
   Goal: Get rescued.
3. ***The Name of the Wind* by Patrick Rothfuss**
   Inciting incident: His family is killed.
   Goal: Get revenge.

4. ***The Hitchhiker's Guide to the Galaxy* by Douglas Adams**
   Inciting incident: Earth is destroyed.
   Goal: Escape Earth and find somewhere else to live.

Plan Your Book: Write an elevator pitch.

Step 1: Answer these five questions.

1. **Working Title:** What could hook your reader?
2. **Main Character:** What is one fascinating detail about them?
3. **Inciting Incident:** What is the event that changes their life?
4. **Goal:** What goal will the main character chase afterward?
5. **Stakes:** What happens if they fail?*

Step 2: Write your elevator pitch.

[Title] is about [Main Character] who [Inciting Incident] and must [Goal] or [Stakes].

Busy Writer Recap and Reward: Days 1–4

You brainstormed your story, and now it's time for the reward! Taking the first step to chase any goal is often the hardest part, and you've done it. Your ideas are no longer just taking up space in your brain: They're on the page. You've not only figured out your story idea, but you've also chosen your protagonist, perspective, and POV. You're off to a great start. Reward yourself every time you complete a four-day section in the guide. This is a challenging practice for many artists, but I encourage you to think of what would be a reward for you. For example, I just bought jazz tickets for myself and some family members in the basement of a coffee shop to celebrate finishing edits on this guide. Fifteen dollars each. No big deal. Treat yourself today.

---

* Adapted from *Save the Cat* by Blake Snyder.

Nurture Your Creativity

Start a Creativity Ritual

A creativity ritual transitions you into writing mode. Many authors have their own special rituals. Jandy Nelson has a writing blanket. A. S. King listens to a specific song. I drink black tea with milk. Maybe yours is a bite of chocolate or lighting a specific candle. Whatever it is, use it only during writing time so your brain learns: This signal means it's time to write.

Busy Writer Road Map Days 5–8: Characters and World

In this section, you'll be further exploring your cast of characters and their relationship to their world. Try to write for at least fifteen minutes every day to develop that writing habit—if you don't have time to fully dive into a "Day," you can always flip to page 2 for 15 Magic Minutes inspiration. You're building up your writing muscles, even in this brainstorming period. Some of these planning days could be split up into two or more days. You do you!

Day 5: Embodying Your Character

Today, learn more about your main character by imagining what it's like to be in their physical body. The body holds past experiences, both good and bad. So if you embody your protagonist, you'll get to know them in a deeper way, you'll understand how they move, why they make the choices they make, and how they see the world.

In the following experiment, you'll answer questions designed around the energetic chakras, where we tend to hold experiences in the body. For example, we hold fear in our belly and groin; if you've ever stood on the edge of a cliff, you've probably felt the tightening in that region. This will also prepare you for writing from the protagonist's perspective, from within their body, while drafting your novel. You'll be able to share all of the senses and your character's thoughts, and in doing so, you'll transport the reader so that they feel like it's happening to them. They won't be able to put your book down.

Plan Your Book: Learn about your character.

Step 1: Draw your character.

I know, I know—you're a writer, not an illustrator. This doesn't have to be beautiful; you're not going to show it to anyone. A stick figure is fine. You'll be writing all around this drawing, so it'll be messy in the end in any case. Add any distinguishing characteristics to your character. Dress them in what you think they'll wear at the beginning of the story. Write a paragraph in their voice about what they think about their appearance and clothing.

Step 2: Draw a line from each corresponding body part and then answer the questions for that body part.

Any body part: Do they have any insecurities? Is there anything they love? Do they have any unusual body parts, like six toes?

Scars: What are their memories associated with their scars, physical and emotional?

Legs/Feet: What sports/exercise do they do? Why? How do they walk? Fast or slow? Aggressive or cautious? Why? Do they jiggle their feet or knees when nervous?

Hips: What is their gender and sexuality? Have they had traumatic sexual experiences? What do they yearn for? What is their deeper ambition?

Belly: What are they afraid of? Why? What makes them angry? Why? What do they believe in their gut to be true about people or themselves?

Heart: What do they love? Who do they love? Have they experienced heartbreak?

Arms/Hands: What physical skills do they have? How did they learn those skills? What do they do with their hands when they're nervous?

Throat/Neck: What is their secret? What are they afraid to say?

Mouth/Tongue: What expressions do they choose? How do they talk? How do they kiss? What do they eat? How do they eat? What is their appetite? Do they have any food allergies?

Nose: What are their favorite smells? What's their least favorite? Why?

Ears: What music do they like? Why? What sounds bug them? Why?

Brain: Do they have any neurodivergences? Do they have mental health issues? Do they have ADHD, ASD, dyslexia, bipolar disorder, migraines, or anxiety? What do they think about?

Top of the head: What do they know a lot about? What is their religion? What are their beliefs? What are their superstitions?

Day 6: Multidimensional Characters

Yesterday, a woman showed up to my book club in strange socks with silver baubles like tree ornaments. She was a fashion designer who wanted to start a nonprofit for homeless youth, and she wore big black-rimmed glasses and had blunt, funky bangs. Her slouchy body language whispered *cool.* I loved her socks, but also, I wondered: Don't they bug her? Bounce, bounce, bounce. How long could I wear those without being bugged?

See how the above description reveals something about *both* the person being observed and the observer? When you meet people in the world, notice the unique things about them. Ask questions.

Today, let's explore the obvious and the hidden elements of your characters. Maybe they have a moral weakness in one area and a moral strength in another. A gang member who once did a drive-by shooting now braids his five-year-old daughter's hair while listening to opera. Someone "normal" keeps a box of thirty rabbit heads in their closet. (People collect those. Really.)

Ultimately, your plot will be influenced by the dynamics among characters—the more unique and well developed they are, the more intriguing your plot will be. This is important. Make your characters different enough to keep the story interesting and add conflict. Give them a range of skills, strengths, weaknesses, backgrounds, and personality types. If you don't plan this intentionally, you may have four versions of the same person, who is basically you.

Also consider who's going to cause problems in the story. Ever had a difficult neighbor? If so, you know all the problems they can cause. We've had a neighbor who walked around with a machete, a downstairs neighbor who wanted us to carry our two-year-old daughter inside the apartment so he wouldn't hear her running, and a neighbor who burst into our house and said his son was trying to kill him. Neighbors can cause problems in life and in stories—after one sketchy neighbor stole our recycling bin, I started imagining a scenario in which he stole our cat, who loved to go into his yard. What would I do? How could I prove he had my cat?

Think about any character who can cause problems or possibly help your protagonist.

How many characters should you have in a book? If you're writing a fantasy book, you might have up to eight main characters, but be careful about adding too many. It can be hard for the reader to keep them straight. Most books have three to five main characters. That obviously doesn't include the butler, the server, or the dog walker. If a couple of key characters serve the same purpose, combine their traits into one character.

Finally, to avoid reader confusion, the characters' names should start with different letters. We don't need an Annabel, Amanda, Anika, and Astoria in the same scene. Also, please don't give us a bunch of lengthy names plus the nicknames. Just whatever the protagonist calls them. The nineteenth-century Russian novelists got away with a bunch of names for each person, but we're not in the nineteenth century. Different rules for different times.

Plan Your Book: Learn about your characters.

Step 1: List your key characters.

In *The Hero with a Thousand Faces,* Joseph Campbell detailed character archetypes, and these were later narrowed down to eight archetypes by Christopher Vogler in *The Writer's Journey.* Here's Vogler's list, but choose what works for your story.[1]

1. **Hero:** the protagonist or main character
2. **Mentor:** a wise character who shares knowledge and trains the protagonist
3. **Ally or allies:** characters who help the protagonist with the goal
4. **Herald:** a character who transitions them to the new world
5. **Shadow:** main antagonist or villain
6. **Trickster:** the comic-relief character, usually an ally
7. **Shape-shifter:** a character whose allegiances are unclear, planting doubt in the reader's mind
8. **Threshold Guardian:** a character who tests the hero early and creates the first obstacle (it may be the rule or obstacle itself)

Step 2: Basics

Write down the basic facts for each of your key characters.

1. **Name, age, physical appearance:** For appearance, hair color and eye color are less important than details that reveal something about the character, like weird socks or a machete they carry everywhere they go. Think of those details now.
2. **Personality:** Think of a few key traits. Are they an extrovert or an introvert? Are they a joker, cynic, intellectual, straight shooter, or peacekeeper? Can you think of two opposing traits? For example, the class clown who secretly reads Nietzsche, using humor to deflect his inner despair.

3. **Family:** Do they have brothers or sisters? Do they have parents? Who's important to them? Why?
4. **Home:** Where do they live?

Step 3: Character Prompts

Explore these questions for your protagonist and any other characters. This isn't a checklist: Answer whatever inspires you or save them for 15 Magic Minutes.

1. **Core desire:** What do they want more than anything at the beginning of the story?
2. **Contrast:** What is something about them that nobody would expect? For example, maybe he's a football player who collects ceramic dolls or she's a PTA mom who is slowly poisoning her husband with his favorite chocolate-chip cookies.
3. **Fear:** What do they fear? Any phobias? Think of emotional fears (public speaking, embarrassment), physical fears (heights, spiders), and weird fears (dirt under one's nails).
4. **Failures:** What is their biggest failure at school/work or in their personal life? How do they feel about it?
5. **Strengths:** What are they good at? Think of knowledge, skills, interpersonal abilities.
6. **Skill plus weakness:** What is a big skill they have in one area, plus a weakness that stands in their way? For example, a skilled surgeon who has a terrible bedside manner.
7. **Knowledge:** Do they have any unique specialized knowledge? For example, They know everything about opening a safe or eighteenth-century architecture.
8. **Core impulse:** Do they naturally fight, flee, freeze, or fawn? (Fawning is a trait of the peacekeeper, a character who instinctively tries to calm everyone and help them get along.)

9. **Pet peeves:** What annoys them but doesn't annoy everyone? Examples: people who interrupt, loud chewing, lateness, slow walkers, scraping noises.
10. **Values and beliefs:** What is their religion? What are their politics? Do they have a moral code? What are their core beliefs? Why do they believe this?
11. **Backstory:** What is a key event that shaped who they are?
12. **Secrets:** What are they hiding? What would embarrass them if people found out? What are they ashamed of?
13. **Speech:** How do they talk? What are their favorite expressions? Are they quiet or talkative?
14. **Core identities:** What are their roles in their family and community (mother, sister, lawyer, swimmer)? What is their top skill and biggest weakness for each of these identities? What are their hopes or goals for each one of these identities?
15. **Love:** Who and what do they love? Why? Who likes and loves them? Why?
16. **Trauma and misbelief:** What bad thing happened to them and what self-sabotaging belief about themselves, or others, do they have due to that trauma?

Day 7: Worldbuilding and Settings

Before you write a single word, step into your protagonist's world and their home. Are dogs in uniforms guarding the streets outside? Are Mafia guys tracking bets in a back room? Maybe a drone is delivering a package to their front door. Perhaps they wouldn't open the door because the air is filled with a poisonous yellow gas. You need to know.

Worldbuilding is important in every novel, from contemporary, to fantasy, to sci-fi.

Today, I encourage you to draw a map of your protagonist's neighborhood or a floor plan of their house to help you imagine the scenes before writing them.

You may have two or more distinct worlds in your book. Often, after the inciting incident, your protagonist will transition to a new world. For instance, the first world in *Harry Potter and the Sorcerer's Stone* by J. K. Rowling is London and Privet Drive; the second world is Hogwarts School of Witchcraft and Wizardry and the magical world, including places like the Ministry of Magic. In Sylvia Plath's *The Bell Jar,* the first world is New York City, and then she goes to the secondary world of the mental hospital. No matter what, every world has different places and its own customs and rules, and this will be important to examine before you start writing.

Plan Your Book: Develop your world.

Step 1: Draw a map. (It doesn't have to look good.)

This could be the map of their childhood village, the secondary location, a neighborhood, a town, nature, or magical kingdoms—whatever might be relevant to your story. You can create several maps if you like, but let's start with one. Mark important locations in a city or town where you might want to set a scene—school, work, a bakery, stores, landmarks, city hall, central square, the homes where each of the characters live, and any key natural landmarks like rivers and mountains. Mark distances between areas so that you know the time it takes to travel to each place.

Step 2: Add memories, opinions, and rules to your map.

This prompt is inspired by Amy McNamara's gorgeous novel *A Flicker in the Clarity,* in which the main character maps her memories. Look at your map, imagine being the character, and think about whatever key memories may pop up connected to the various places . . . where she kissed her first boyfriend, where they had that wild bush party, or where Joe found his missing brother's shoe. Jot down any memory. Does your protagonist have any opinions about any place or the people in that place? Are there any unusual rules they must follow in this world? Where do these rules apply? For example, perhaps there is a forbidden forest.

Step 3: Draw a floor plan of the protagonist's house and add important objects.

A floor plan helps you avoid continuity errors—if the kitchen is upstairs in one scene and then you forget and suddenly it's downstairs, your reader will be confused. It also needs to make sense for the region: You don't want a bedroom in a basement in Los Angeles, where most homes don't have basements. First, decide where the rooms will be, and then add any key objects and furniture. The objects in our homes can show a great deal about us. For example, if I walk around in my house, I see an almond Hershey's bar wrapper next to the bed, a photoshopped image of a half-giraffe/half-man in my office, and an oddly placed can of mosquito spray on the bookshelf next to pink books. All of these objects tell something about me, for better or for worse. (I love almond chocolate bars, I color-coded that bookshelf, I like weird art, and I'm terribly allergic to mosquitoes.) What objects in your protagonist's home reveal something about them? Do this for any homes or indoor locations, like a family store, a palace, or a school.

Day 8: So You Want to Write an Early Flashback or a Prologue?

I suggest avoiding both, at least for now.

Writers often torture themselves over trying to perfect their prologue, rewriting it over and over, never accepting that some (most) prologues are inherently boring. The problem isn't with the writer; it's with the kind of prologue they're attempting.

Worldbuilding prologues are an old convention from back when readers had more patience—the author would explain everything about the world, and readers would fall asleep, but there was far less content in the world, so they'd keep reading. In modern fiction, an info dump doesn't work. You have to grab the reader.

Worldbuilding is like salt; sprinkle it lightly throughout your scenes, rather than dumping the whole container into your story stew. Instead of an info dump, start with a *scene* that captures the reader within the first two pages, especially if you want to hook a literary agent or publisher.

An Early Flashback

Perhaps you're thinking about including a flashback—a traumatic event from your protagonist's past. This is their origin story.

Every character has a defining event that shaped them; otherwise, we wouldn't write about them. This trauma has given them flaws and misbeliefs, and your story will explore how they'll grow beyond them.

Writers sometimes feel the reader *must* see this terrible moment right away, but it's often more powerful if we meet the character as they are now, and then become curious about what made them this way. In the first half of the book, you can drop hints about the past, build tension, and reveal it later for a greater emotional impact. We'll include flashbacks here as a discussion, but even if you feel tempted to draft one, I encourage you to save it for later in the narrative.

If You Must Write a Prologue . . .

I'll walk you through how to do it well, using examples from bestselling novels in different genres. The best prologues are *scenes* with high-stakes, character-driven action, multisensory description, and line-by-line tension.

First, look at your mentor book—one of your favorite novels in your genre, published within the last thirty years. Does it have a prologue or early flashback? If it does, how did it hook you? If not, perhaps you should avoid it in your own novel as well.

Thrillers or Whodunits

A gripping scene foreshadows the coming drama and teases the mystery. It might flash forward or backward to a murder. Often, it's told from another perspective, like a killer's or an omniscient narrator's perspective.

The Housemaid by Freida McFadden

This psychological thriller opens with a flash-forward to the book's ending.

> If I leave this house, it will be in handcuffs.
>
> I should have run for it while I had the chance. Now my shot is gone. Now that the police officers are in the house and they've discovered what's upstairs, there's no turning back.[2]

Literary, Historical, or Contemporary Fiction Novels

Again, write a short, vivid scene. Avoid a historical info dump. Readers won't remember it.

The Frozen River by Ariel Lawhon

This literary historical novel uses an omniscient prologue in which a fox discovers a dead body.

> The body floats downstream. But it is late November, and the Kennebec River is starting to freeze, large chunks of ice swirling and tumbling through the water, collecting in mounds while clear, cold fingers of ice stretch out from either bank, reaching into the current, grabbing hold of all that passes by.[3]

Notice the hook and the gorgeous personification of the ice.

Fantasy or Speculative Fiction

These genres often tempt writers to start with an info dump. Don't. *You* need to know the details; readers don't—not yet. Start with an action-packed scene, often in omniscient POV.

The Cruel Prince by Holly Black

A man knocks on the door, kills the parents, and takes the daughters to the fae world.

> On a drowsy Sunday afternoon, a man in a long dark coat hesitated in front of a house on a tree-lined street. He hadn't parked a car, nor had he come by taxi. No neighbor had seen him strolling along the sidewalk. He simply appeared, as if stepping between one shadow and the next.[4]

Plan Your Book: Write a flashback and/or prologue.

Step 1: List these five elements: difficult experience, need, flaw, misbelief, theme. Fill them in for your protagonist and any other main character.

Step 2: Write a flashback to develop your protagonist.

In your journal, write about the protagonist's wounding experience. Make it a gripping scene in their perspective and from your chosen POV. This experience is an essential part of their backstory, because it creates a deeper need, a flaw, and a misbelief about the world. The protagonist will transform in the story, and this transformation will often tie in to your theme.

Step 3: Write a prologue (optional).

Try to write an actual scene, like the examples above. If you still want to write a worldbuilding prologue, listing *all* the key information about your world, do it right now. Write this in a journal so you aren't tempted to bore the reader at the start or rewrite it a bunch of times. If, after your first draft, you still think you need it, revisit it then (and find ways to make it interesting).

Busy Writer Recap and Reward: Days 5–8

You're now eight days into the guide. You've brainstormed your characters and world. You're further ahead than all the writers who don't brainstorm anything and write with zero planning—they jumped into their car, but they didn't fill it with gas, and now they're stuck in the middle of the desert, sweating and hungry. You, on the other hand, are prepared. You're coasting along—you've got a full tank and plenty of snacks. You've just saved yourself months of rewrites and potential bouts of writer's block. Congratulations! Now let's talk about the possible reward.

Nurture Your Creativity

Take a Very Long "Idea Bath"

I know a TV writer who takes three-hour baths, emptying the water and refilling it to think up ideas and jokes for a late-night talk show. I love that idea. A notepad next to the bath. So nurturing. You can come up with ideas for your story in the bath. (You could voice it into your phone.) If you can't stand baths, your version might be a long walk or sketching the sunset or using a coloring book. Slow, relaxing activities can distract your body so your mind can run free. The point is you don't need to sit at your desk to come up with ideas and turn it into "work." Do it from a relaxed place. Let yourself daydream a little. Take the pressure off.

Andy Weir (***The Martian***)

on Developing Your World

"The first question I had to ask was the economics . . . If you have your lunar colony, why do people live there? . . . There has to be an economic foundation for everything . . . So I turned back to history and said, 'Why do people go settle new places in the first place?' "[5]

Lisa McMann (***The Unwanteds***)

on Knowing Your Characters First

"It's really important to know who your characters were before the story starts. . . . Even if their backstories never come out in the book, YOU need to know what life was like for them leading up to this moment."[6]

Busy Writer Road Map Days 9–12: Your Story Architecture

For the next four days, we'll be working on a loose framework for your novel. Whether you're a "pantser" or a "plotter" or somewhere in between, you'll be able to develop your story in a way that works for you. First, you'll explore the character arc, or how your character will grow throughout the story. Then you'll plan four pivotal scenes. Finally, you'll dive into more detailed plotting, creating a fun sticky-note wall and a few fully brainstormed scenes to get off to a strong start.

Day 9: Character Arc

We're all changed by shocking life events like death, divorce, and war. Your character arc explores that change. But what comes first: character or plot? You can't have one without the other. In a plot, a big event disrupts a character's life and they pursue a goal because of it; but in my opinion, one of the key questions that defines a plot is *why* your protagonist pursues one goal over another. If aliens attacked Earth, the scientist protagonist might either try to destroy them or befriend them—the choice comes down to the character.

The protagonist's personality, goals, choices, and reactions create the plot. You can't just wave your magic wand and make a car accident happen; you need to show cause and effect. Maybe a couple argues over who will take their kid to school. The mom ends up driving, texts while speeding, and—*bang*—she crashes. Their daughter is in a coma. That's your setup. Now you explore her goal, her struggle, and her growth: in other words, her character arc. By the end, she will be different from who she was on page one.

Three Types of Character Arcs

1. **Positive Change Arc**
   The plot pushes the protagonist to grow. This is the most common arc—you'll find this in most bestselling novels. As author Emma Kress says, "Books [can be] hope sparklers . . . we need them to light our way during those dark days."[1]
2. **Negative Change Arc**
   The protagonist becomes worse and may even turn into the villain. In *Crime and Punishment* by Fyodor Dostoevsky, Raskolnikov's feeling of superiority drives him to murder, and the guilt consumes him. He glimpses the truth that he was wrong but digs his heels in and refuses to accept it, deteriorating throughout the novel to the very end.
3. **Neutral Arc**
   The protagonist doesn't change, but others do through their influence. Sherlock Holmes has a solid moral compass and logic to guide him, but others around him, like Watson, evolve.

Character arcs mirror real life. We all face challenges that break us, forcing us to grow . . . or harden. Readers love positive arcs because they remind us that we, too, can make it through the hard times. As Lisa Cron explains in *Wired for Story*, "Neuroscientists believe the reason our already overloaded brain devotes so much precious time and space to allowing us to get lost in a story is that without stories, we'd be toast. Stories allow us to simulate intense experiences without actually having to live through them."[2] Your story may not involve saber-toothed tigers, but your characters will face monsters of their own—emotional or physical—and come out the other side transformed in a meaningful way.

Plan Your Book: Design your character arc.

Step 1: Journal about your protagonist's life situation, flaws, and yearnings at the beginning. Where do they start before the big inciting incident sets off their transformation?

Step 2: Write about how you want them to change. By the end, what realization will they make? What will they learn about themselves, humanity, and life?

Day 10: Story Architecture

Today, we'll design the basic architecture for your story: four pivotal scenes in four acts. Acts are major sections in a story, each with a turning point that propels the story forward.

Your character takes actions that lead toward each of the four pivotal events, and then they react to those events. Focus on the pivotal scene in each act: the four pillars that hold up your story like the corners of a house. You've already mapped out the first one back on Day 4: the inciting incident. Now you'll plan three more. That's it—three scenes. You've got this.

Act One: The Inciting Incident

Most novels begin with a character's problem: the assistant with a nasty boss, the once-famous actor working at Trader Joe's, the bullied kid. We see the protagonist's yearning, and then—*boom*—something happens that changes their situation and creates their goal.

Act Two: The Midpoint Shock

This act is often called the *success* act. The protagonist pursues their goal in a new world, gaining skills, allies, and enemies, mostly progressing toward their primary goal. Then they hit the Midpoint Shock: a betrayal, death, breakup, or major loss. This varies, of course, depending on the genre. In a romance, the midpoint is typically the declaration of love, or it may be a false victory. Either way, the story hits a screeching sharp right turn. Now we're heading down that unknown alley, and the second half feels new and unpredictable, keeping both you and the reader hooked.

Act Three: The All-Is-Lost Moment

Life gets hard. Think of those brutal times in life when everything goes wrong—your new girlfriend dumps you, then your dog Woof-Woof tears up the expensive Room & Board comforter, and the next day a gas leak blows up your car. It's not all downhill; you still want to alternate between success and failure scenes, but your protagonist is facing bigger failures and mistakes, leading them to the All-Is-Lost Moment, when they'll have to face themselves.

Act Four: The Climax

From the low point comes clarity. The protagonist experiences an epiphany—a Lightbulb Moment—that allows them to confront their flaw or misbelief. They recommit to their goal or choose one that fits their new mindset. Then comes the climax, in which we see their true growth. Like the Rolling Stones song, they "can't always get what they want," but they just might get what they need.

Plan Your Book: Build your story's architecture.

Today, think about the four major events for your story. Answer the questions below for each and then plan out the scenes as much as you can: setting and character details, the protagonist's goal at the start of the scene, the action heading into the scene, and the first big obstacle of the scene.

Step 1: Plan the Inciting Incident. You've already brainstormed this, but you can flesh it out more here. What happens leading into this scene?

Step 2: Plan the Midpoint Shock. How does your protagonist pursue their new goal after the inciting incident? What major event will flip the story in the middle?

Step 3: Plan the All-Is-Lost Moment. What mistake or bad plan after the midpoint drives them to confront their flaws or misbeliefs, forcing internal change?

Step 4: Plan the Climax. What realization will prepare them for this final challenge? What will happen?

Day 11: The Busy Writer Plot—Four Acts, 22 Plot Points

Did I say plot? Yes, but I whispered it.

If the thought of *plotting* makes you want to run away and eat a big slice of chocolate cake, go ahead, eat the cake first. Then think of your plot like a recipe.

My Opa was a baker. I spent hours watching him mix ingredients with his thick, strong arms. He rarely looked at a recipe, but that didn't mean he didn't have one. He'd simply memorized it. If it was a chocolate or a lemon cake, he adjusted as needed. Plot is like that.

Some writers, like Stephen King, have the basic recipe within them. They adjust as needed. Maybe you, too, have naturally internalized story through your life experience. Perhaps you listened to family members share hilarious tales around the dinner table. But most of us had to chew with our mouths closed and get our elbows off the table. We need a recipe.

A loose plot keeps you writing instead of staring at rain snaking across the window.

The Busy Writer Plot gives you 22 Plot Points within a four-act structure—a common structure for bestselling and award-winning novels. It avoids a slow middle and ensures strong pacing. Think of these plot points as flexible guideposts. Adjust as needed. Go ahead—add broccoli to the cake!

If you prefer not to plan ahead, no problem. You can still improve your storytelling craft. I'll share ideas and examples for each plot point throughout this guide—take what helps you, and skip what doesn't. Next, you'll see a list of the main plot points; they may represent several scenes or chapters. Percentages show you roughly where you are in your novel.

Abraham Verghese *(The Covenant of Water)*

on Writing a Detailed Plan

"I thought I had a detailed plan when I began: my blueprint was on a huge whiteboard occupying one wall of my writing office. . . . Every few months I had to erase the whiteboard (photographing it before I did) and draw a brand-new blueprint to reflect the new reality of the story."[3]

Jennifer Castle (*The Beginning of After*)

on Creating a Rough Plan

"I need to know where I'm starting, where I'm going to be halfway through a story, and where I want to end up. I don't like to outline the whole thing, because I want to leave breathing room for the characters to evolve as I write them. I'll usually map out 50 pages at a time."[4]

The Busy Writer Plot: Beat Sheet

Act One

Plot Point 1: The Imperfect Life (0–5%): The main character deals with regular life.

Plot Point 2: The Inciting Incident (5–10%): A big event changes everything.

Plot Point 3: First Response (10–12%): They react to the inciting incident.

Plot Point 4: The New Goal (13–15%): They pursue a new goal because of the inciting incident.

Act Two

Plot Point 5: New World and Allies (15–20%): They explore the new world and meet allies.

Plot Point 6: The Antagonist Threatens (20–25%): They face the enemy or the first big obstacle.

Plot Point 7: Skills and Information (25–30%): They learn new skills and information.

Plot Point 8: Subplot Challenge (30–35%): A side problem (theirs or an ally's) interferes.

Plot Point 9: Escalating Obstacles (35–45%): Tension, problems, and stakes increase.

Plot Point 10: False Hope (45–50%): They have a victory or joyful moment.

Plot Point 11: The Midpoint Shock (50–55%): A big twist or betrayal changes everything.

Act Three

Plot Point 12: Reaction to the Midpoint (55–58%): They react to the Midpoint Shock.

Plot Point 13: The Fuse (58–60%): Time pressure, stakes, and danger increase.

Plot Point 14: Flawed Plan (60–65%): The characters make a risky or impulsive plan.

Plot Point 15: Subplot Complications (65–70%): A side problem interferes with their goal.

Plot Point 16: A Near Win (70–75%): The main character almost succeeds in reaching their goal.

Plot Point 17: The Big Mistake (75–80%): A devastating mistake causes a big loss.

Plot Point 18: The All-Is-Lost Moment (80–83%): The protagonist hits rock bottom.

Act Four

Plot Point 19: The Lightbulb Moment (83–85%): They make a realization and grow.

Plot Point 20: The Climax (85–95%): They face the final battle or test to get what they want.

Plot Point 21: Aftermath (95–97%): They deal with the fallout from the climax.

Plot Point 22: The Ending (97–100%): They demonstrate their transformation.

Plan Your Book: Answer the questions for each plot point.
You now have your story's architecture—time to fill in some ideas for scenes. Answer these prompts with your protagonist in mind: their personality, impulses, strengths, and flaws.

Step 1: Plan Act One

1. **The Imperfect Life:** How can you show their initial problems or yearning?
2. **The Inciting Incident:** What big event changes their life?
3. **First Response:** How do they react to the inciting incident?
4. **The New Goal:** What goal do they pursue based on what's happened?

Step 2: Plan Act Two

5. **New World and Allies:** How do they explore this new world or challenge?
6. **The Antagonist Threatens:** What does the protagonist's enemy do to threaten them?
7. **Skills and Information:** What skills or information does the protagonist pursue?
8. **Subplot Challenge:** What side problem complicates the main story?
9. **Escalating Obstacles:** How can you make things harder?
10. **False Hope:** What moment of happiness or success could lower their guard?
11. **The Midpoint Shock:** What twist or betrayal happens in the middle?

Step 3: Plan Act Three

12. **Reaction to the Midpoint:** How will they respond emotionally to the shock?
13. **The Fuse:** How can you raise the stakes or add time pressure?
14. **Flawed Plan:** What bad plan do they make?
15. **Subplot Complications:** How does the subplot interfere with their goal?
16. **A Near Win:** How do they almost succeed and then fail?
17. **The Big Mistake:** What action directly causes the disaster?
18. **The All-Is-Lost Moment:** How do they suffer or lose hope?

Step 4: Plan Act Four

19. **The Lightbulb Moment:** What is their realization or growth moment?
20. **The Climax:** What final dramatic test shows what they've learned?
21. **Aftermath:** What will be the consequence or negative impact of the climax?
22. **The Ending:** How will you show the protagonist's growth?

Day 12: Planning Your Scenes

You've already mapped out your character arc, story architecture, and big-picture plot points—this is your final day of planning! Before you start drafting your novel, let's focus on three key storytelling tools that will guide you in every scene you write: scene-sequel, success-failure, and opposites.

Three Elements to Remember When Planning a Novel

1. Scene-Sequel

This is an essential concept to master, whether you're a character-first or plot-first writer.

A scene is the action. The protagonist pursues a scene goal, taking action that leads to an obstacle. You can amplify the obstacle with a mistake or complication to make it worse. The protagonist either succeeds or fails in dealing with the obstacle. Now they react.

A sequel is the reaction. It's your transition between scenes. The protagonist faces a new choice or dilemma, they make a decision, and they pursue the next scene goal.

Every scene needs a goal and an obstacle. The goal should be something so specific you could film it. "Be happy" is not a good scene goal, even if it's a good life goal. It requires action so that they would hit an obstacle. Maybe they want a friend. The action: Meet someone in the cafeteria. Next, you need the obstacle, creating conflict. It could be intense shyness or a mean girl at their chosen table. No conflict? No scene.

2. Success-Failure

In some scenes, the protagonist overcomes the obstacle—this would be a success. In other scenes, they don't—this would be a failure. Alternate wins and losses. Not every scene ends in disaster. You need to give the poor reader a break and add some hope. Tension grows when readers wonder what will happen. A failure scene doesn't need to be devastating; it could simply be an embarrassment, like a girl's tutu falling down in the middle of a performance. Remember, this is all about character. In the sequel or reaction, does she quit ballet or does she continue dancing without a tutu? What causes your protagonist to succeed or fail? What skill do they use? What fear, flaw, or misbelief comes into play? Each result reveals character.

Success–Failure plotting in *Gone Girl* by Gillian Flynn

Failure Scene: On the night of Amy's disappearance, Nick gets drunk and argues with police.

Success Scene: Amy's parents arrive, and Nick worries they'll blame him, but they're kind.

Failure Scene: In a news interview, he looks drunk and uncaring.

Success Scene: The cops show him a wrapped box. Amy always gives him a treasure hunt on their anniversary—it's a romantic treasure hunt that makes him look good.

3. Opposites

Opposite settings keep readers on their toes and add electricity to your writing. From one scene to the next, create contrast: hot to cold, bright to dark, crowded to empty, country to city. Choose your settings for maximum impact so that each location amplifies the tension in the scene. Instead of a conversation with a friend in a kitchen or thoughtful pondering while alone in their bedroom, two friends could talk, or the protagonist could think, while scaling a cliff.

In *The Hunger Games* by Suzanne Collins, chapter one alone moves through several contrasting locations, including Katniss's safe home, the dangerous woods, the dirty Hob shopping area, the luxurious mayor's house, and the bright, crowded square for the reaping.

Plan Your Book: Planning your scenes.

Step 1: Create a Sticky-Note Wall. Now it's time to play. Grab sticky notes (Post-its or a similar type of note) and get ready to build your story visually on your wall. Label four sections: Act One, Act Two, Act Three, Act Four. Put scene ideas on sticky notes under each act. Follow the plot points. Do it fast. Fifteen minutes. In *The Sticky Note Plot,* David Macinnis Gill describes it best: "This method thrives in the space between the known and unknown. Say Yes to everything. After all, it's just a sticky note, and stickies can easily be tossed."[5]

Step 2: Brainstorm your scenes in detail. Use the checklist below. If nothing else, just brainstorm your first scene. You can also take a picture of this checklist and do it on the go. This is perfect for 15 Magic Minutes, so maybe you want to bookmark or take a photo of this page and continue to come back to it. You can think about scenes in line at the grocery store, on the treadmill at the gym, or on the subway to work.

Checklist: 6 Key Elements for Any Scene

1. **Purpose:** What is the purpose of this scene? What are you trying to reveal? How does the scene move the story forward?
2. **Setting:** Where will you start? Time? Danger? Multisensory details?
3. **Characters:** Who's in the scene? Description? What just happened to them? How are they feeling and why?
4. **Goal:** What does the protagonist want to do right now? What do others want? Does anyone have a conflicting goal?
5. **Actions:** What physical actions do the characters take to pursue their goal?
6. **Conflict:** What is their internal conflict, fear, insecurity, or worry? What is their external problem or obstacle?

Step 3 (alternative): Create a chart: If you're more visual, you may want to write the six key elements in the checklist on the top of a chart and the scenes along the side. Then fill in the squares.

Busy Writer Recap and Reward: Days 9–12

You've designed a rough or detailed plot for your book. This is no easy task, and you did it. As you move through the guide, I'll give you more examples and ideas for each plot point in case you want to add extra scenes or change your course. For now, you've created a basic road map so that you don't get stuck; you're ready to jump into that writing convertible with a map in hand. But remember, you can always change your map. If you happen to see a doughnut shop in the middle of the desert playing heavy metal, go ahead, have a doughnut, rock out, and meet that wild man or woman with the dinosaur tattoo. Then, adjust your sticky-note wall and continue on. (Speaking of that, if you have little kids or dogs, take a picture of the wall. They may get sticky-note happy.)

This is your storytelling journey. Have fun!

Nurture Your Creativity

Shake It Out: Your Creativity Dance

Think of a song that could represent your character's life at this point. Play it on repeat to get into the mood of this scene. While you listen and before you write, shake out the tension in your body to release the stress of the rest of your life or go ahead and dance with wild abandon. You can let it be a dark or dramatic dance like in *All Fours* by Miranda July. Loosen up energy blocks, move the parts of you that are stuck, add in some hip gyration, toss your head, scream. If you do this and put it on social media, please tag me. I would love to see your creativity dance.

ACT ONE

You're about to write your draft. Facing the blank page can be terrifying—many writers worry that they'll do it wrong. But there is no right or wrong. Take a deep breath and let go of perfectionism. You've got this. Have fun and follow the yellow brick road.

Plot Point 1: The Imperfect Life (0–5%)

Plot Point 2: The Inciting Incident (5–10%)

Plot Point 3: First Response (10–12%)

Plot Point 4: The New Goal (13–15%)

Meg Medina (***Merci Suárez Changes Gears***)

on Finding a Supportive Community

"Sometimes in writing it feels like you're walking on a tightrope between two skyscrapers, and you need the people around you who are going to keep you calm and say, 'Come across. You can do it. Don't look down, just look at me. Just keep walking.'"[1]

Amy Poehler (***Yes Please***)

on Writing a Book Even When It Is Hard

"Well, the first thing we do is take our brain out and put it in a drawer. Stick it somewhere and let it tantrum until it wears itself out. You may still hear the brain and all the shitty things it is saying to you, but it will be muffled, and just the fact that it is not in your head anymore will make things seem clearer. And then you just do it. You just dig in and write it."[2]

Busy Writer Road Map Days 13–16: A Riveting Beginning

Your job in the first few pages (ideally the first few paragraphs) is simple: Hook the reader and make us care. We'll be working on a strong opening for your novel. But no pressure! Please don't revise and rewrite this beginning a million times. Remember, you don't need to get it right this time around; you'll refine the writing in future drafts. Entertain yourself and have fun.

Act One, Plot Point 1: The Imperfect Life

Most stories open up with a scene showing the protagonist's regular, flawed life, before the Inciting Incident in which everything changes. This might just be a few paragraphs or it might be a couple scenes. Below are some ideas and examples of this plot point in popular novels.

Ideas and Examples

1. Divorcing your spouse (*Fleishman Is in Trouble* by Taffy Brodesser-Akner)
2. Experiencing grief and/or suicidal ideation (*A Man Called Ove* by Fredrik Backman)
3. Being bullied (*The Lightning Thief* by Rick Riordan)
4. Facing poverty or looming starvation (*The Hunger Games* by Suzanne Collins)
5. Working under a nightmare boss (*The Devil Wears Prada* by Lauren Weisberger)

Day 13: Hooking the Reader

From the first page, aim to hook the reader. Make them curious about the character and their situation. In *Writing the Breakout Novel Workbook*, literary agent Donald Maass says, "The number one reason my agency rejects manuscripts is insufficient tension or conflict, especially in the opening pages."[3]

Here's what author Rick Riordan says about the start of a novel:

Beginning writers tend to believe they must "set things up" before they get into the real meat of the novel. They want to introduce characters, history, and setting before they start on the central dilemma. Chapter one is often limp, because of this. Even worse, some writers are so hesitant to get to the point in chapter one that they put off the action even further by writing a prologue.[4]

So, get to the point.

8 Hooks to Pull in Any Reader

1. Foreshadowing: Direct

Everything I Never Told You by Celeste Ng

Lydia is dead. But they don't know this yet.[5]

2. Foreshadowing: Indirect

The Giver by Lois Lowry

It was almost December, and Jonas was beginning to be frightened.[6]

3. Action

I'll Give You the Sun by Jandy Nelson

This is how it all begins.

With Zephyr and Fry—reigning neighborhood sociopaths—torpedoing after me and the whole forest floor shaking under my feet as I blast through air, trees, this white-hot panic.[7]

4. Strangeness—a weird character, behavior, or object

Desert Star by Michael Connelly

Bosch had the pills lined up on the table ready to go.[8]

5. Mysterious Dialogue

The Seven Husbands of Evelyn Hugo by Taylor Jenkins Reid

"Can you come into my office?"[9]

6. A Forbidden or Dangerous Setting

The Golden Compass by Philip Pullman

Lyra and her daemon moved through the darkening hall, taking care to keep to one side, out of sight of the kitchen.[10]

7. Funny Opinions About Anything or Anyone

Angus, Thongs and Full-Frontal Snogging by Louise Rennison

If Uncle Eddie (who is bald as a coot) says to me one more time, Should bald heads be buttered? I may kill myself.[11]

8. Danger—Emotional or Physical

It Ends with Us by Colleen Hoover

As I sit here with one foot on either side of the ledge, looking down from twelve stories above the streets of Boston, I can't help but think about suicide.

Not my own.[12]

Hooking with Action, Characterization, and Details

After you've hooked them in the first line, is that it? Are you all good?

Sadly, no. You've got to make us care deeply about your main character, and you can't bore us with a bunch of backstory. Sometimes a writer will tell me, "Oh, don't worry, it gets good later." You don't have *later*. You've got two pages to make us *fall in love*.

Keep hooking us throughout the entire first chapter. Stay in the scene! Show us your protagonist's personality through the voice and description, and put them in the middle of action.

Fourth Wing by Rebecca Yarros

In the opening scene, Violet is carrying a heavy backpack, preparing to enter the dangerous war college that trains dragon riders. Her mother is forcing her, though she's not dragon rider material. She's an intellectual, and she has a physical disability. In the first scene, her sister is trying to convince their mom that she's too weak and she'll die. High stakes!

Write Your Book: Hook the reader.

Act One, Plot Point 1: The Imperfect Life

Step 1: Before you start writing any scene, including this first scene, imagine where your character is. Put them in an interesting location—ideally, one that creates the possibility for tension and conflict. See the place through their eyes. Go through all the senses. For this opening scene, avoid starting with a dream, a boring wake-up, an alone thinking scene, or a flashback.

Step 2: Choose one of the hooks above and start writing! It doesn't need to be perfect. Stick with your chosen POV and verb tense. Put your protagonist in the middle of action.

Day 14: Multisensory Descriptions with Personality

Have you ever walked down a street or a hiking trail with a family member and realized that you don't notice the same things? When my daughters and I used to walk down the street in Brooklyn, one daughter would comment on weird-looking people ("That man's eyebrows look like caterpillars"), and the other would notice intricate carvings at the tops of buildings or the lion sculptures at the entrance to Prospect Park (she called them Emma and Danger). I, on the other hand, would notice the very sweaty, red-faced mom trying to manage a baby and a three-year-old spilling Goldfish like confetti.

Descriptions work best when you imagine your protagonist's way of seeing the world. Their perceptions are shaped by their emotions and experiences, especially those in their recent past. If you're in a good mood, you see the world differently from how you'd see it if you were in a bad mood.

Use all the senses to transport the reader so they're wearing the too-tight boots and breathing in the smell of pizza when a truck rattles down the street and splashes freezing-cold puddle water on their bare legs.

4 Top Description Tips

1. Add all the senses.

Stolen by Lucy Christopher

Gemma is in a café at the airport in Thailand, drinking coffee with her future kidnapper.

> There was a swarm of nameless faces slowly being drawn toward the drinks counter. People, people, everywhere. The grind and hum of the coffee machine. The squeal of small children. The smell of eucalyptus coming off your checkered shirt.[13]

2. Reveal dangerous details to build tension.

The Lovely Bones by Alice Sebold

But on December 6, 1973, it was snowing, and I took a shortcut through the cornfield back from the junior high. It was dark out because the days were shorter in winter, and I remember how the broken cornstalks made my walk more difficult. The snow was falling lightly, like a flurry of small hands . . .[14]

3. Show how the protagonist sees the setting.

The Paper Palace by Miranda Cowley Heller

On the far side of the pond, beyond the break of pine and shrub oak, the ocean is furious, roaring. It must be carrying a storm in its belly from somewhere out at sea. But here, at the edge of the pond, the air is honey-still.[15]

4. Show how the protagonist sees themselves or others.

Gone Girl by Gillian Flynn

Go is slender and strange-faced, which is not to say unattractive. Her features just take a moment to make sense: the broad jaw; the pinched, pretty nose; the dark globe eyes. If this were a period movie, a man would tilt back his fedora, whistle at the sight of her, and say, "Now, there's a helluva *broad*!"[16]

Write Your Book: Describe through the protagonist's lens.

Act One, Plot Point 1—The Imperfect Life

Step 1: Plant yourself in the character's body and imagine all the senses. Ask yourself: *What would your protagonist notice, based on their mood?*

Step 2: As you add to your word count today, show what they're experiencing and what they notice about the setting and the other characters.

Use descriptions to show the judgment they pass on the world around them (yes, even in the third person POV).

Day 15: A Captivating Voice and Dialogue

You've now worked on hooking the reader and adding multisensory description with personality. Two more core skills are dialogue and voice, essentially the main character's opinions and thoughts. Your protagonist needs to be either likable or fascinating in some way. If you nail their voice and dialogue, people will fall in love with your main character and keep reading, even if they're just clipping their toenails. Below, I'll give you a few ideas for how to do this.

1. Humor: Could they have a funny take on something?

Furiously Happy by Jenny Lawson

Everyone has human heads in their closet. Sometimes the heads are secrets, or unsaid confessions, or quiet fears. This book is one of those severed heads. You are holding my severed head in your hands.[17]

2. Expressions and Vocabulary: How does word choice show who they are?

The Catcher in the Rye by J. D. Salinger

If you really want to hear about it, the first thing you'll probably want to know is where I was born, and what my lousy childhood was like, and how my parents were occupied and all before they had me, and all that David Copperfield kind of crap, but I don't feel like going into it, if you want to know the truth.[18]

Holden's expressions show his personality and make us curious.

3. Syntax: Do they use contractions, long/short sentences, run-ons, fragments?

The Curious Incident of the Dog in the Night-Time
by Mark Haddon

A boy with autism has found the neighbor's dog with a garden fork in it. Notice the voice of this character: He doesn't use contractions, and his tone is matter-of-fact, making the scene even more poignant as he describes the dead dog.

> I pulled the fork out of the dog and lifted him into my arms and hugged him. He was leaking blood from the fork holes.
>
> I like dogs. You always know what a dog is thinking. It has four moods. Happy, sad, cross and concentrating. Also, dogs are faithful and they do not tell lies because they cannot talk.[19]

4. Grammar and Dialect: How does it show their education and background?

Haircut by Ring Lardner

> I got another barber that comes over from Carterville and helps me out Saturdays, but the rest of the time I can get along all right alone. You can see for yourself that this ain't no New York City and besides that, most of the boys works all day and don't have no leisure to drop in here and get themselves prettied up.[20]

5. Opinions: What do they notice and how do they feel about it?

A Brief History of Seven Killings by Marlon James

> Hey I'm nothing if not adventurous, my wife would say crazy. It was a humongous glass jar of mashed pepper paste. I dipped the

> chicken in and swallowed the piece whole. You know that part in Road Runner where Wile E. Coyote's bomb goes off right after he swallows it, and smoke comes out of his ears and nose? Or that dipstick, first time at the sushi bar thinking damn right I can swallow a teaspoon of wasabi? That was me.[21]

6. Imagination and Exaggeration: Where does their mind go?

Insignificant Events in the Life of a Cactus by Dusti Bowling

The protagonist, who was born with no arms, starts to lie about how she lost her arms:

> I knew from the first moment I told a girl my arms had burned off in a fire, I had found a great hobby: making up stories.[22]

7. Dialogue: What do they talk about?

Think about what the characters could be doing and saying to reveal their personality while also adding tension. In John Steinbeck's classic *Of Mice and Men,* we see the humanity in both men and George's gentleness with Lennie, despite the fact that he's killed a mouse. Here is the advice John Steinbeck gave on writing dialogue: "If you are using dialogue—say it aloud as you write it. Only then will it have the sound of speech."[23] I suggest reading Steinbeck's dialogue below aloud to see how it flows.

Of Mice and Men by John Steinbeck

> "What you got in your hand—hidin' it?"
>
> "I ain't got nothin', George. Honest."
>
> "Come on, give it here."
>
> Lennie held his closed hand away from George's direction. "It's on'y a mouse, George."
>
> "A mouse? A live mouse?"

"Uh-uh. Jus' a dead mouse, George. I didn' kill it. Honest! I found it. I found it dead."[24]

Steinbeck cuts most of the description and dialogue tags here, allowing the dialogue and actions to pop. Notice the character development. We learn that Lennie likes to pet the mouse, and we guess he probably killed it by accident. This serves the purpose of foreshadowing a scene later in the book, when Lennie accidentally kills Curley's wife. The conflict between the two brothers is both on the surface and in the subtext. Lennie clearly has some mental challenges, and George's reaction to the mouse adds subtext—he throws the mouse away, as if throwing it away will eliminate the underlying issue of his brother's accidental violence.

Write Your Book: Captivate the reader with the protagonist's voice and dialogue.

Act One, Plot Point 1: The Imperfect Life

Step 1: Decide how you'll help the reader connect to the main character emotionally and develop sympathy for what they're experiencing. The protagonist's voice is one way to achieve this. Dialogue is another, but the same principle applies—make it interesting. What opinion could the main character share? What could they talk about with another character?

Step 2: Continue writing the first plot point; show the protagonist's personality through their humor, expressions, wisdom, opinions, and observations. Show their goals, yearning, fears, and insecurities.

Day 16: Kindness, Advice & Theme

As you show the character moving through their imperfect life before the inciting event, try to hit two key beats: a kindness moment and an advice moment, often called theme-stated.

1. Kindness Moment: Save the Cat

What I'm referring to as a Kindness Moment was originally called "save the cat" because in old movies, the protagonist would save a cat . . . or walk an old lady across the street. At some point in your beginning pages, you want to show the character's inner kindness, but you don't need to "save a cat," obviously. In this moment, simply show they're good at heart, so that even if they're externally grumpy, the reader sees their inner kindness.

2. Advice Moment: Theme-Stated

In *Save the Cat! Writes a Novel,* Jessica Brody refers to the advice moment near the beginning of a book as "theme stated"—essentially, whatever the character needs to learn over the course of the book. This can often come in the form of advice that they reject or choose to ignore, because they must learn it for themselves. This is your theme.

A Man Called Ove by Fredrik Backman

> [Ove's wife] believed in destiny. That all the roads you walk in life, in one way or another, "lead toward what has been predetermined for you."[25]

3. Theme and Counter-Theme

Many writers don't know their theme when they start, so if you have no idea, don't worry. Theme is basically whatever idea you have about humanity that you want to explore in the course of the story, and it often ties in to the theme-stated moment, whatever your protagonist needs to learn. To decide on a theme, think about a statement of your own beliefs that might connect to this story. For example: "Kindness to others overcomes financial hardship." Expand it to add a reason to the statement: "Kindness to others overcomes financial hardship because you will have what you need and plenty of people to love you." Now think of the counter-theme, whatever would be the opposite. Often, your antagonist will embody the counter-theme. Perhaps it would be: "Money alone keeps you safe and secure; kindness cannot put food in your belly."

Write Your Book: Add a kindness or advice moment to demonstrate theme.

Act One, Plot Point 1: The Imperfect Life

Step 1: Identify your theme. If you're not quite sure, think about how you want the main character to grow throughout the book. This might demonstrate the theme. Who could give them some advice in this scene? How can you show their inner kindness?

Step 2: Look at what you've already written and notice what you utilize the most—description, thoughts, actions, or dialogue. Aim for a balance. Whatever you do the most, decrease that today; whatever you do the least, increase it.

Busy Writer Recap and Reward: Days 13–16

Act One, Plot Point 1: The Imperfect Life

You've finished your first scene. Congratulations! You've now hooked the reader and pulled us into a gripping story with a fascinating main character. This is huge, people! Remember, every four days you're finishing a plot point—this may be one or more scenes or chapters, but either way, we're moving on to the next plot point. Get ready: This snowball is gathering speed. Keep going! Now for the reward: I'm going to suggest a nice neck massage or foot massage and some ramen . . . *really* slurp that ramen. Let those noodles slap your face. *Mmmm.*

Nurture Your Creativity

One-Minute Meditation

The key to success is starting small . . . this is also true for meditation. If you've never meditated, try it for just one minute simply by focusing on your breathing. Use it as a transition in the car before you drive and when you arrive. Try it now. One minute. Breathe deeply into your belly. That's roughly five deep inhales and exhales. You can do this any time you need a fast reset or whenever you feel dysregulated, stressed, or anxious. You can also use this tool to set the intention to have a peaceful interaction with someone.

Jacqueline Woodson ***(Brown Girl Dreaming)***

on Writing Without Worry

"I always start writing saying no one is ever going to see this. . . . That way, I'm freed up to put on the page what I might not if I thought someone was going to read it. Then I read it out loud so I'm able to identify what I feel safe putting into the world. That gets me to the next step."[26]

Busy Writer Road Map Days 17-20: Tension

Tension is not just for fight scenes or car crashes; you need it in every scene even if it's just a hint of danger coming to spark the reader's curiosity and to signal a change. If you were verbally telling this story, would your listener lean in or yawn? Use the tools in this section to avoid being like your old uncle Herbert droning on at Thanksgiving.

Act One, Plot Point 2: The Inciting Incident

The Inciting Incident is the big life-changing moment in the character's life, the whole reason for your book. I think (and hope) everyone will have brainstormed this by now, unless you skipped the entire planning section in this book. If you did, it's not too late. Plan it now.

Ideas and Examples

1. Receiving a lot of money (*The Inheritance Games* by Jennifer Lynn Barnes)
2. Being invited to a special school (*Harry Potter and the Sorcerer's Stone* by J. K. Rowling)
3. Starting a new job (*The Silent Patient* by Alex Michaelides)
4. Hurting a loved one (*The Kite Runner* by Khaled Hosseini)
5. Meeting the love interest (*Lessons in Chemistry* by Bonnie Garmus)

Day 17: Foreshadowing

Have you ever had an itch in the back of your mind, the sense that something bad was about to happen? You walk into a party and something feels off. You hear the crunch of a beer can in a dark parking lot. You're on a date and they hold your hand too tightly. How do you react?

In real life, there's foreshadowing everywhere. We just don't always notice it. In fiction, those same warnings and red flags build tension, especially if the protagonist ignores them.

You don't need to resort to clichés like "It was a dark and stormy night." Foreshadowing can be anywhere: at the start, in the middle, or in the cliffhanger. It's also not just for thrillers or horror; every genre uses it to signal that something bad is coming. But to use it effectively, you must know what's ahead. That's why planning matters.

10 Types of Foreshadowing to Hook Your Reader

#1: Direct Foreshadowing

The Beginning of After by Jennifer Castle

> Anyone who's had something truly crappy happen to them will tell you: It's all about Before and After. What I'm talking about here is the ka-pow, shake-you-to-your-core-and-turn-your-bones-to-plastic kind of crappy. One part of your life unyokes from the other.[1]

#2: A Bad Feeling

The Scorpio Races by Maggie Stiefvater

> She is my mare and my best friend, and I keep waiting for something bad to happen to her, because I love her too much.[2]

#3: A Lack of a Bad Feeling

Daughter of Smoke & Bone by Laini Taylor

> Walking to school over the snow-muffled cobbles, Karou had no sinister premonitions about the day.[3]

#4: Suspicious Behavior and Bad Weather

Something Wicked This Way Comes by Ray Bradbury

> The seller of lightning rods arrived just ahead of the storm. He came along the street of Green Town, Illinois, in the late cloudy October day, sneaking glances over his shoulder. Somewhere not so far

back, vast lightnings stomped the earth. Somewhere, a storm like a great beast with terrible teeth could not be denied.[4]

In this case, nearly every line displays a form of foreshadowing.

#5: Ignoring Red Flags or Early Signs of Danger

The Shining by Stephen King: Jack's job interview to be a caretaker at a hotel is filled with red flags he ignores: isolation, strange noises in the attic, and the story of a previous caretaker who killed his family. Jack keeps saying it'll be fine, and the reader just thinks, *Oh, no, you are all dead.*

#6: A Dream

Moby-Dick by Herman Melville: Captain Ahab dreams of his own death.

#7: A Prophesy

Romeo and Juliet by William Shakespeare: In the prologue's chorus, we learn that the star-crossed lovers will take their own lives.

#8: A Dangerous Object or Protective Object (Chekhov's Gun)

Anton Chekhov said: "If in the first act you have hung a pistol on the wall, then in the following one it should be fired."[5]

The Fellowship of the Ring by J. R. R. Tolkien: Bilbo gives Frodo a chain mail shirt that later protects him against an orc attack.

#9: Warnings from Nature—Strange Animal Behavior or a Storm

Leave the World Behind by Rumaan Alam: Early deer sightings become more frequent, until the girl, Rose, sees dozens. The narrator reveals:

> Had she been up higher, she'd have understood there were hundreds, more than a thousand, more than that, even.[6]

Thousands? Run, Rose, run!

#10: Symbolism—Use of an Object, Color, Event, or Image to Foreshadow

Lord of the Flies by William Golding: The boys kill a pig and put the head on a stake. This foreshadows the death of one of the boys.

Write Your Book: Add foreshadowing.

Act One, Plot Point 2: The Inciting Incident

Step 1: If you haven't fully brainstormed the inciting incident, do that now. Jot down notes on setting, characters, goals, and conflict. Then close your eyes and drop into your protagonist's body. What are they doing physically?

Step 2: Hook the reader with foreshadowing and write fast. Use all the tools we've worked on previously: scene structure, hooks, details, and voice. We're scaffolding skills as you continue, adding each new skill rather than ignoring the earlier skills.

Remember: You don't need to finish a scene or chapter every day. A plot point may extend across a couple of scenes or just one. The plot points are here to guide and inspire you, not to restrain you. Some writers find it helpful to stop for the day in the middle of a scene so their imagination keeps working at it while they're not writing. (If you do this, I recommend leaving yourself a note so you can pick right back up again tomorrow.)

Day 18: Scene Questions

Yesterday I discovered a bite on our goldendoodle's butt. All the hair was ripped off, and something had broken the skin. The mystery is what bit him. He'd had no recent interactions with other dogs. Did a coyote get into the backyard? A rabid raccoon? An opossum? A scene question is the mysterious butt bite in your book, a line or detail that makes the reader wonder.

After the first hook, draw the reader through the scene with scene questions, which you can think of as mini hooks within your chapter. You make the reader wonder and then you answer the question in their mind; and then you plant a new question.

Drop details like breadcrumbs so that the reader follows the trail you're laying for them; you want to pose questions so intriguing they *have* to keep reading to find out the answer. Examples of scene questions are: "Why did he look at the housekeeper that way?" "Why is a tall black hat sitting on the sofa?" "Where is the daughter hiding?" "What is that sound in the closet?" If you're working in the mystery/thriller space, you may want to have more breadcrumbs, or even misleading details (called red herrings); but you need scene questions no matter what type of fiction you're writing—from romance, to fantasy, to contemporary fiction.

Gone Girl by Gillian Flynn

When Nick enters his apparently "burglarized" home, he notices that his wife's favorite vase is on the ground, intact. He notes that she always put it away when the cleaners came, so it wouldn't get smashed. Besides the major scene question of what's happened to Amy, we wonder: *Why is the vase not broken?*

The Handmaid's Tale by Margaret Atwood

Offred describes Nick and shows she's both attracted to him and suspicious of him, which makes the reader suspicious.

> He's too casual, he's not servile enough. It may be stupidity, but I don't think so. Smells fishy, they used to say; or, I smell a rat. Misfit as odor. Despite myself, I think of how he might smell. Not fish or decaying rat; tanned skin, moist in the sun, filmed with smoke.[7]

Write Your Book: Add a scene question.

Act One, Plot Point 2: The Inciting Incident

Step 1: Your protagonist may notice something strange about another character or something mysterious in the setting. An out-of-place object like an alarm clock in the woods, a strange sound like a loud pop at a swimming pool, or suspicious body language—two people give each other a look or a man glances over his shoulder.

Step 2: As you continue, add more mysterious details. Plant the question and answer it. Lead the reader forward, like you're sprinkling breadcrumbs along a path.

Day 19: Internal and External Conflict

You've built tension in the inciting incident by foreshadowing what's to come and making the reader curious by planting scene questions. Now it's time for that pivotal moment that changes your protagonist's life.

Your task is to create a riveting scene by weaving together internal and external conflict. This doesn't always mean explosions or fights—it depends on the genre—but every inciting incident contains both internal struggle and external obstacles.

Internal conflict is the protagonist's private struggle—fears, insecurities, decisions.

External conflict is whatever stands in the way of their goal.

Symptoms of Being Human by Jeff Garvin

This novel is about a gender-fluid teen's experience at a new school after a previous bullying situation. In the inciting incident, they start at a new school.

Internal Conflict: Riley's walking into the school, and their goal is directly stated:

I want to be invisible.[8]

External Conflict: Some girls are mean.
Internal Conflict: Riley runs to the bathroom and reacts:

I haven't been here five minutes, and the harassment has already started.[9]

Riley has to make a choice about what to do next, stay in the bathroom or go to their first class. They choose to get to the class quickly in order to find a good seat.

Charlie and the Chocolate Factory by Roald Dahl

Internal conflict: Charlie finds money and struggles over a decision about whether to buy chocolate for a chance to get the winning ticket or to save the money for his family. He buys the chocolate and gets a Golden Ticket. This is great news, but he has a strong emotional internal reaction and freezes.
External Conflict: People surround Charlie, trying to buy the winning ticket:

Charlie hadn't moved. He hadn't even unwrapped the Golden Ticket from around the candy bar. He was standing very still, holding it tightly with both hands while the crowd pushed and shouted all around him. He felt quite dizzy.[10]

As you can see, the conflict jumps between internal conflict and external conflict. Even in fast-paced action, don't skip the internal conflict. It's common to forget thoughts, mental reactions, fears, or insecurities in this type of scene, but we need both.

Your job is to transport the reader into the protagonist's mind *and* body. If the main character is cornered in a fight, we should flinch when a thick fist swings toward them. We should hear their fears and their decisions. If a little boy is running through a crowd, searching for his mom, the reader should be that boy, dodging hips and handbags, breathing in perfume and body odor, and feeling the thwack of a lady's hair, while deciding which way to go, terrified that Mom is gone forever.

Write Your Book: Add internal and external conflict.

Act One, Plot Point 2: The Inciting Incident

Step 1: Dive into the protagonist's thoughts, worries, fears, and decision-making. Begin by writing what's in their mind to show internal conflict.

Step 2: Describe where they are, activating all the senses. Embody the protagonist so that you feel like you've become the character. In this way, the reader will also be transported into the scene. If you're writing a high-action scene, focus on the sense of touch to transport the reader into the protagonist's body. Also use tight language—short sentences and fragments to speed up the pacing of the scene. Make sure you add internal and external conflict.

Day 20: Cliffhangers and Curiosity

Do you need a strung-out drug dealer to point a gun at your accountant protagonist to create a satisfying cliffhanger? In short, no. A cliffhanger merely makes the reader curious enough that they want to keep reading. Look at chapter endings in your mentor book; I'm sure that every chapter doesn't end with life-or-death stakes, but the end of the chapter usually makes the reader curious enough to move on to the next chapter.

Remember, the end of the chapter is not an actual ending to your story—you're opening narrative pathways, not resolving them. Think of it more like a stop in the middle of the action. Make the reader desperate to turn the page, but avoid cheesy life-and-death cliffhangers like getting knocked out or fainting. It shouldn't feel like a trick, but more like you're stopping at a moment of decision or revelation or danger.

To demonstrate that cliffhangers are necessary for all books, even literary novels, I'm going to give you actual chapter endings in the following literary bestseller.

The Seven Husbands of Evelyn Hugo by Taylor Jenkins Reid

Who the hell was Evelyn Hugo in love with?[11]

"Yes, ready. Go for it. What happened next?"[12]

We were married for two months before he started hitting me.[13]

"Celia St. James is going to ruin everything."[14]

That's when I started to take a liking to Celia St. James.[15]

And now I'm finally starting to suspect that I should be scared.[16]

Common Mistakes for Chapter Endings

1. **Putting your characters to sleep.**

   The reader is likely to go to sleep, too, and they may forget to pick your book back up. If you put your character to sleep, you may have less fire to keep writing the next day. In Henry Miller's 11 Commandments on Writing, he said writers need to end their writing in the middle of a scene so that they know what they're going to write next. (I've mentioned this trick above.)

2. **Adding a final summary paragraph.**

   If you summarize the chapter or how they feel about the day, this is the opposite of a cliffhanger. We have no questions. Author Tim Wynne-Jones shared this trick with me from one of his editors: "Lay a ruler under the last line of your chapter and then move the ruler up the page to see if you've already written a better chapter ending."

3. **Ending on description.**

   In this case, you're simply describing for the sake of the description—a character staring out at the sunset or the rain. If you end on description, make sure there's something mysterious that the protagonist notices. Keep our curiosity.

4. **Ending on reflection.**

   Too much internal monologue or too many thoughts at the end of a scene can also feel like a summary. If we don't have a question in our head, we may not keep reading.

Write Your Book: End your chapter with a cliffhanger.

Act One, Plot Point 2: The Inciting Incident

Step 1: In the scene you're working on now, build the action, conflict, and tension with the tools we've learned so far. Draft through to the end of your current chapter.

Step 2: End with a cliffhanger. For this particular plot point, we're often left wondering how your protagonist will react to what's just happened; or you could leave us with more of a danger-based cliffhanger in which we're left with a life-or-death question.

Busy Writer Recap and Reward: Days 17–20

Act One, Plot Point 2: The Inciting Incident

You're speeding along! In the last four days, you finished the inciting incident. You worked on tension, conflict, scene questions, foreshadowing, and cliffhangers. Remember: forward movement. Don't go back and fix the beginning. By the time you finish this draft, you may want to rewrite the opening anyway, so *onward*. Give yourself a reward! Eat a giant pickle or pet a frog. (Don't eat the pet frog.)

Nurture Your Creativity

Meditation: What Are You Thinking?

For five minutes, breathe, clear your mind, and observe your thoughts. You're not judging the thoughts or trying not to think. Meditation is about awareness. Notice each thought as it passes and label it: a worry thought, future fear, plan, regret, imagination, judgment, observation. Then let it go. Maybe you remember you forgot to switch the laundry—label it "planning thought." Come back to the breath. You may find it impossible to stay blank. That's the point. Meditation helps you become *aware* of your thoughts. Next, you remember that dumb thing you said to your sister-in-law about the mac and cheese (regret thought). Return to the breath. A few seconds later, you're imagining a man with a knife chasing you (imagination thought). Now you know where your thoughts go. . . . So, next, consider: Where do your protagonist's thoughts go?

Busy Writer Road Map Days 21–24: Character Reactions

The way everyone responds to the inciting incident will show who they are at their core. We all face hardship, criticism, and tragedy, but how we react in the face of crisis depends on core impulses, backgrounds, experiences, fears, strengths, weaknesses, and limiting beliefs. This is your chance to show these layers of your characters' personalities.

Act One, Plot Point 3: First Response

For this plot point, focus on what your protagonist feels and how they react. When faced with the inciting incident, do they act heroically? Do they freeze? Why? The other characters will also react, so make sure you show what they do and say—this is how we'll get to know who they are.

Ideas and Examples

1. Avoiding the future love interest (*Twilight* by Stephenie Meyer)
2. Refusing the case (*Murder on the Orient Express* by Agatha Christie)
3. Calling the police or getting help (*Gone Girl* by Gillian Flynn)
4. Escaping to survive (*The Bourne Identity* by Robert Ludlum)
5. Pretending compliance (*The Handmaid's Tale* by Margaret Atwood)

Day 21: Core Impulse

If a man in a ski mask bursts into your house and demands your valuables, how do you respond? Your response shows a lot about you, for better or for worse. In stressful moments, our core impulse kicks in—we freeze, fight, flee, or fawn. You may freeze. Your kid might flee (let's hope). Your great-aunt may fight the intruder with an umbrella, which, surprisingly, has a secret knife in the tip. Your brother might bargain, "Take anything, just please let us go." That's the fawn response, typical of the peacekeeper.

Remember to question gendered responses; it's not necessarily the man who will choose to fight. Question any biases you might have as you write this novel, and let yourself be surprised by your characters. Show the main character's thoughts, as well as everyone else's actions and dialogue, to reveal more about their personalities.

Next, consider what each character would perceive as a threat. If the intruder is a little girl in a chicken costume, they may react differently . . . unless demons in this world typically look like little girls in chicken costumes. Characters perceive danger based on their past experiences, fears, family history, and triggers.

The Hunger Games by Suzanne Collins

When Katniss's sister is chosen for the Hunger Games, Katniss freezes. She compares it to falling out of a tree:

> It was as if the impact had knocked every wisp of air from my lungs, and I lay there struggling to inhale, to exhale, to do anything.[1]

Others react around her. A boy grabs her arm. The crowd is murmuring. Then Collins zooms in:

> I see the back of her blouse has become untucked and hangs out over her shirt. It's this detail, the untucked blouse forming a ducktail, that brings me back to myself.[2]

The tiny detail unfreezes Katniss; she runs after her sister and volunteers to go instead.

Write Your Book: Portray the characters' core impulses.

Act One, Plot Point 3: First Response

Step 1: First, imagine the setting, characters, scene goal, and obstacle. Decide how each character will respond based on their personality and core impulse.

Step 2: To start your scene, focus on the immediate, core impulse response in your protagonist. You can even try a simile or metaphor to capture the core impulse. Then zoom in on a detail that represents the chaos of this moment. On Day 22, you'll be exploring how characters react and why they react the way they do.

Day 22: Backstory

On a subway platform, a woman has just been stabbed in her thigh. Your teen protagonist runs up. His past will play a role in whether he knows what to do or panics. If he has training or experience, he'll point at a bystander, instruct them to call 911 and report back to him; then he'll apply pressure to the wound and elevate it. From years of lifeguarding and lifeguarding competitions in my teens and twenties, I still have a mantra in my brain for these situations: PIE—pressure, ice, elevation.

A person with no first aid experience or training may panic. Their lizard brain and core impulse will kick in. A person with trauma involving blood, even a car accident, may go into shock and pass out. If they tend to avoid taking responsibility, maybe that wasn't safe when they were a kid. This is why you need to know the backstory for each character to understand how they'll react.

As author Margaret Atwood says in her MasterClass, we have to consider "all of these interactions that change us, that reveal us to ourselves, that reveal us to other people, and therefore to the reader. So, somebody, let's give them an automobile accident, they run over their neighbor's cat, do they tell? Do they pretend somebody else did it? Do they dispose of the body?"[3] What they do no doubt depends on how they were raised or what they've learned since their childhood.

Write Your Book: Show the reactions.

Act One, Plot Point 3: First Response

Step 1: You've gone over the protagonist's reaction. Now think about other characters in the scene. Consider each character's backstory to decide how they'll react to what just happened.

Step 2: As you draft, show their reactions. Do not give us a big flashback scene, even if the protagonist is triggered. At most, it might be a short paragraph. Let it show up in the dialogue, actions, or in the protagonist's thoughts for a line or two. We want to save flashbacks for later, once we know them better. Try to stay in the current scene.

Step 3: Remember to add a balance of dialogue, action, description, and thoughts to the scene.

Day 23: Comfort & Discomfort Body Language

Does your detective bite the end of his pencil when working a case? This is called a pacifying gesture. We all have our favorites. For example, you may squeeze your earlobe, rub your legs, bite your nails, lick your lips, rub your eyes, mess around with an object, adjust your bra strap or tie, apply lip gloss, or click a pen. The more anxious we are, the more often we do these pacifying gestures, and sometimes we don't even know we're doing them.

Eighty percent of communication is nonverbal, so it's important to understand the science of body language to avoid clichés. Many writers struggle with body language, often resorting to repetitive actions like shrugs or nods, which, if you act them out, would feel odd within the scene. One easy way to avoid many of the clichés is to get away from facial body language—wincing, smirking, winking, glaring, narrowing your eyes. Instead, think of neck-down body language. What could they do with an object? What are their hands and feet doing?

If you get the body language right, your reader will feel whatever your protagonist is feeling because their mirror neurons are triggered.

These empathy neurons are why we want to cry when our friend is crying.

Comfort Body Language

Think about what you do when you're comfortable with someone. You lean toward them. Hug them. You might mirror their body language without even realizing it. Your body relaxes.

The Mysterious Benedict Society and the Perilous Journey
by Trenton Lee Stewart

> Kate's greeting, delivered at full tilt, was more of a football tackle than a hug . . . [4]

Discomfort Body Language

When you're uncomfortable or nervous, you show that discomfort in your body, even if your face is masking it. You tense up, fidget with your hands or with an object, or move away from the source of discomfort. Your feet may point in the direction of the door. You may shield yourself with your arms or with an object.

The Goldfinch by Donna Tartt

> . . . her hands were shaky as she re-tied her scarf . . . [5]

Joey Pigza Loses Control by Jack Gantos

> . . . Mom was driving with both hands clamped tightly around the wheel as if she had me by the neck. I had been snapping my seat belt on and off and driving her nuts by asking a hundred *what-ifs* about Dad.[6]

Write Your Book: Show comfort or discomfort body language.

Act One, Plot Point 3: First Response

Step 1: Picture the other characters in the scene from the protagonist's perspective. What are they doing with their bodies? Are their feet tapping? Are they clenching the steering wheel? How does the protagonist interpret these actions?

Step 2: As you write your scene, show what other people do, physically, as they discuss the inciting incident. Show who feels comfortable or uncomfortable.

Day 24: Who's in Control?

Is your protagonist a bag floating in the wind or are they the wind?

If they're not the wind, *who* or *what* is?

"Locus of control" is a psychological concept to explain how we respond to the events in our lives, and whether we feel we have control over what happens to us. We have either an internal or an external locus of control, and I think this is an important concept to explore, not only for our protagonists, but also for ourselves.

Internal Locus of Control: "I'm in charge of my destiny."

In modern bestsellers, protagonists often believe their success or failure depends on them, and they attempt to change their situation. They're able to handle stress, rejection, and failure, and they're motivated to make a change. Obviously, this is a typical hero or heroine—they have a sense of agency, taking meaningful actions toward their goals.

***The Hunger Games* by Suzanne Collins**: From chapter one, Katniss Everdeen hunts in the woods to feed her mom and sister, even though it's forbidden, and when her sister's name is called, she volunteers. At that point, she doesn't give up; she plans to win.

External Locus of Control: "I have no say. Others control my life."

For the external locus of control, the protagonist believes others are in charge of what happens. As a result, they're passive and resist taking action to change their situation. They might resist what Joseph Campbell refers to as "the call to action" after the inciting incident. In a positive change arc, they move from being passive to being active, from victim to hero.

***The Catcher in the Rye* by J. D. Salinger**: Holden Caulfield believes he has no control over his life at the beginning. He dislikes his school and doesn't feel that he has the power to change his situation. When a teacher encourages him to play a game, he says it's fun only if you're with the "hot-shots."[7] He doesn't feel he can control whether he wins or not, and he doesn't want to try. This novel has a positive change arc, so he transforms to having an internal locus of control.

***The Metamorphosis* by Franz Kafka**: Gregor Samsa works as a traveling salesman and complains about the extra hardship, the bad food, and the lack of friendships. Most of all, he blames his parents.

> If I didn't hold back for my parents' sake, I'd have quit ages ago.[8]

This novel features a negative change arc; Gregor turns into a cockroach and, in the end, he dies.

Write Your Book: Show who's in control.

Act One, Plot Point 3: First Response

Step 1: Think about your protagonist's sense of empowerment. Do they feel motivated to act, or do they feel like they're powerless?

Step 2: Show your protagonist's feelings about their own sense of control through their thoughts and dialogue. Show who or what urges them forward. If someone else is in control, show this in their thoughts and actions.

Busy Writer Recap and Reward: Days 21–24

Act One, Plot Point 3: First Response

Your book is on fire! Well, I hope not literally on fire like in *Fahrenheit 451,* but you're doing great. You're coming to the end of Act One. That's a big deal. Keep working on those skills and following the road. Consider your own locus of control. Do you believe you're in charge of your own success? I do. I *know* you can achieve your goal if you just keep writing every day and working on improving your craft. Writing a novel is no different from any other hard-earned goal. You are in charge of your success. Another plot point done: How will you reward yourself? Reward suggestions: fifty-seven M&M's or concert tickets (cheap seats are fun too).

Nurture Your Creativity

A Power Pose + A Countdown

Reach your arms out right now in a V above your head. Clench your fists with your thumbs pointed toward each other. Breathe in and out through your nose, pumping your belly. Do this for one minute. At the end, take in a deep breath, hold, and exhale. This will not only release stress, it will also expand your personal aura and your ability to do hard things. Now give yourself the 5 Second Challenge. This concept is detailed in Mel Robbins's book *The 5 Second Rule*. You count down from 5 to 1 and then you do whatever you intend to do. No more procrastination. 5-4-3-2-1. Now let's get ready to write!

John Steinbeck shared some writing advice in a letter to Robert Wallsten in February 1962.

You can find his original advice in the 1979 book Steinbeck: A Life in Letters, *but here's what stood out to me:*

1. Steinbeck recommends you adjust your expectations, aiming not to finish but to just write one page per day, and let yourself be surprised when you find yourself with 400 drafted pages.
2. Avoid the urge to edit or rewrite while you're drafting.
3. And write to an "ideal reader."[9]

Busy Writer Road Map Days 25–28: Goals and Obstacles

A basic element of scene design is that every chapter is its own mini novel or story and has a beginning, middle, and end. Every scene must move the story forward in some way; goals and obstacles are an essential part of that design. In the next four days, we'll be working on the big-picture goal versus the scene goal, the reasons why the characters pursue one goal over another, and how to choose obstacles that might stand in their way.

Act One, Plot Point 4: The New Goal

After the inciting incident, your protagonist commits to a concrete, external goal. They'll pursue this goal for at least the first half of the book, when their end goal may change. This book goal must have stakes—it must carry real consequences for failure.

Ideas and Examples

1. Rescuing a loved one (*The Princess Bride* by William Goldman)
2. Making friends at a new school (*Symptoms of Being Human* by Jeff Garvin)
3. Solving a case (*Murder on the Orient Express* by Agatha Christie)
4. Saving Earth (*Project Hail Mary* by Andy Weir)
5. Reaching safety during an apocalypse (*The Road* by Cormac McCarthy)

Day 25: Book Goal Versus Scene Goal

After the inciting incident, the main character will generally have a new book goal—this is different from a scene goal. The book goal is what they're fighting to achieve by the end, hitting obstacles along the way. In a two-goal plot, that big-picture goal shifts at the midpoint. Avoid vague goals like "be happy." Even in a romance, the goal isn't necessarily to fall in love; in fact, it may be to *avoid* falling in love to keep a job or satisfy family pressures, as in *Romeo and Juliet*. A more nuanced goal will make for a more intriguing plot.

You also have a big-picture goal: to write a novel! Like any difficult goal, you'll need smaller daily goals: a regular practice of writing, which is essentially your scene goal.

This is true for anyone with a goal. A soccer player who's trying to win a soccer championship needs to practice multiple times a week. A pianist who wants to play Carnegie Hall needs to practice piano every day. These experts do not ask themselves whether they feel like practicing. They make it a priority.

You'll achieve your goal in the same way. Move forward in your novel each day by following this guide or doing 15 Magic Minutes. Essentially, this is *your* scene goal. If you aren't writing frequently, ask yourself why, because it will inform what might be holding your character back.

You may be facing external obstacles, but in my experience, the internal obstacles are our real barriers. Examine any subconscious goals that may conflict with your big goal. Look at the fears or insecurities standing in your way. Maybe you want to avoid criticism. That's natural. This is why a habit is essential—this way, you don't give that fear a voice. You just do it, like brushing your teeth. (It's a rough draft. Don't worry. Nobody ever needs to see it.)

Now let's turn to your protagonist. What's their big goal and what's interfering with their scene goal? Usually, it's tied to their fear, misbelief, and/or flaw.

In a detective story, the big-picture goal is to find the murderer, but in each scene, the detective will have a scene goal—she wants to interview the neighbor or scour the internet for a suspect's alternate identity.

In a magic school story, the big-picture goal is to become a witch or a wizard; but maybe the kid will have smaller scene goals, like mastering a spell or learning to ride a broom or controlling their power.

Key Points to Remember for the Big-Picture Goal

1. The inciting incident triggers the character's new goal.
2. They have reasons to pursue this goal, which should be apparent to the reader (or become apparent as the plot progresses).
3. There's a big reward for getting what they want and a consequence if they don't.
4. The protagonist and antagonist will oppose each other in their pursuit of their goals.
5. What the protagonist wants should be hard to get—this is essential for tension.

Scene Goals

Author Kurt Vonnegut talked about the importance of a goal in every scene, even something trivial. He told writers to make sure their characters want something right away,

> even if it's only a glass of water. . . . One of my students wrote a story about a nun who got a piece of dental floss stuck between her lower left molars, and who couldn't get it out all day long.[1]

The scene goal is a concrete, short-term objective your character is pursuing in this particular scene, and for a reason.

Goal: Find a place to sit at the lunch table.

Reason: Avoid looking like a nerd.

The other characters also have scene goals; tension rises when those goals conflict. This creates subtext in the dialogue, because the other characters may be hiding what they want, pretending to go along with what the protagonist wants, when really they have another agenda.

***Murder on the Orient Express* by Agatha Christie**

Inciting Incident: A passenger on the train is dead.

Book Goal: Detective Poirot wants to find the murderer.

Let's look at the scene goals and obstacles leading up to the inciting incident.

Scene 1 Goal: The detective, Poirot, wants an uneventful trip to Istanbul.

Obstacle: A telegram forces him back to London immediately.

Scene 2 Goal: On the train, Poirot is hoping to remain unnoticed.

Obstacle: Ratchett wants to hire him for protection. Poirot refuses.

Scene 3 Goal: Poirot wants to sleep; the killer wants to kill; the conductor wants order.

Obstacle: A bell, a thud, and a voice wakes up Poirot.

Is this pattern of scene goal–obstacle just for thrillers or high-octane fantasy? No. This is useful in any novel. Let's look at a bestselling YA romance. It's not as high stakes, but there is a directionality to the scenes.

***The Summer I Turned Pretty* by Jenny Han**

Inciting Incident: Isabel arrives at the vacation house.

Book Goal: She wants to make it the best summer ever and get a boyfriend.

Scene 1 Goal: She wants to get to the vacation house.

Obstacle: Her brother is driving too slowly.

Scene 2 Goal: They arrive, and she wants to look at her two former crushes without them noticing her . . . an easy goal, she thinks.

Obstacle: They notice her, and treat her differently.

Write Your Book: Show the big-picture goal and a scene goal.

Act One, Plot Point 4: The New Goal

Step 1: Brainstorm the six key elements of your scene if you didn't do this yet (at least mentally): purpose, setting, characters, goal, action, conflict.

Step 2: As you write this plot point, show the protagonist's thoughts and fears about the big-picture goal and maybe let them discuss it with someone else. Remember, the other characters have their own conflicting goals.

Day 26: Trauma, Wants, Needs, Yearning

Have you ever wanted something very badly, like a car, a relationship, better grades, or a promotion, but then you got it and that happy feeling faded? That's because the external reward is just a temporary dopamine hit. You haven't satisfied an inner need or yearning. The following example shows the protagonist's inner yearning.

Fear of Flying by Erica Jong

And what about those other longings which marriage stifled? Those longings to hit the open road from time to time, to discover whether you could still live alone inside your own head, to discover whether you could manage to survive in a cabin in the woods without going mad; to discover, in short, whether you were still whole after so many years of being half of something (like the back two legs of a horse outfit on the vaudeville stage).[2]

We all *want* things on a surface level, driven by fear, pride, or the belief that success will make us happy. But we *need* things on a deeper level—and this is where we find that true fulfillment. Lasting contentment doesn't come from achievement; it comes from growth, and that's exactly what your protagonist must discover.

What stands in the way of us getting what we deeply yearn for? Usually, it's our trauma, flaw, and misbelief. Our characters are exactly the same. Below are two examples of trauma and the resulting wants and needs.

Trauma: A boy's brother is murdered.

Misbeliefs: Revenge will heal his pain. The death is his fault, since he was supposed to be there.

Surface Want: Now he *wants* revenge—this is his surface goal. We all know the death of someone else is not going to bring him happiness. He still won't have his brother.

Deeper Need: If you look at the feeling under the feeling, you may find it easier to figure out what he actually *needs*. Under the rage, the boy is sad. He *needs* to forgive himself and possibly his brother's killer.

Trauma: Her best friend dumped her in a vulnerable moment.

Misbeliefs: She is not lovable. She can't trust anyone.

Surface Want: Now she wants a partner. She scours the dating sites: "It's a numbers game!" But every time she dates someone, she becomes jealous and sabotages the relationship.

Deeper Need: What she *needs* is self-love. I know, sorry, that's cheesy, but it's real. If she doesn't learn this, she'll repeat the same patterns.

When you explore your character's desire line, you allow the reader to connect to your character. Even if we think we just want to pick up a fun beach read or a page-turning thriller, deep down we all want to learn just a bit more about ourselves and the world. The yearning and hope under the surface is where the heat of your story burns.

Write Your Book: Show your character's inner yearning.

Act One, Plot Point 4: The New Goal

Step 1: Show what your protagonist longs for as you continue to write in their thoughts and observations. What makes them think about this longing? Often, they'll notice someone else who seems to have what they want, representing that inner yearning. An object may symbolize that yearning.

Step 2: Write quickly to tap into the raw emotion. Let it be a bit of a dump, a free-association type of writing, fragments, or run-ons . . . surprise yourself. Then dive into their imagination. What do they imagine life would be like if they could get what they crave and need?

Day 27: Obstacles

In The Worst-Case Scenario Card Game (which I recommend for writers—it's based on the bestselling book series), you put down five cards featuring terrible situations. One person chooses their order for what is the worst. The others guess what that person's answers would be. The person who has the most correct guesses wins, but people rarely guess correctly. Why? One person's worst-case scenario is no big deal for someone else, and it's hard to imagine someone you know and love would rather grow an unremovable tail versus wrestle an alligator, or vice-versa.

Various obstacles represent different levels of challenge to each individual. Some people faint at the sight of a needle, while others willingly spend hundreds of dollars to go to an acupuncturist. One person might happily jump out of a plane on a random Tuesday, but for others, even the thought of getting on a plane has them curled up in the corner of the airport's Starbucks.

Your character's worst-case scenario might not be physical; it may be emotional. For example, they may fear rejection, losing a family member, failing a test, or public speaking. They'd rather be covered in tarantulas, get stuck underwater in a car, or snowboard over a hundred-foot cliff than suffer a heartbreak or be mocked on social media.

What would your character perceive as the highest form of danger? Would it be emotional or physical? This can inform the challenges you place in front of them. As they pursue their scene goal today, make sure they hit an obstacle that is especially difficult for them, based on their personal fears and insecurities.

Examples of Challenging Obstacles

1. **Physical attack:** an antagonist or trusted person hurts them
2. **Environment:** natural disaster, blackout, poisonous air or water
3. **Entrapment:** in a collapsing building, in the trunk of a car, in an elevator, in a bank vault
4. **Legal:** an arrest, a missing passport, a lawsuit, a permit issue
5. **Shortage:** food, money, oxygen, device power, electricity, time
6. **Fear:** heights, spiders, dogs, crowds, public speaking
7. **Verbal or emotional abuse:** rudeness, insults, hostility, neglect
8. **Coercion:** harming someone or doing something wrong under threat
9. **Communication:** language barrier, misunderstanding, tech breakdown
10. **Medical:** heart attack, mental health, cancer, asthma, allergic reaction

Write Your Book: Add a challenging obstacle.

Act One, Plot Point 4: The New Goal

Step 1: Set your timer for the amount of time you choose. Time is your obstacle, so write quickly, and don't edit. Your ultimate goal is to write a novel, not perfect a paragraph.

Step 2: As you write this scene, show your character actively pursuing their goal. Then throw a challenging obstacle into their path. It's not random, but something that happens as a result of their choices. This obstacle should be difficult for your character and interfere with their scene goal.

Day 28: Agency = Decisions + Actions

Agency is how your character pursues a scene goal through their decisions and actions. First, they have a goal; then they choose how to go after it; finally, they take action. Now they'll hit an obstacle, which they'll need to overcome. They'll make choices and then act.

In every scene, your protagonist takes steps to pursue their scene goal. Sometimes they succeed and sometimes they fail. Then they respond, reevaluate, and take the next action. The important element here is that they're *choosing* their next steps; that's agency.

Stuff can't just randomly happen *to* them. You don't want a story filled with coincidences. That's like watching a soccer game with no goals or goalies, just players running around on the field, dodging random lightning strikes.

Let's say your protagonist, Jack, is thirteen and he's at home alone at night for the first time. He's aiming to relax and watch TV, but then he hears a growling, otherworldly noise in the backyard. His parents said not to open the door, but he thinks it's some neighborhood kids trying to freak him out. He's got three options and a decision to make.

Option 1: Call his parents.
Option 2: Grab a kitchen knife.
Option 3: Open the door to prove he isn't scared.

As he evaluates the pros and cons, the reader will decide—should he open the door? He makes the decision: open the door. He wants to figure out who's messing with him and show them he's not afraid. (Has he *never* watched a horror movie?)

By showing his possible choices, the pros and cons, and the decision-making process before he takes a physical action, the reader has a chance to become a cocreator of the story. When the protagonist actively *chooses* a course of action, the reader becomes involved and thinks: *What would I do?* We argue mentally for the choice we think the character should make, and we keep reading to find out the result.

Make it clear that your character is making the decisions. They have agency; events aren't random. They aren't just a leaf being blown about in the wind. They *are* the wind.

Write Your Book: The protagonist takes decisive action.

Act One, Plot Point 4: The New Goal

Step 1: Start with your protagonist's thoughts about what they want in this scene.

Step 2: Show them taking actions to achieve it. They may make a mistake, misjudging other characters or the risks involved. What happens next is a result of the choices they've made. Show the decision-making on the page, so the reader is immersed in the scene and argues for what they think your character should do.

Busy Writer Recap and Reward: Days 25–28

Act One, Plot Point 4: The New Goal

You've finished Act One! I'm spinning for you just like one of those hippie girls at a Grateful Dead cover band concert. Now you're headed into Act Two. You're on a solid path. People with no plan and no writing guide often never get to this point. Reward suggestion: Get a tie-dye shirt and go to a Grateful Dead show . . . or a live show of any type. And eat street food.

Nurture Your Creativity

Plant Yourself in the Senses

This is a fast reset, often used for anxiety, but especially useful for us writers, since you will need to be able to transport yourself into your character's sensual experience.

1. Plant your feet on the ground. Breathe in. Identify the texture of the floor under your feet. Exhale. Now you're in your body.
2. Breathe in. Identify one specific thing you see. Exhale.
3. Breathe in. Identify something you hear. Exhale.
4. Breathe in. Identify a smell. Exhale.
5. Breathe in. Identify any area of tension in your body. Exhale. Let the tension go.

V. E. Schwab ***(The Invisible Life of Addie LaRue)***

on Writing the First Draft

For me, writing a first draft is one long doubt-ridden roller coaster, punctuated by brief moments of hope and long swells of you-suck-you-suck-you-suck.[3]

ACT TWO

You're into the second act, writers! First act done. Keep going! This act is all about the protagonist pushing toward their big goal. Get that draft down. Remember, it doesn't have to be perfect. Just have fun diving into your imagination.

Plot Point 5: New World and Allies (15–20%)

Plot Point 6: The Antagonist Threatens (20–25%)

Plot Point 7: Skills and Information (25–30%)

Plot Point 8: Subplot Challenge (30–35%)

Plot Point 9: Escalating Obstacles (35–45%)

Plot Point 10: False Hope (45–50%)

Plot Point 11: The Midpoint Shock (50–55%)

Busy Writer Road Map Days 29–32: Multisensory Descriptions

Now let's focus on descriptions, using all the senses to plant the reader in the scene and describing with the similes and metaphors what your protagonist would choose. As the protagonist enters this new or changed world post–inciting incident, you'll show the specific details *your main character* would notice, based on their life experience and way of seeing the world.

Act Two, Plot Point 5: New World and Allies

Once the protagonist commits to their goal, either they step into the new world or their regular world shifts. Sometimes, as in a portal story, the new world is the inciting incident. In this case, the goal happens afterward. In *The Wonderful Wizard of Oz* by L. Frank Baum, Dorothy doesn't have a goal until she steps into the new world and discovers she's not in Kansas. In this changed world, they usually experience a new location and meet new allies, enemies, and mentors. However, it may be that their world hasn't changed but their viewpoint of the world or the way people view them has changed.

Ideas and Examples

1. Taking strange transportation (*The Hunger Games* by Suzanne Collins)
2. Staying in the same world, but people see the protagonist differently (*Gone Girl* by Gillian Flynn)
3. Shopping in the new world (*Harry Potter and the Sorcerer's Stone* by J. K. Rowling)
4. Dealing with a new workplace culture (*The Firm* by John Grisham)
5. Exploring multiple worlds (*The Midnight Library* by Matt Haig)

Day 29: Sound and Touch

Sound and touch are powerful senses to show the contrast from the old world to the new, like in *The Wonderful Wizard of Oz* by L. Frank Baum, when Dorothy is transported through the roar of the Kansas tornado to the bright world of Oz filled with the sounds of the nearby waterfall.

Hooking with Sound

A mysterious sound can instantly hook the reader. Begin with the unexpected: a scratching sound in the closet, the beat of dragon wings, or the clatter of a dog's metal dish. Avoid familiar sounds, such as an alarm clock or a school bell. They feel like clichés and don't capture the reader's attention. Instead, choose a weird or ominous noise, something harder to identify. The reader's mind will get busy trying to figure out what it is.

Onomatopoeia

Onomatopoeia is the literary device in which the word sounds like the actual noise. *Bang! Crash! Hiss!* Onomatopoeia can be used in any book, not just kids' books.

Indian Shoes by Cynthia Leitich Smith

> Ray tracked Grampa's steps, danced to the *rat-a-tat-a-clang* of a trash-can band, and skipped beneath the ruffling branches.[1]

Ambient Noise

When you move somewhere new, every sound feels strange. After college, I moved to Seoul, and on my first day, an air-raid siren filled the air. I nearly dove for cover while locals strolled past me, not even *noticing* the sound. Later, in Los Angeles, police helicopters circled overhead, and I was sure a killer was lurking in my backyard. In New York City, truck brakes outside our apartment woke up the baby every night. Once we get used to these sounds, we may not even notice them. Go ahead, listen to your surroundings right now. My old Lab, Lola, is snoring, and our air-conditioning is humming. I didn't notice these sounds until now. However, since everything is new to your protagonist, they'll notice everything.

The Name of the Wind by Patrick Rothfuss

Silence adds suspense:

> It was quiet, as if everyone in the troupe was listening for something. As if they were all holding their breath.[2]

Music

I tend to forget music, but it can make a big impact on a scene, just as it can make a big impact on a room. Think about how it influences mood: country music in a nearly empty bar versus loud hip-hop at a crowded party.

Every Day by David Levithan

Consider the way your protagonist interprets the sound to reveal their personality:

> Justin listens to loud and obnoxious music on a loud and obnoxious station where loud and obnoxious DJs make loud and obnoxious jokes as a way of getting through the morning.[3]

Touch

Imagine yourself in your character's body. What are they stepping on—leaves, mud, or concrete? What does the hamburger feel like in their mouth—dry, juicy, or slimy? What are they touching with their hands—a cold wall or a baby's wiggling toes? Are they wearing an itchy wool sweater, a silk shirt, or soft flannel? Are they carrying anything? Do they feel any pain—an aching back or the sharp pain of a bleeding, ripped-off toenail?

The Maze Runner by James Dashner

Limit lighting and amplify sounds and the sense of touch:

> Metal ground against metal; a lurching shudder shook the floor beneath him. He fell down at the sudden movement and shuffled backward on his hands and feet, drops of sweat beading on his forehead despite the cool air.[4]

If I Ever Get Out of Here by Eric Gansworth

Show what your protagonist is touching:

> I left a few minutes later, starting my long walk home across half the reservation, still gripping the hank of hair. I opened my fingers a little every few yards to let the August breeze take some for the birds.[5]

Lord of the Flies by William Golding

Consider temperature and weight:

> He jumped down from the terrace. The sand was thick over his black shoes and the heat hit him. He became conscious of the weight of clothes . . .[6]

Write Your Book: Hook with sound and transport with touch.

Act Two, Plot Point 5: New World and Allies

Step 1: Listen to your character's new world. What sounds define it? Music, language, accents, slang, or dialect can put your characters on unstable footing. Everyday noises increase tension or hint at danger—loud neighbors, barking dogs, or a midnight chainsaw. Imagine these sounds before writing. What music is playing and how does that reflect their mood? Try listening to this music as you write.

Step 2: Hook the reader with a mysterious sound—a creak, a whisper, silence. Then layer in ambient noises, using them to heighten emotion and ground the reader in this place.

Day 30: Lighting and Color

Is your protagonist squinting in the bright sun in the middle of a baseball field? Huddled in a dark basement prison? Lying in a hospital bed under fluorescent ceiling lights? Relaxing next to the fireplace in their cozy cabin? Holding a torch?

You're the lighting designer of the movie you're creating in your reader's head.

You're also the set designer. You paint the colors that will pop on the page.

Lighting

Lighting sets the mood and adds tension and visual detail. In this new world, the lighting may be different from that in the old world, or the protagonist may perceive it differently. Their mood will affect how they perceive everything.

Sorcery of Thorns by Margaret Rogerson

Night fell as death rode into the Great Library of Summershall. It arrived within a carriage. Elizabeth stood in the courtyard and watched the horses thunder wild-eyed through the gates, throwing froth from their mouths. High above, the last of the sunset blazed on the Great Library's tower windows, as if the rooms inside had been set on fire—but the light retreated swiftly, shrinking upward, drawing long fingers of shadow from the angels and gargoyles who guarded the library's rain-streaked parapets.[7]

Color: Setting

Be specific. In *Writing Fiction*, Janet Burroway says: "A detail is *concrete* if it appeals to one of the five senses; it is *significant* if it also conveys an idea or a judgment or both. The windowsill was green is concrete, because we can see it. The *windowsill was shedding flakes of fungus-green paint* is concrete and also significant because it conveys the idea that the paint is old and suggests the judgments that the color is ugly."[8]

The colors of a place are an important part of the worldbuilding; every place has a different color palette—San Francisco is famous for its colorful homes built on steep hills, whereas Santorini, Greece, is dotted with whitewashed homes build on cliffs overlooking the bright blue of the Aegean Sea. Consider the color palette of this new world, and zoom in on anything that might be unique or characteristic of this place or the people within it. You won't always mention the dirt if it's the same as the dirt everywhere; however, as William Zinsser states in *On Writing Well*: "If you're in a part of the country where the dirt is red, feel free to mention the red dirt."[9]

The Namesake by Jhumpa Lahiri

Her swollen feet ache against speckled gray linoleum. Her pelvis aches from the baby's weight. She opens a cupboard, the shelves lined with a grimy yellow-and-white-checkered paper she's been meaning to replace, and reaches for another onion, frowning as she pulls at its crisp magenta skin.[10]

Kafka on the Shore by Haruki Murakami

There's no sun there, no moon, no direction, no sense of time. Just fine white sand swirling up into the sky like pulverized bones.[11]

Color: Clothing, Eyes, Hair

In terms of your characters, a common mistake is to simply state the color of your character's hair or eyes—truly, the reader won't remember, since this doesn't tend to show anything unique about them. However, if someone is wearing an all-beige pantsuit or they have bangs as pink as cotton candy, please let us know.

The Mysterious Benedict Society and the Perilous Journey
by Trenton Lee Stewart

She had coal-black skin; hair so long she could have tied it around her waist (and yes, it truly was green); and an extraordinarily puffy white dress that gave you the impression she was standing in a cloud.[12]

Metaphorical Colors or Simile Colors

You know when you go to the hardware store for paint and they have those cards with colors on them? You're choosing between pickle green and olive green for your wall; this is a metaphorical color. The noun is in front of the color. You can also write colors like similes, using "like" or "as" with the comparison noun after the color. Her face was as green as an olive. Her shirt was the color of one of my mom's pickles.

Here is a challenge: The next time you go to the hardware store, get a few of those paint chips, or, even better, tell your kid or your partner to pick one out for you—then, when you write, you've got to include that color.

Write Your Book: Describe the lighting and colors in this place.

Act Two, Plot Point 5: New World and Allies

Step 1: Describe the nature of the light as you continue to write this plot point. We often describe the light near the start of the scene, but if you aren't starting a new scene, the lighting may also change within the scene, shifting the mood.

Step 2: Also add a color simile or a metaphorical color, but be judicious about what colors you share and make sure they set the mood or show something about the place or the characters in it.

Day 31: Smell and Taste

When my Oma passed away, I kept her housedress. She often wore it while making me tea and a Dutch breakfast of rusk with Gouda cheese. Even years later, her sweet smell remained on that housedress. I could picture her alive, sitting across the table, talking in her strong Dutch accent, voice further muffled by the dentures she hadn't yet put in.

The Sense of Smell

Why did I remember these details because of the smell of an old housedress? Because smell is the sense most closely tied to memory—it's processed in a different part of the brain, triggering earlier and more specific recollections. This is called the Proustian Memory Effect, named after Marcel Proust, who wrote about how the smell of madeleines dipped in tea brought back memories.

The Lightning Thief by Rick Riordan

The smell of a person:

He had thinning hair and a scruffy beard and a frayed tweed jacket, which always smelled like coffee.[13]

If I Was Your Girl by Meredith Russo

The smell of a place:

The bus smelled of mildew, machine oil, and sweat.[14]

The Sense of Taste and Food

Taste isn't limited to food—it's also hair, bad breath, medicine, or glue on an envelope. Though I do love food in a book. Including food is not just about making the reader hungry; it's about evoking a feeling from the food—nostalgia, a memory, a desire, a loss.

The Doughnut Fix by Jessie Janowitz

Use comparisons in your food descriptions:

The eggs are so creamy, they taste like custard, and the onions are so sweet, you'd swear they were cooked in maple syrup.[15]

Eat, Pray, Love by Elizabeth Gilbert

Describe appearance and texture:

. . . the intestines had a kind of . . . well . . . *intestinal* consistency. Kind of like liver, but mushier. I did well with them until I started to think how I would describe this dish, and I thought, *it doesn't look like intestines. It actually looks like tapeworms.*[16]

The Underground Railroad by Colson Whitehead

Their mouth may have a taste even without food:

Her mouth was an old dustpan after the rain of flying grit in the tunnel.[17]

Write Your Book: Add the senses of smell and taste.

Act Two, Plot Point 5: New World and Allies

Step 1: First, focus on the sense of smell. Imagine being in your protagonist's body. Close your eyes. Breathe in. What do they smell? What do they think of the smell? What memories does it evoke? How does it make them feel? Next, consider the food in the scene. Can you think of some specific foods that might be unique to this new world? Do your protagonist's new allies introduce them to a new food? Or is there something else they can taste?

Step 2: As you write, focus on the senses of taste and smell. This does not need to be food. If no food exists in the current scene, show the smell or taste of something else. Or, you could have them think about the old food they miss.

Day 32: Similes and Metaphors

Today let's do the writer's version of a backflip off the high diving board: an original simile or metaphor. Your protagonist is exploring the new world and meeting new characters, so make sure you describe this place and the people through *their* lens, with their sarcasm, humor, life experience, and intelligence. That way, you've done double duty, showing something not only about the person being described, but also about who's doing the describing.

Similes and metaphors have the power to transform descriptions from the mundane to the extraordinary. When you compare someone's nose to an eraser, a banana, or a branch on an oak tree, you've given the reader an image to truly picture that nose, and you've also shown how your protagonist sees them.

What is the difference between a simile and a metaphor? Who cares. Yep, I told you not to care. Terminology doesn't matter—what matters is *how* you use them. I think terminology can become one of those elitist guardrails that make people think they can't possibly tell a story, which is total nonsense. You're just comparing two unlike things.

In any case, I'll define them here in case you want to know . . .

Simile: a comparison of two different things using "like" or "as."

Metaphor: a comparison of two different things *without* using "like" or "as."

"She is like a mountain" versus "She is a mountain." It's that simple. Do either.

But don't write a boring or clichéd simile. If you've heard it before, stop yourself. Don't write, "Her face was as red as a tomato." Instead, think of what the character would think of as red in their world—maybe kimchi. Elevate common ones beyond the ordinary. "Her face was an *overripe* tomato," or "Her face was a tomato that had been squished under her mother's stiletto."

We Have Always Lived in the Castle by Shirley Jackson

Use hyperbole or exaggeration:

I always stood perfectly straight and stiff when the children came close, because I was afraid of them. I was afraid that they might touch me and the mothers would come at me like a flock of taloned hawks; that was always the picture I had in my mind—birds descending, striking, gashing with razor claws.[18]

Dear Martin by Nic Stone

The mood of the comparison should match the mood of the scene:

She's missing a shoe, and the contents of her purse are scattered around her like the guts of a pulled party popper.[19]

Write Your Book: Add original similes and metaphors.

Act Two, Plot Point 5: New World and Allies

Step 1: Before you write, imagine your protagonist exploring their new world. What do they think about the world and the people in it? If they haven't met a new ally yet, now's the time. How would your protagonist describe them? Can you think of a metaphor or simile they'd use?

Step 2: As you begin your scene, describe the setting and the other characters through the protagonist's perspective, with original similes and metaphors. Push your imagination. Use the protagonist's voice, humor, and unique expressions.

Step 3: Remember, though it seems that we're just working on description here, in every scene, they're still pursuing a scene goal and running into ever-increasing problems. Ratchet up that tension!

Note: If you've just realized you write with a lot of clichés, don't worry about it. Whatever you do, don't go back and fix old descriptions; just move forward with this new skill.

Busy Writer Recap and Reward: Days 29–32

Act Two, Plot Point 5: New World and Allies

In this plot point, your characters have explored their world, and they've met allies to help with their goal. Time for the reward . . . How about a big tub of that baseball gum Big League Chew or tickets to a Major League Baseball game? Or your favorite deli sandwich.

Nurture Your Creativity

Imagination as an Anti-Anxiety Tool

If you have anxiety, you can use your imagination to decrease it. In *Beyond Anxiety: Curiosity, Creativity, and Finding Your Life's Purpose,* Martha Beck talks about the toggle effect of creativity and anxiety—when one is up, the other is down. So, writing will help. But how can you get yourself to sit when anxiety hits? Here are some of her suggestions: Do art, color, or dance. Do something unusual with your body (I do pretend synchronized swimming in my living room) or give your anxiety a silly name. (Mine? Panic Puppy.)[20]

In *The Anti-Anxiety Toolkit,* Melissa Tiers recommends using your imagination to decrease your anxiety. Picture what your anxiety looks like and then use your imagination to counter it. If it's spiraling inside you, look at the direction it spirals and imagine it spinning the opposite way. One of her clients imagined "a cauldron boiling over," and they cooled it down with ice.[21] What does your anxiety look like?

Busy Writer Road Map Days 33–36: Conflict

In the next four days, we'll work on conflict, especially any challenges, threats, or conflicts with the antagonist or a systemic antagonist (and we'll dive into defining these as well). If your protagonist is alone or their journey is more of an internal one, they may be experiencing inner conflict, or the conflict may be with nature or an enemy who isn't physically there but who's still a threat.

Act Two, Plot Point 6: The Antagonist Threatens

In this plot point, the protagonist faces their first big challenge in the new world, usually in the form of the antagonist, who stands in the way of the protagonist's goal.

Ideas and Examples

1. Facing the antagonist during training (*The Hunger Games* by Suzanne Collins)
2. Witnessing the antagonist punishing someone (*The Handmaid's Tale* by Margaret Atwood)
3. Watching the antagonist's show of advanced magic (*Mistborn* by Brandon Sanderson)
4. Facing the antagonist's threat to kill them (*Life of Pi* by Yann Martel)
5. Witnessing the antagonist's violent side (*It Ends with Us* by Colleen Hoover)

Day 33: The Multidimensional Antagonist

We need an antagonist who feels real so that they can be a mirror to your protagonist. Show what makes the antagonist dangerous and bad, but also show their strengths and any aspects of their personality that humanize them. Make them a multidimensional character, or explore a systemic issue (racism, poverty, homophobia) and how it manifests as an opposing force.

Can a character be their own antagonist? It's true, many of us can be our own worst enemy. This is why we explore internal conflict and limiting beliefs. However, an external force that your protagonist needs to push against will ensure more action and less moping.

The Classic Antagonist

This is your straightforward, old-fashioned bad guy. Stephen King said this about antagonists: "Writers must be fair and remember even bad guys (most of them, anyway) see themselves as good—they are the heroes of their own lives. Giving them a fair chance as characters can create some interesting shades of gray—and shades of gray are also a part of life."[1] If the antagonist feels real, the reader will think of the antagonist in their own life, and you'll get the reader–character connection that's essential for any story.

Then She Was Gone by Lisa Jewell

In this novel, we have a classic antagonist, Noelle, a math tutor who kidnaps and kills her student.

> Ellie struggled against the cuffs around her ankles, pounded her feet against the end of the bed. She roared and thrashed, and Noelle stood and watched her, her arms folded, shaking her head slowly. "Now, now, now," she said. "This isn't going to work. The longer you behave like this, the worse it will be and the longer you'll be here."[2]

Noelle is evil, for sure, but author Lisa Jewell adds complexity to her villain; in the story, we learn that Noelle's sister died when she was younger and she was never the same.

The Systemic Antagonist

If your antagonist is more of a systemic oppressor, it's still useful to give your protagonist some tangible opponent who represents the bigger problem: a leader who is the face of an evil movement, or a character who embodies misogynistic beliefs. In the case of the systemic antagonist, the stakes are higher and the challenge is greater because even if the protagonist overcomes the threat of this singular opponent, the systemic issue will still remain. They'll have to fight against the rules of the system or build a bigger resistance to overturn the government. The big threats of racism, poverty, homophobia, and global warming don't have easy solutions. The representatives of the systemic antagonist will also fight back and adjust, changing rules and structures to adapt, making the issue harder to overcome.

***The Handmaid's Tale* by Margaret Atwood:** Enforcement (The Eyes—the secret police), rigid dress codes (handmaids wear red cloaks with hoods that shield their hair and face), and punishments (bodies on the wall).

***Fahrenheit 451* by Ray Bradbury:** After he witnesses an older woman choosing to die in the flames with her books, the protagonist realizes he is not the hero but the antagonist who represents the corrupt system of oppression, and he switches sides.

The Symbolic Antagonist

The symbolic antagonist often involves a world restriction in which an aspect of a world takes on the role of an antagonist. It may not be outright evil; more than anything, it helps the character grow.

***Before the Coffee Gets Cold* by Toshikazu Kawaguchi:** The basic premise in this book is that you can use the café to travel into the past to change something you regret, but you must return before the coffee gets cold. The café becomes both the portal and the antagonist, due to the restrictions.

***Hatchet* by Gary Paulsen:** Brian's plane goes down in northern Canada and he needs to fight against nature to survive.

The Emotional Antagonist

This person will challenge your protagonist to grow, usually through psychological pressure, and we may even think this person is the real villain. They shape the protagonist's character arc through criticism.

> ***Harry Potter* by J. K. Rowling:** Severus Snape puts Harry down, makes him question his worth, and stands in the way of his goals.
> ***Anne of Green Gables* by L. M. Montgomery:** Anne's foster mother, Marilla, serves as an emotional antagonist, creating strict rules and withholding affection, standing in sharp contrast to Anne's warm personality.

Write Your Book: Portray a multidimensional antagonist.

Act Two, Plot Point 6: The Antagonist Threatens

Step 1: Choose a setting with potential danger. Add foreshadowing or a detail that shows the heat of the impending conflict—potentially the first real challenge your protagonist will face in your plot. Reflect their specific fears, insecurity, and even their sense of humor. Let them discuss or think about the threat of the antagonist before we see them.

Step 2: Introduce the antagonist. If you've already introduced them, show the threat. What does your protagonist notice about them? Let them describe the antagonist physically, and maybe compare the antagonist to something they dislike or something humorous to downplay the threat.

Day 34: Internal Conflict

Internal conflict is the inner turmoil within all of us: the competing desires or loyalties, fears, worries, insecurities, and secrets—categories we'll explore in this section. In every scene, your character will be experiencing some degree of internal conflict if you're to have any tension at all. The potential for external conflict with the antagonist can also increase the internal conflict—think of the kid who lives with an abusive parent; often, they'll do anything to avoid this parent.

Competing Desires or Loyalties

In any moment, we all have things we'd like to do and things we need to do. We have people who want our help and we also have our own desires. Your friends want you to go out with them tonight, but you promised your mom you'd help her paint the bathroom in her house, so do you choose Mom or the friends? This decision-making process adds internal conflict. Let's take a look at this issue in a popular classic.

> ***Hatchet* by Gary Paulsen:** Brian knows the "secret" of why his mom is divorcing his dad, and he's on his dad's side. When they arrive at the airport, she gives him a hatchet to put on his belt. He wants to refuse it, but "her voice was thin, had a sound like something thin that would break if you touched it, and he felt bad for not speaking to her."[3]

Fear

Most successful storytelling has some degree of emotional or physical danger, resulting in a fear that something could go wrong. Emotional danger could be a reactive boss, rejection from a romantic interest, or ridicule about bad bangs. Physical danger could look like a big fall from a height, a bear attack, or zombies. The threat—implied or obvious—is a key part of tension. Show the protagonist's fear through their thoughts and imagination about what *could* go wrong.

Secrets

A secret can be a great way to add tension, stakes, and internal conflict to your narrative, particularly if your protagonist shares their secret, adding a potential for betrayal. We want to trust people, but deciding who to trust with our secrets can cause internal conflict.

> ***All Fours* by Miranda July:** The protagonist tells her family she's driving across the country, but instead stays in a motel forty-five minutes away. Feeling bad about her deception, she tells her best friend, but then her best friend experiences internal conflict due to her mixed loyalties.

Insecurities

Pretty much every person has an insecurity, typically stemming from a past difficulty or trauma. No insecurity is too small to talk about in a book. In fact, sometimes it's in the mundane that we land on that relatable, raw insecurity. People think they're bad at a whole host of things: small talk, running fast, kissing, mental math, making money, doing their hair. Show this insecurity in your protagonist's thoughts.

The Way of Kings by Brandon Sanderson

> He hated that he felt some of that same paranoia that the others showed. How could he not, after eight months of beatings, deprivation, and brutality?[4]

Wings of Fire: The Dragonet Prophesy by Tui T. Sutherland

> Clay felt about as dangerous as cauliflower.[5]

Write Your Book: Show the internal conflict.

Act Two, Plot Point 6: The Antagonist Threatens

Step 1: Brainstorm the source of your protagonist's internal conflict. Are they torn between loyalties to two people? Do they have to make a tough decision? What is their insecurity in this moment? Any worries? Fears? Secrets? How about the other characters? Could an ally or family member be acting in a way that might demonstrate they're struggling mentally or they're planning a betrayal? What fear do they have regarding the antagonist?

Step 2: Write your scene, showing the internal conflict in the main character's thoughts and within other characters through what they say and do.

Day 35: External Conflict

A screaming fight with a cheating spouse. Two wild dogs fighting. A bottle thrown across the living room. A bat swung against a car window. Heavy metal booming from the neighbor's house at three in the morning. External conflict is anything pushing against your protagonist's goal—nature, technology, society, racism, homophobia, AI, ignorance, patriarchy. It doesn't have to be a fight. It could be a woman finding vodka hidden behind the toilet or a CEO receiving a blackmail letter.

Now the character needs to react. Does the woman confront her husband? Does the CEO give the money? Do they fight, flee, freeze, or fawn? You'll need to show their internal conflict before they react, and then we'll see more external conflict.

You may be thinking that external conflict is for a thriller or a fast-paced adventure story, but you need it in every genre.

Whatever happens, the protagonist stands to lose something. They have to face the problem and do something about it, unlike internal conflict, which can rot and fester. In today's scene, this external conflict will likely involve the antagonist.

Write Your Book: Add an external conflict.

Act Two, Plot Point 6: The Antagonist Threatens

Step 1: Consider the stakes in this conflict with the antagonist. What could your protagonist lose? How will this particular problem challenge your protagonist's insecurities or fears? What is their scene goal and the first obstacle? Can you increase the stakes with an added complication?

Step 2: As you write your scene, add some fast-paced action. When dealing with this problem, the protagonist may also face external conflict with allies who have different solutions.

Step 3: *Now* add another complication—maybe there's a time limit or an added environmental challenge like exhaustion, heat, bugs, or a storm.

Melanie Jacobson (*The Fall Back Plan*)

on Writing Romance with Conflict

"The key to structuring a strong romance is that the central conflict can't be solved by a conversation you're refusing to let your characters have. If they could solve it by talking it out, your conflict isn't strong enough. Romance needs a strong internal and external conflict, and you increase the tension and stakes if the conflict will ultimately require one or both of the characters to make a major sacrifice."[6]

Day 36: Power Dynamics and Body Language

Scenes are often about power—who has it and who wants it. Since you're working through a conflict with the antagonist, now is a good time to focus on how your antagonist might demonstrate their power and how the protagonist may show a lack of power at this point. I'll share some of the research behind the body language of power that you can use to reveal the relative power of the characters in your scene.

The body language of power is one of those underrated tools in a writer's toolbox that has the ability to trigger the reader's mirror neurons so they feel that it's happening to them. For example, if you show a boss intimidating the female accountant by resting his thick, hot hand on her shoulder or leaning over her while she's sitting, breathing on her hair, we're going to cringe inwardly and think, *Get away from her.*

1. Expanding versus Contracting

   Power—expanding: The character with more power might stretch their arms, kick their feet up on a table, make big gestures, manspread, or point.

   No power—contracting or freezing: The character with less power will cross their legs, make themselves small, or tighten in a ball. They may freeze, stop moving their feet, or pin their arms. Sadly, this is one way to see if a child is being abused. Their arms will stiffen at their sides near the abuser.

Speak by Laurie Halse Anderson

I stop on a frozen puddle. Maybe he won't notice me if I stand still. That's how rabbits survive; they freeze in the presence of predators.[7]

2. Spreading or Touching Belongings versus Holding Belongings

   Power—spreading/touching/destroying: People with power not only expand their bodies, but their belongings also become an extension of that power. They might fling a jacket over a chair, toss their keys into a dish, or spread papers all over a table, claiming territory. They also touch other people's objects or move their glass or bag, rearrange items in the way that they like them to be. They may destroy someone's treasured thing. Or pick up something private, like a phone or a journal.

   No power—holding/containing: These characters will try to limit their impact on a space, keeping their personal belongings close. On the bus, they might keep their backpack on their lap. A kid who lives in a strict home might not throw their stuff everywhere, but rather put it in their room to avoid punishment. A woman might walk down the street clinging to her purse, sometimes out of fear, but also to protect a secret item like a letter, thereby revealing she has something to hide.

I Am Here Now by Barbara Bottner

She tears up my sketch into small newsprint flakes that float over my carpet. "There's your creativity!"[8]

3. Unshielding versus Shielding

   Power—unshielding: They step around furniture, lower their glass, or remove clothing. Men may remove shirts to fight. If someone turns their back and walks away, they show they're unafraid of an attack from behind.

   No power—shielding: They hold an object in front of their body, like a book or a teddy bear, or they step behind furniture, as a form of protection.

   ***A Clash of Kings* by George R. R. Martin:** The villain, Ramsay Bolton, forces his captive, Reek, to shave his adoptive father, Roose Bolton, demonstrating Ramsay's total control over him. Roose places himself in a vulnerable position, unshielding himself; Reek has the power to slit his neck, but he does not. (In the TV adaptation, he shaves Ramsay.)

4. Taking Space versus Clearing Space

   Power—taking space: They block exits, stand in the doorway, block people from leaving, and don't move out of the way for others.

   No power—clearing space: They let people pass; they jump out of the way.

5. Higher Position versus Lower Position

   Power—higher position: They seek a higher position over others, sitting on top of the desk, standing on a higher step, raising a leg up on a chair, or standing over someone, crowding them.

   No power—lower position: They might sit on the ground or take the lower chair.

6. Excessive Touching versus Avoiding Touch

   Power—excessive touching: They'll move too close or touch a person too much, even inappropriately. They don't have to grab someone's butt; you can show them touching a less obvious vulnerable part of the body, like the wrist or the neck, and we'll still feel creeped out. Imagine someone you don't know touching your hair.

   No power—avoiding touch: They move away, flinch, dodge a touch, or experience a subconscious response like blushing or heart racing.

The Golden Compass by Philip Pullman

As she passed her on the way to the armchair, Mrs. Coulter touched Lyra's hair briefly, and Lyra felt a current of warmth flow into her, and blushed.[9]

Write Your Book: Show who has power and who doesn't.

Act Two, Plot Point 6: The Antagonist Threatens

Step 1: Think about your protagonist's relative power in the scene—usually they will feel less powerful when facing the antagonist. Imagine what each character is doing with an object in the scene to show their relative feelings of power or lack thereof.

Step 2: As you write, show the antagonist or some other power-tripping character demonstrating their power. Write about what the protagonist thinks about their antagonist or aggressor—perhaps you can even let their imagination loose and show what they wish they could do to this antagonist or power-tripping person. Exaggerate. Have fun with this. Let their imagination go wild.

Busy Writer Recap and Reward: Days 33–36

Act Two, Plot Point 6: The Antagonist Threatens

You wrote some conflict. Jump up and down. Shake it out. You did it. Lots more conflict to come. Balance that out with fun and humor and success scenes. Now it's reward time—well, the reward honestly is in the writing, but just as you suck on an orange when running a marathon, let's suck on a metaphorical orange in our creative marathon too. That's my first reward suggestion: Go eat a juicy orange or make freshly squeezed orange juice. You don't like oranges? What are you, a maniac? Okay, watermelon. The second reward idea is to do zero housework for the next twenty-four hours. Lie on the floor. Do nothing. Order in.

Nurture Your Creativity

Meet a Stranger

For today's creativity challenge, meet a stranger. Then here's an extra challenge: Put this stranger in your book. In his MasterClass, writer David Sedaris talks about how he hates small talk, but he doesn't stare at his phone in lines or on elevators. Instead, he has a list of strange questions he typically asks strangers to get them sharing details of their life: "Do you know many people in wheelchairs?" "Do you know a lot of doctors?" "Have you ever run for office?" "When was the last time you touched a monkey?"[10] Try this regularly and you could end up feeding your novel with unique details and fascinating insights into humanity.

Literary Agent Donald Maass (*Writing the Breakout Novel*)

on Emotions

"Heighten it. Make it bigger, funnier, more shocking, more vulgar, more out of bounds, more over the top, more violent, more insightful, more wildly romantic, more active, more *anything*."[11]

Cassandra Clare (*City of Bones*)

on Writing Dialogue

"Listen to the way people actually talk. To an extent, all written dialogue is stylized where we take out the *ums* and the *sort ofs* and the minimizing language. And remember that there is a rhythm. That the back-and-forth of talking is rhythmic: Somebody gives information, somebody else reacts."[12]

Busy Writer Road Map Days 37–40: Dialogue

In the next four days, we'll work on writing tight, interesting dialogue that hooks the reader, reveals character, and drives the plot forward.

Act Two, Plot Point 7: Skills and Information

For this plot point, your character is learning, training, doing research, and finding mentors. What skills or information does your protagonist need for the coming conflict? It often depends on the genre. In sci-fi, they need scientific skills. In a thriller, they need investigative skills. In fantasy, they need to perform magic. In a romance, they may need to learn how to dance before the ball or, if it's a fake dating situation, they'll set up the rules for their fake relationship.

Ideas and Examples

1. Learning how to fight (*The Hunger Games* by Suzanne Collins)
2. Practicing a spell (*Harry Potter and the Sorcerer's Stone* by J. K. Rowling)
3. Learning how to survive in the wilderness (*Hatchet* by Gary Paulsen)
4. Researching a threat (*World War Z* by Max Brooks)
5. Taking on a false identity (*How to Kill Your Family* by Bella Mackie)

Day 37: Dialogue Hooks

A dialogue hook can be an effective way to start your chapter; it'll throw the reader off-balance and make them curious about who's talking or why they're saying it.

Tips to Hook the Reader with Dialogue

1. Add mystery and make the reader wonder.
   A Thousand Splendid Suns by Khaled Hosseini
   "I need to speak to your parents, *dohtar jan*," he said when Laila opened the door.[1]

2. Show someone's goal through an offer, a refusal, or a threat.
   Caraval by Stephanie Garber
   "This way." Julian tugged her toward a corridor lined in bricks and lit with glowing spiderwebs.[2]

3. Show power, either being conceded or taken.
   The Tiger's Wife by Téa Obreht
   "No," Duré said to Fra Antun, "No, I don't want her, get me someone else."[3]

4. Reveal an opposing goal, a hidden fear, or a lie.
   The Giver by Lois Lowry
   "You slept soundly, Jonas?" his mother asked at the morning meal. "No dreams?"
   Jonas simply smiled and nodded, not ready to lie, not willing to tell the truth.[4]

(In *The Giver*, one of the rules is that he can't tell his dreams to anyone.)

Write Your Book: Hook the reader with dialogue.

Act Two, Plot Point 7: Skills and Information

Step 1: Brainstorm your scene mentally. Where can you place this scene for maximum tension? Try to make the setting different from the last setting in some way. Get into your protagonist's body. How are they feeling? What do they notice? What do they smell? Hear? How's the lighting?

What do they want to do right now? What will be their first actions? Before you start writing, think about the other characters. Where did they just come from? How are they feeling? Goals?

Step 2: Dialogue hooks can be a challenge because, by their very nature, they require jumping into the middle of things. You aren't giving us the boring beginning or the introductions, just the meat of the conversation. After you hook the reader, show any reactions to what has just been said, and then catch us up with the other details of the scene. You don't need to finish it today. Stop partway through, providing your imagination with the impetus to sit down tomorrow.

Day 38: Tighten the Dialogue

When you're writing dialogue, it shouldn't be exactly like real life, which can be boring—we've all run into talkative Tracy or Bob the blowhard. As a result, some writers have far too much dialogue. Published novels usually have roughly 25 percent each of description, thought, action, and dialogue, depending on genre. Most authors favor one of them, but I've found that dialogue is the one that's often overused.

If your writing is being dominated by any single one of these at the expense of the others, then perhaps you're out of balance. Today, we'll work on tightening the dialogue. If your dialogue is already spare, then perhaps some other element is overused.

Within your dialogue, you can have thoughts, actions, and description, and this can help the reader feel more engaged. Otherwise, you may have a situation called floating voices or talking heads—we hear your characters, but we can't see them.

Midnight's Children by Salmon Rushdie

Note the use of body language here together with the dialogue.

"Now that I'm getting married," Emerald told Mumtaz, "it'll be very rude of you if you don't even try to have a good time. And you should be giving me advice and everything." At the time, although Mumtaz smiled at her younger sister, she had thought it a great cheek on Emerald's part to say this; and, unintentionally perhaps, had increased the pressure of the pencil with which she was applying henna tracery to the soles of her sister's feet. "Hey!" Emerald squealed, "No need to get mad! I just thought we should try to be friends."[5]

Tips for Tightening the Dialogue

1. **Start in the middle.** You don't need to give the entire conversation. Just the interesting parts.
2. **Use fragments and interruptions.** In real life, dialogue is distracted and disjointed. People ignore each other. They walk away in the middle of a conversation. They interrupt each other. They switch subjects randomly.
3. **Leave some things unsaid.** People often don't say what they mean. We hide our feelings, secrets, and desires. Make sure it's not too on the nose.
4. **Avoid info dumps.** Avoid long stories in dialogue. Most people don't talk like that, and if they do, we're bored. Dialogue is a conversation. If you want to show that someone is long-winded, you can summarize it in the protagonist's thoughts. Avoid two people talking about something they both know for the reader's benefit, just to impart information. "As you know . . ."
5. **Avoid extending dialogue unnecessarily.** Often, one or two lines will suffice.

Write Your Book: Work on balance between dialogue, action, description, and thoughts.

Act Two, Plot Point 7: Skills and Information

Step 1: Decide what characters need to say and how it will move the story forward. Imagine the scene before you write to ensure you also include description, thoughts, and actions.

Step 2: Aim for tight dialogue as you write this scene. Make sure that you're avoiding on-the-nose dialogue. Let most of it go unsaid, and make the reader curious.

Day 39: Common Dialogue Mistakes

Mistake #1: Too many dialogue tags.

Back in elementary school, you may have been told "said is dead." You were instructed to avoid "said" and use a wide variety of dialogue tags, like "exclaimed," "retorted," and "spat," along with adverbs like "angrily" or "sadly." Today, it's time to unlearn that.

Most literary and bestselling novels do not use a bunch of different dialogue tags and adverbs. Why? Strange dialogue tags like "enunciated" and "cogitated" make you sound like you took a nosedive into a thesaurus, and other dialogue tags like "boasted" *tell*, after you've *shown;* therefore, they're unnecessary.

Fix #1: Mostly, use "said" or no tags when it's clear who's talking.

Elmore Leonard, widely recognized as a master of dialogue, advised writers to "never use a verb other than 'said' to carry dialogue and never use an adverb to modify the verb said."[6] Rick Riordan agrees: "Leave your characters alone and let them talk."[7] Stephen King recommends that writers stick to "said," and he has the following to say about adverbs in dialogue: "I can be a good sport about adverbs, though. Yes I can.

With one exception: dialogue attribution. I insist that you use the adverb in dialogue attribution only in the rarest and most special of occasions . . . and not even then, if you can avoid it."[8]

In the classic craft book *Writing Fiction,* Janet Burroway writes: "While unintentional repetition usually makes for awkward style, the word *said* is as invisible as punctuation; when we're reading, we're scarcely aware of it, whereas we are forced to be aware of *wailed*."[9]

After two people begin talking, you can cut the dialogue tags altogether. It just goes back and forth. Use paragraph breaks. See below.

All My Rage by Sabaa Tahir

"Re-remember when she told you to dress up as a terrorist for Halloween?"

"Sixth grade. Never trusted her again."

We glare at Jamie's retreating back. For a moment we're kids again. Unified against an invisible evil.[10]

Mistake #2: Using too many adverbs or adverb clauses.

Adding adverbs to those tags just makes for clumsy sentences. Most important, the combination of strange dialogue tags and adverbs distracts from the dialogue itself. The good news is that it's easy to fix.

Fix #2: Cut dialogue tags. Replace them with actions.

Most adverbs can be cut, but keep them if they add to the sentence because they contradict the verb. For example: "Get out of here," she whispered loudly. "Loudly" contradicts "whispered," so you'd keep it. However, if you look at the weak example below, you don't need any of the adverbs or the final adverb clause. In the strong example, adding an action gives the reader more to imagine.

Weak

"I don't like peanut butter," her brother proclaimed **angrily.**

"You could have jam," she soothed, **gently.**

"Jam tastes like slime licked off a sidewalk," he grumbled **with great annoyance.**

Stronger

"I don't like peanut butter," her brother said.

"You could have jam." **She bumped his shoulder.** "Or honey."

"Jam tastes like slime licked off a sidewalk."

Write Your Book: Decrease dialogue tags and adverbs.

Act Two, Plot Point 7: Skills and Information

Step 1: As your protagonist tries to learn a particular skill or gain information, show them hitting an obstacle, which they will either overcome or not.

Step 2: Use dialogue to make your scene feel more alive and immediate. Aim to decrease the wide variety of dialogue tags and adverbs, and try to use fewer words for tighter storytelling.

Day 40: Character Reveals in Dialogue

What do I mean by revealing character? Should the character tell another character about themselves? You can do this in a more intimate moment, but keep it tight to avoid overly direct, on-the-nose dialogue. Instead, you can use the dialogue to reveal their background, mood, and relationships with others.

One way to improve this skill is to listen closely to how people talk to different people, exactly what words they choose, what they reveal, how they shut down, how they puff themselves up, and how they use language to show their power over others.

1. Reveal who the characters are by how they speak.

   Writers usually connect with their main character, but sometimes they forget their side characters; as a result, the dialogue may feel flat. Learn what expressions they use, where they come from.

2. Use dialogue to shift relationships.

   Conversations should move the narrative forward and add tension, serving to either bring people together or move them apart. A spouse who normally stays quiet says, "Well, you're no picnic either." *Boom.* Now we have a shift. Vulnerability, on the other hand, can bring characters together as you'll see in the following scene.

Lessons in Chemistry by Bonnie Garmus

"A brother," she said. "You?"

"None." His voice was flat.

She lay very still, taking in his tone. "Was it lonely?" she asked.

"Yes," he said bluntly.

"I'm sorry," she said, taking his hand under the sheets.[11]

3. Add conflict through opposing goals.

   In a conflict-adjacent dialogue, each speaker wants something. When one tactic doesn't work, they try another: bribery, flattery, insults, accusations, lies, or threats. Some people will use all the tools in their arsenal to get the other person on their side. Those tools become their weapons.

The Lovely Bones by Alice Sebold

In this novel, Susie Salmon is dead, in heaven, and she becomes the omniscient narrator, telling the events of what happened before and after her murder. In the following scene, her father talks to the mom of the kid suspected of killing Susie. The boy did not kill her; he had a crush on her. Notice the tension from the two parents with opposing goals: Susie's dad wants information, and the mom wants to protect her son.

"That must be why you've come," she continued.

"Yes," he said, "I want to talk to him."

"He's at school right now," she said. "You know that." Her legs in the gold pants were tucked to her side. The nails on her toes were long and unpolished; their surface gnarled from years of dancing.

"I wanted to come by and assure you I mean him no harm," my father said.[12]

4. Show how everyone reacts to what has been said.

   When someone says something surprising, shocking, or offensive, the characters must react. This reaction moment can shift the story, but if you miss it, you've missed a major beat and your reader may be pulled out, thinking, *Why didn't they react?*

Write Your Book: Reveal your characters' truth in dialogue.

Act Two, Plot Point 7: Skills and Information

Step 1: To make sure everyone's dialogue shows their individuality, think about each character's background, speech patterns, vocabulary, sentence structure, and expressions.

Step 2: Use dialogue to advance relationships along. What do the characters talk about? Can you reveal something about them? Maybe a secret, a lie, a funny opinion? How do they react?

Busy Writer Recap and Reward: Days 37–40

Act Two, Plot Point 7: Skills and Information

Just as your characters are gaining skills and information, you've probably noticed your own skills are improving. I hope your creative confidence is growing as you continue to write. Now it's time for a treat. Today, it's dessert before dinner, all the while whispering, in an evil accent, "Because I'm the boss."

Nurture Your Creativity

Watch Movies with Lots of Popcorn

Cozy up under a blanket and watch a great movie. Let yourself relax. Focus on these five questions for the dialogue:

Subtext: Focus on what is *not* said. What do the characters really mean?
Tension: How does the dialogue reveal underlying problems?
Characterization: How does the dialogue show the characters' personalities and interests?
Decisions: What decisions does the character make based on what's said—and not said?
Exposition: What information do you learn from the dialogue?

Busy Writer Road Map Days 41–44: Character Development

Character development lies at the heart of your novel; this is what will make your story stick with readers long after they've finished reading. The characters drive the story, and the secondary problems in the subplot will help them grow.

Act Two, Plot Point 8: Subplot Challenge

The subplot (or B storyline) is the protagonist's secondary problem or another character's problem that complicates your protagonist's main goal. Subplots add emotional depth to character development and complicate the main storyline, forcing tough choices.

Ideas and Examples

1. Struggling with addiction (*The Girl on the Train* by Paula Hawkins)
2. Competing with a sibling (*The Nightingale* by Kristin Hannah)
3. Helping a sick friend (*The Fault in Our Stars* by John Green)
4. Reliving past trauma (*Six of Crows* by Leigh Bardugo—both Kaz and Inej)
5. Navigating family pressures (*The Sun Is Also a Star* by Nicola Yoon)

Day 41: Conflicting Identities and Roles

Have you ever been torn among the roles you play in your life? We all have different identities and roles we play—I am a mother, a daughter, a sister, a teacher, a writer—and these roles sometimes conflict. Tonight, for example, my daughter has a performance, and I teach a writing class from home until 7:00. If I time everything right, I can race over to her school and still catch her singing. My roles as a teacher and parent are colliding—if this were a movie, it would be a car accident waiting to happen, right when she hits the high note.

In stories, just as in life, the protagonist's identities will conflict.

Remember to give some attention to these other roles and the people in their lives, because this is where the plot thickens, no matter what type of story you're writing. Under each identity, they have different desires and responsibilities, creating dilemmas and hard choices.

If you show the choices on the page, the reader will have an opinion: This triggers the reader–character connection that is so essential to storytelling.

The Tobacco Wives by Adele Myers

Maddie is a teenager, a niece, and a seamstress in a tobacco town, making dresses for all the rich women. Her identities collide because she's still a teen and wants to fit in with the other teens, but she has to work, which means she can't really fit in.

Write Your Book: Show conflicting identities causing problems.

Act Two, Plot Point 8: Subplot Challenge

Step 1: Hook the reader with a dilemma involving a clash of identities, an essential part of character development. You could start the scene with an argument, or you could show the character's internal conflict regarding their dilemma.

Step 2: Show the subplot in the protagonist's interactions with other characters—later in the story, you'll be adding more complications to this subplot.

Day 42: The Four Faces of Your Character

Is your character a liar?

I sure hope they are. At least, they should lie to themselves about something—this is a key part of your character arc, and this is what we're exploring today. What is their public face versus their personal and private faces? That's the lie they tell the world. What is their hidden face? That's the lie they tell themselves.

Public: The first face is the face they show the world.
Personal: The second face is the one they show their close friends and family.
Private: The third face is the one they show themselves.
Hidden: The fourth face is the one they may not recognize or acknowledge, but which can nonetheless cause havoc in their life.

First you should know these for your main character, but also any other significant character, especially because the subplot usually involves an issue with another character. In this scene, you'll be showing that others have their own private and hidden faces.

The Fault in Our Stars by John Green

Public face: Hazel Grace tries to put on an "I'm okay" face to the world.
Personal face: She shows her mom and dad that she's feeling depressed.
Private face: She doesn't tell her family about how guilty she feels for making them worry or how she thinks she's an unsafe person to love—this is her misbelief.
Hidden face: She doesn't let herself love or get close to anyone because she doesn't want to hurt anyone else.
The subplot: The problems of other people in the story are the subplot, but these problems are hidden from her—they all have their own faces. Her mom has secretly gone back to school, Augustus is dealing with his own health issue, and their friend Isaac breaks up with his girlfriend and loses an eye.

Write Your Book: Reveal the protagonist's private face.

Act Two, Plot Point 8: Subplot Challenge

Step 1: Before you start writing, think about the four faces of your protagonist. How does their personal or private face conflict with their public face?

Step 2: Portray the contrast among what the protagonist says, thinks, and does. Show their private face in their thoughts as they think about the challenge of the subplot. At this point, the hidden face usually remains hidden from the protagonist and the reader—this will become apparent in Act Three.

Day 43: The Wound

Your character has a past trauma that still shapes them. Now let's explore the effect of this trauma: the fear, the need, and the misbelief. This wound leaves them vulnerable to triggers in their environment and leads to reactive choices.

Then She Was Gone by Lisa Jewell

Laurel is cleaning the home of her adult daughter, Hanna. Her trauma or origin story is that her other daughter, Ellie, disappeared when she was a teenager. Her fear is that she'll lose Hanna, and her misbelief is that it's her fault that she didn't protect Ellie and nobody is safe. Notice her perceptions and internal reactions based on that backstory.

> It looked as though Hanna hadn't been home the night before. There was no cereal bowl in the sink, no milk splashes on the work surface, no tube of mascara left half-open by the magnifying makeup mirror on the windowsill. A plume of ice went down Laurel's spine. Hanna always came home.[1]

Write Your Book: Reveal the effect of the wound.

Act Two, Plot Point 8: Subplot Challenge

Step 1: Identify the protagonist's fear, deep need, and core misbelief. They may not be aware of this need or misbelief, yet, but you'll hint at it through their thoughts, observations, and actions.

Step 2: Show something that might trigger the protagonist. Reflect their fear in their physical actions and responses.

Day 44: The Third Rail and the Subplot

In *Angela's Ashes,* Frank McCourt writes: "When I look back on my childhood I wonder how I survived it at all. It was, of course, a miserable childhood: the happy childhood is hardly worth your while."[2] The same goes for our characters. We worked on the wound on Day 43; now let's look at how it plays a role in the subplot.

Your character's past is the engine of the subplot. It created their flaws and misbeliefs. At this point in the story, your protagonist *can't* get what they want because a misbelief stands in the way. "I want a true friend" collides with "I'm not good enough for a true friend."

In *Story Genius,* Lisa Cron calls this internal struggle the third rail, like the electrified rail on a subway track that powers the train. Every scene must touch it. The third rail shows up in the character's perceptions, reactions, and decisions. If you know your character deeply, this will happen naturally. If you don't, the story will fall flat. Cron argues that most rejected manuscripts fail because "they do not have a third rail."[3]

The subplot often involves their past resurfacing and causing problems, forcing the character to grow, as in the examples below.

In the Same Boat by Holly Green

Sadie wants to complete the 265-mile Texas River Odyssey to redeem her failure the previous year. She's been training for a year, planning to race with her brother, but then he ditches her at the last minute. She's forced to pair up with Cully, her former best friend, further complicated by the fact that their families are enemies too. The race is the main plot. In the subplot, her confusing romantic feelings and conflict with her father over choosing to race with Cully add stakes and fighting to the grueling race. Her third rail is clear: She misses Cully, but doesn't trust anyone enough to rely on them, especially not him.

Dangerous Play by Emma Kress

Zoe wants to win the field hockey championship. After she's assaulted at a party, her goal shifts to protecting other girls and seeking vigilante justice. The subplot is her romance with the quarterback, but her trauma stands in the way of trusting him. She yearns for love but believes that boys can't be trusted.

Write Your Book: Show the third rail in the subplot.

Act Two, Plot Point 8: Subplot Challenge

Step 1: Think of the protagonist's trauma and origin story—what exactly happened? What misbelief did it cause? Does someone or something in the current scene remind them of that hard experience? How can the past resurface here to intensify the tension between yearning and the misbelief? Journal on this before you start drafting pages.

Step 2: As you write this scene, show the protagonist's wound in how they think and react to what's happening in the current moment, especially with anyone connected to that trauma. Show where their imagination goes and how the past colors their perceptions. Show other characters reacting to what's happening—maybe they know what the protagonist is going through or maybe they have their own triggers.

Busy Writer Recap and Reward: Days 41–44

Act Two, Plot Point 8: Subplot Challenge

You're now halfway through Act Two! You're doing an excellent job. You've explored your main character's conflicting identities and the faces they show the world. You looked at their trauma and origin story, and the resultant driving misbelief, fear, and need. Your characters have hit some emotional obstacles, and you've revealed the subplot regarding other characters and maybe other secondary problems your protagonist is facing. Reward time: Treat yourself to a massage. Or stand outside in your bare feet, toes on sand, grass, or snow. This grounding exercise will feel nice. Go ahead, try it right now.

Nurture Your Creativity

Give Away Ten Things and Make a Creativity Bag

Do you have a lot of stuff? You're not alone—I've found that many creative people have random things, collections, books, and art supplies, much of which they don't use. Don't worry, I have a fun way to use this stuff in your story. But first, a clear workspace and an organized home can help decrease stress and increase creativity. Notice specific things in your life that might be creating clutter or stopping creative flow. Give ten things away. But don't give away everything. . . . I challenge you to make a creativity bag filled with random quirky objects. Put these weird objects in a creativity box or bag. Anytime you need inspiration, reach in, take out one of the objects, and put it in your next scene.

Brendan Reichs (***Nemesis***)

on Character Flaws

"The trick is you actually plot the entire book based on the character flaw of your main character. I think of a situation and that's how I start my idea, but then I put a person in it and then I ask myself what's wrong with this person that they're going to fail. . . . I don't think characters really pop unless there's something a little bit broken in them. I think, *What is this character's weakness going to be? What has been holding this character back?"*[4]

Busy Writer Road Map Days 45–48: Specificity

Specificity can heighten the tension as you escalate the obstacles in Act Two, providing specific details so that the reader *believes* the story and experiences a scene as if they are right there. Details prove that your story could be real. The dog is not just a dog; it's a rottweiler.

Act Two, Plot Point 9: Escalating Obstacles

What escalating challenges can you throw into the protagonist's path? Do they fear heights, rotten food, needles? Give them whatever they fear. The danger could be emotional, like public speaking or humiliation, but it could also be physical, like an attacking rhino or a house fire. Be specific about the obstacle. Would you rather pick up a garter snake or a Mohave rattlesnake?

Ideas and Examples

1. Getting beaten up (*Divergent* by Veronica Roth)
2. Dodging the police (*The Da Vinci Code* by Dan Brown)
3. Fleeing monsters (*The Maze Runner* by James Dashner)
4. Facing a rival (*Ender's Game* by Orson Scott Card)
5. Trapped in a collapsing building (*Catching Fire* by Suzanne Collins)

Day 45: Specific Verbs and Action Similes

I tend to walk fast and eat fast. I'm not saying this is a good thing—it's infinitely better to chew your food twenty times or stroll down the street with leisure, observing the pink cherry blossoms like a Zen monk. But that's not me. First of all, chewing twenty times feels like the action of a psychopath—by the end, any food feels like refried beans in your mouth. No, I devour a bowl of spaghetti like a starved shelter dog, and I march down the street like I'm being hunted by an assassin, even if I'm going to the dentist.

In the paragraph above, I included specific verbs and action similes, and now we're going to work on this skill in the Escalating Obstacles plot point, since it usually involves action.

Specific Verbs

Verbs are the action words in the sentence; in general, try to choose specific verbs over verb-adverb pairs ("trudged" versus "went slowly") or verb-noun phrases ("decided" versus "made a decision"). A strong verb not only tightens your manuscript, but it also shows your protagonist's mood and/or judgment ("snitched" versus "implicated").

Choose active verbs rather than passive verbs, so that we know who did the action, unless someone's trying to avoid blaming someone else, like a coworker. ("He removed the files" versus "The files were removed.")

The Maze Runner by James Dashner

He lifted the spear above his head, braced his feet—felt them sink into the disgusting blubber—then thrust the spear down and into the monster.[1]

Action Similes

Actions paired with similes can pull the reader into any story because you can add humor and give the reader a specific image. Plus, it'll make the reader curious.

The Midnight Library by Matt Haig

Mrs. Elm had held her, stroking and smoothing the back of her head like a baby, not offering platitudes or false comforts or anything other than concern.[2]

Write Your Book: Use strong verbs and an action simile.

Act Two, Plot Point 9: Escalating Obstacles

Step 1: Your character is attempting to achieve a goal, but the obstacles are escalating, increasing the stakes. Ask your protagonist what their goal is. Now, to brainstorm this scene, list five obstacles. Examples: storm, locked door, wild animal, fire, rival fight, phone/car/computer dies, their big fear, allergies, spilling a drink, police arrest, trapped in an elevator, broken arm, uncontrollable sneezes, friend captured . . .

Step 2: Describe where they are and continue with strong action verbs. Add your protagonist's observation about how someone moves for the action simile. What strange thing could they be doing? How would your protagonist describe them?

Day 46: Specificity and Conflict

It's 9:32 at night, and you're craving your favorite gingersnaps from Ralph's grocery store. Your partner says they'll pick them up. But somehow they get it wrong and bring home shortbread cookies. They shrug. "Well, you said cookies." Are *any* cookies good enough? No, shortbread is not the same thing as those yummy gingersnaps you were craving, with whipped cream (amazing). Now we've got conflict. What if this isn't the first time? What if they always forget your cookies? What if they *never* listen? (If you're also pregnant, your partner is probably taking a trip back to the store.)

Specificity is important, and not just when it comes to cookies. If the nurse from my daughter's school calls and leaves a message on my voicemail telling me that she has a wound, that is *not* enough noun specificity. What cut her? Is it a six-inch knife wound in her thigh, down to the bone, from which she may die in the next hour? Or a paper cut? Add specificity. The details of any story are how we achieve a feeling of verisimilitude, a feeling that the story is real.

Exactly What?

Specific numbers, names, and places are ways to add tension to a scene and make it feel real. If your character's a diamond thief, she'll know the difference between a two-carat type I and a type Ia diamond—and her knowledge may provide the missing piece to the mystery. She'll have tools like a glass cutter for cutting display glass or a plasma torch to get into safes. Maybe she'll target a vault like The Helix Reserve, one of the most difficult diamond exchanges to break into. The specific name matters, and it adds obstacles.

How Many?

Let's talk about numbers. Nobody would say some men broke into their house. If you're in that situation, you'd count the men! Is it four men? Or two? That makes a difference. In your story, you may also use a deadline or a countdown to build tension at this point, like in John Green's *Looking for Alaska,* in which the days count down to the midpoint. As the numbers go down, we know we are moving closer to disaster.

Shatter Me by Tahereh Mafi

From the beginning of this story, the protagonist counts to maintain her sanity.

> I've been locked up for 264 days. I have nothing but a small notebook and a pen and the numbers in my head to keep me company. 1 window. 4 walls. 144 square feet of space. 26 letters in an alphabet I haven't spoken in 264 days of isolation.[3]

When this novel hits the Escalating Obstacles plot point, the boss causes her to hurt a toddler, and she's furious:

> I crush the glass with 10 fingers. I'm clutching a fistful of gravel and a fistful of fabric at Warner's neck and there are 50 different guns pointed at my head.[4]

The numbers make it feel real, intensifying the stakes for the reader. Perhaps a woman is climbing Mount Kilimanjaro and she's counting her steps—12,508 in 8 hours. 5,693 to go. But it's steep, so it'll take 6 hours. On top of that, she has a fear of African tick-bite fever, and her Apple Watch says her temperature is 103.

What *Type*?

We don't care if your character has a random plant in their kitchen, but if they have a beloved prickly pear cactus they've lovingly named Mr. Cactipoo and they learn cacti have bad feng shui (and they're the superstitious type), we wonder what will happen to Mr. Cactipoo.

If a teen is angry and throws a ball at the dinner table, it matters if it's a Ping-Pong ball or a basketball—if it's the latter and he has a volatile mother, now we're worried.

If a man has four Persian cats and his boyfriend brings him flowers, there's no problem. But if the boyfriend brings Stargazer lilies even though lilies are poisonous to cats, we're going to have an issue.

If a sweet ten-year-old girl comes home with a stray dog, there's a big difference if she's returned with a pit bull or a Chihuahua.

Let's say the creepy antagonist is choosing between types of rope at the hardware store. He tells the salesman he needs rope for tying knots.

"You're going to need to get yourself some nylon or polyester rope," says the salesman.

"What's the difference?"

"Nylon's better for adjusting the knots. Polyester'll hold, but you'll never loosen those knots."

"I'll take twenty feet of polyester."

Now the reader is even more worried about the kid the kidnapper's been eyeing. His attention to detail makes us worried that the kid doesn't have a chance.

Write Your Book: Use specific nouns, numbers, and types.

Act Two, Plot Point 9: Escalating Obstacles

Step 1: Think of any names or numbers you might be able to add to your scene. Jot down any real or convincing names to the places—stores, streets, towns, models. Also brainstorm the exact count of soldiers, dollars, minutes, steps, bullets, pizza slices, or whatever is relevant to the scene. Time. Add the specific time or the countdown numbers.

Step 2: Think about your protagonist's fear. Add a number and name to their fear. Add a number or place to a past worry (Mount Kilimanjaro / Apple Watch, fear of the tick-bite fever, plus a rising temperature).

Step 3: Add one more precise detail that makes the obstacle more challenging or dangerous. Perhaps it's an object like a switchblade or a specific type of snake, like a black water moccasin.

Day 47: Listing

The other day, in rowing class, the tall guy next to me dumped his pockets into the little basket: keys, a phone, some Tic Tacs, and a *large pocketknife*. Do not bring a knife to rowing class—especially if you're sitting beside a novelist. My brain galloped. Should I tell the front desk? See something, say something! What if he grabs it? What if he becomes Stabby Man? Do I run? Do I warn everyone? And then I stared at the white Tic Tacs. Would a rower who tosses a knife in with Tic Tacs turn into Stabby Man? Probably not. (Orange Tic Tacs would have been more reassuring.) He did not go psycho. We just rowed. I rowed harder than normal.

Even without knives, our stuff tells a great deal about us. Dump your own bag—what does it reveal? Here's mine: a Ziploc bag with multicolored hair streaks, an empty candy wrapper from a recent strange massage, an Apple AirTag.

What assumptions can you make about me based on these objects? I'm around schools and kids a lot. I lose my stuff easily, thanks to my distractable, ADHD brain. I love a good massage, but maybe I go for the more affordable option with a masseuse who gets me to drink five cups of goji berry tea.

What problems can these objects cause? Maybe someone steals my bag and my AirTag leads me on a wild-goose chase across town to retrieve it, where I stumble upon a crime in action.

List specific objects; add at least one item that could cause problems.

Let's say your character looks in the backpack of their new love interest. They find a burner phone, a small baggie with white pills, a slip of paper with a phone number on it, and hemorrhoid cream. Do you think they'll keep dating this person?

In Cold Blood by Truman Capote

Perry picks up his suitcase. It contains clothes,

> "a box of aspirin, a bottle of tequila, scissors, a safety razor, and a fingernail file."[5]

This list of items he's carrying reveals information that could lead to escalating conflict, and indeed it does: Perry already has pain; the tequila shows how he deals with stress; the scissors, razor, and fingernail file show he's uptight about his appearance (especially the file), and this characteristic will cause conflict with his swaggering, freewheeling partner, Dick.

List the main character's opinion about the best or worst ways to do something; then let them do it wrong.

High Fidelity by Nick Hornby

> Here's how not to plan a career: (a) split up with girlfriend; (b) junk college; (c) go to work in record shop; (d) stay in record shops for rest of life.[6]

List the rules; rules are meant to be broken.

When you list rules, the reader is now worried because the protagonist will probably break them . . . especially if they're strange rules or rules that anyone would want to break.

***The Giver* by Lois Lowry:** When Jonas becomes the community's future "Giver," he receives eight new rules, all of which have the potential for causing problems. He's now not allowed to talk about dreams, even though he always talks to his parents about dreams, and he *can* now lie, though lying was previously forbidden, so it's very hard for him.

Write Your Book: Add a list of objects, rules, or opinions.

Act Two, Plot Point 9: Escalating Obstacles

Step 1: Pick the type of list you want to reveal in this scene that might best escalate obstacles: a list of objects, a list of the best or worst ways to do something, a list of rules.

Step 2: Add the list early on and show your protagonist's mental reaction to it before you show how they respond.

Day 48: Clincher Details and Cliffhangers

Today, work on ending both your paragraphs and your chapter in a gripping way, with a powerful image or a detail that nails a character, place, or the feeling of the scene in just a few words. Clincher details are how you tug on the reader's emotions and make them ache for your character . . . and keep reading.

Ideas for Clincher Details

1. Foreshadow with a Strange Detail or Simile
   Everything I Never Told You by Celeste Ng

Still, the small of her back prickles, like beetles marching down her spine.[7]

2. Mirror the Protagonist's Emotion with the Setting
   Dig by A. S. King

Before he took the car home, he drove all the way across town to the automatic car wash. During the spray cycle he'd cried.[8]

3. Show their Body Language or Emotion with a Simile
   A Man Called Ove by Fredrik Backman

He has to sort of struggle for a mouthful of air, like a fish in an overturned bowl.[9]

Write Your Book: Add clincher details.

Act Two, Plot Point 9: Escalating Obstacles

Step 1: First, list the setting details. Next, go through all the characters in the scene and decide how they're feeling so that you can use imagery and similes to demonstrate these feelings; perhaps they manifest in the scenery. Finally, decide what twist and clincher detail will end the chapter.

Step 2: As you write, use specificity to make every paragraph pop, and end the chapter itself on a powerful note. Your obstacles escalate throughout this plot point, so let's end this chapter with a shock or a twist, using the details to create the twist.

Busy Writer Recap and Reward: Days 45–48

Act Two, Plot Point 9: Escalating Obstacles

You're two plot points from the midpoint. Over the last four days, you wrote the Escalating Obstacles plot point, working on raising stakes with specificity. Random reward time: Cuddle a dog, a cat, or your furry animal of choice; just really sink into that experience. Food? Maybe pizza with pineapples or anything unusual . . . Take the road less traveled.

Nurture Your Creativity

Make a Meal from Your Story

First, go to the grocery store and buy things your character would buy. Then go home, prepare their favorite meal, and eat it, imagining that you are your character. The False Hope plot point (next) often includes food. Can characters share a meal? Food can also add a problem: crunching Cheetos during an interview or licking the Tajín rim on a margarita glass while their friend is unpacking trauma. I was doing a reading at an author event in New Paltz, New York, along with fellow authors Jennifer Castle and Nova Ren Suma, when a guy sat in the front row and started slurping his noodle soup and asking questions. Very hard not to look at him and start giggling. I'm not even sure if I made any sense—this is an example of a real-life food/eating complication.

Adele Myers (*Tobacco Wives*)

on Perseverance

"I was invited to be a part of a writers' group with a couple of other women. . . . And the feedback from them really encouraged me, you know, they said, 'We think you can get this published.' . . . It was a long journey. That sounds kind of cliché, but it really was . . . it takes a lot of perseverance. . . . Just keep at it. Just keep working towards it."[10]

(P.S. This was my writers' group, and this book really was fabulous from the beginning.)

Busy Writer Road Map Days 49–52: Beautiful Language

Our skill focus in the next four days is to mirror the protagonist's hope and joy before the midpoint twist in how they see the world through literary language: imagery, metaphors, personification, repetition, and alliteration. Vivid writing can make any scene come alive, but this isn't a time to be "perfect." Treat this as a time to play.

Act Two, Plot Point 10: False Hope

You know that moment in a horror movie: They're all laughing around the campfire, roasting marshmallows, but it's the middle of the movie and you realize, *Oh, no, someone's going to die.* The contrast is why this scene works—it builds the suspense.

Ideas and Examples

1. Gaining someone's trust (*The Hunger Games* by Suzanne Collins)
2. Falling in love (*The Fault in Our Stars* by John Green)
3. Gaining a key resource, like potatoes on Mars (*The Martian* by Andy Weir)
4. Winning a big battle (*Red Rising* by Pierce Brown)
5. Bonding over breaking rules (*The Librarian of Auschwitz* by Antonio Iturbe)

Day 49: Imagery and Contrast

The False Hope scene gives readers a break while also adding tension by foreshadowing something bad that's around the corner. We're leading up to the midpoint shift, which is often a negative shock, so a positive scene, often involving love and bonding, heightens the shock. But remember, these plot points aren't ironclad, and your story might have some differences: Sometimes the False Hope *is* the actual midpoint shift.

Create some imagery and then add contrast, something out of place or surprising. For instance, in a zombie story, a father and his son have found an empty house where they eat cold beans and laugh because beans used to be gross. The sunlight glows on the kid's face, and then they hear a rattle from the attic. *Oh, no: zombies.*

The Emperor of Any Place by Tim Wynne-Jones

Note the contrast of the beautiful sky and the devil boats:

> I saw the boat first. It was early morning, first light. The sea was dead calm. The sky blue with pure white cirrocumulus clouds five miles up. A herringbone sky. The boat was anchored two hundred yards offshore at the inner edge of the heart's eastern shoulder. A small American gunship. The kind we called "devil boats."[1]

Write Your Book: Add contrasting imagery to your scene.

Act Two, Plot Point 10: False Hope

Step 1: This is a reminder to brainstorm each scene before writing it, at least the basics: purpose, setting, characters, scene goal, action, conflict. Also, keep in mind the use of opposites—we want setting opposites and success-failure opposites throughout the book, but especially in this plot point. In terms of setting opposites, if the last scene was in a field of sunflowers in the middle of a bright, sunny day, maybe this one is in a bustling Times Square at night.

Step 2: As you start writing today, hook us with a funny thought or opinion, a strange sound, a mysterious object like a square box tucked in the man's jacket. Then describe the setting, adding contrast. Within the moment of hope, plant a darker element to foreshadow the midpoint. Joy and then despair. Love and then violence. Birth and then death.

Day 50: Alliteration and Repetition

Alliteration

Today, your writing will not go slug-slow; it'll go fire-engine fast. Alliteration is the repetition of the first consonant of two or more words in a row or near one another. You can use this device to elevate your prose and amplify the emotion of the False Hope scene. National Youth Poet Laureate Amanda Gorman said, "I always use alliteration for the moments that I want people to remember most in my poems. It's a great memory device."[2]

A Man Called Ove by Fredrik Backman

You can't trust bloody buses. The drivers are always drunks.[3]

Note the alliteration: bloody buses, drivers . . . drunks.

Intentional Repetition

I'm not talking about accidental repetition where you repeat words like "the girl" on the same page—you want to avoid this, and you can catch this type of accidental repetition of words by reading your writing out loud in the second draft. For now, think of an emotion you'd like to amplify and then repeat a word or phrase that could hold this emotion.

The Absolutely True Diary of a Part-Time Indian

by Sherman Alexie

At this point in the story, Junior wins a basketball game against his old reservation team and feels shame.

> I knew that seven or eight of those Indians lived with drunken mothers and fathers.
>
> I knew that one of those Indians had a father who dealt crack and meth.

> I knew two of those Indians had fathers in prison.
> I knew that none of them was going to college.[4]

Negative Repetition

In this case, you talk about what does not exist, and this can be an effective way to show either yearning for whatever's missing or relief over an escape from the bad experience.

> ***The Bluest Eye*** by Toni Morrison
>
> No zinc tub, no buckets of stove-heated water, no flaky, stiff, grayish towels washed in a kitchen sink, dried in a dusty backyard, no tangled black puffs of rough wool to comb.[5]

Write Your Book: Add alliteration and repetition.

Act Two, Plot Point 10: False Hope

Step 1: Now that you've reached a peak moment of emotion in your story, add some alliteration.

Step 2: Next, add intentional repetition to amplify that emotion. You could also use negative repetition: Explore what does *not* exist in this moment.

Day 51: The Rule of Threes

Let's have a little fun with the rule of threes right now: Think of three things that show something about you, and make the last one surprising. For example, I like popcorn, pizza, and parties where I can leave after five minutes. The rule of threes works by repeating a word, phrase, image, or structure three times. Grouping in threes adds rhythm and makes writing more memorable.

In a sentence or paragraph, you might repeat:

1. **Three nouns:** In the Declaration of Independence, it's used for rhythm and to make it more memorable—life, liberty, and the pursuit of happiness. Elsewhere, it's often used for items in description: The grass was dotted with dandelions, random rocks, and candy wrappers.
2. **Three adjectives:** She was tall, wild, and frizzy-haired.
3. **Three actions or sounds:** Upstairs, the dishes clattered, my mom yelled at my brother to help with the dishes, and footsteps creaked down the hall. Notice how the third action is out of place; this can add tension to your paragraph.
4. **The exact same word:** There was no food in the cupboard. No food in the fridge. And no food in my belly.

In the beginning, middle, and end of the book, you might repeat:

1. **A symbol, image, or place:** It has a different meaning at each point in the story or the characters interact with it in a new way. In *The Outsiders* by S. E. Hinton, the repeated image is a sunset.
2. **An object:** It's not the object as much as the character's interaction with that object, like a lucky penny or a notebook. In *The Goldfinch* by Donna Tartt, the repeated image is a painting of a goldfinch, which the protagonist steals, hides, and then returns.
3. **An experience:** Show how the main character is changing through their interaction with this revisited moment. Maybe they ride three taxis or get bullied in these three moments and we see how they respond differently each time.

Write Your Book: Repeat an opening image, object, or experience.

Act Two, Plot Point 10: False Hope

Step 1: You're heading into the midpoint, so now is a good time to look at what object, image, location, or experience you could repeat from the beginning of your novel. It may be used in this hopeful scene or in the midpoint if you'd like it to have a dark twist. Either way, you'll show how the character is changing through their interaction with this revisited moment. Also consider how this could be used in the ending, and put that on your sticky-note wall for later.

Step 2: As you write, show the change in the main character's emotional or physical responses to this symbol or object, and show a change in the way they describe it. Show their thoughts or worries—maybe the object foreshadows what's to come.

Day 52: Personification and Zoomorphism

Your writing chair is whispering for you to sit down. Your computer is growling because you haven't fed it. Let's use personification and zoomorphism when you write today.

Personification is when you give human attributes and actions to an object, building, animal, plant, or the weather.

The Book Thief by Markus Zusak

Voices climbed over shoulders and the smell of pure German sweat struggled at first, then poured out.[6]

Zoomorphism is the same as personification, except it's an animal action. The girl galloped. The wind howled. The fire slithered across the dry grass.

Write Your Book: Add personification or zoomorphism.

Act Two, Plot Point 10: False Hope

Step 1: Personify an object or the weather as you finish the False Hope plot point. Perhaps the beach is smiling at a strolling couple, or the beer bottles are dancing after the battle.

Step 2: End this scene with some foreshadowing of the Midpoint Shock, which will be coming next. Could you add some zoomorphism here? Perhaps the grandmother's picture is barking at them, or old pipes are hissing.

Busy Writer Recap and Reward: Days 49–52

Act Two, Plot Point 10: False Hope

You're now hitting the midpoint, people! You're heading into the middle scene of your book. We're more or less at the 50 percent mark of your narrative. Don't worry too much about this now, but ideally your midpoint will fall roughly at the halfway point of your word count.

You've worked on beautiful language for the last four days, focusing on imagery, alliteration, repetition, personification, and the rule of three. You're accomplishing a big goal—you're already at the middle. That's a fabulous thing. Give yourself a treat: perhaps lying on a hammock or in front of a fire with your drink of choice. Stay hydrated. Be happy.

Nurture Your Creativity

Do a Four-Count Meditation

As we head into the next tense scene, let's release some tension. This meditation will help release stress, especially after real-life conflict, and prepare you for your writing this week. You can do it anytime, anywhere. Breathe in and then just count the exhale: 4-3-2-1. You can also count the inhale, but apparently there is a bigger calming effect if you focus on that slow exhale. Relax the body. Pretend you're a bag of sand. Do this for five minutes. At the end, breathe in deeply, squeeze your whole body tight, and then release. Try it right now (even just five breaths . . . or one)!

Douglas Adams

(The Hitchhiker's Guide to the Galaxy)

in an encouraging note to himself

(Yes, write encouraging notes to yourself!)

"Forget about the worry, just press on. Don't be embarrassed about the bad bits."[7]

Busy Writer Road Map Days 53–56: Twists and Turns

The next four days focus on twists and turns as you write the Midpoint Shock, the next pivotal plot point. This will substantially change the second half of your book. Open your favorite novel to the middle, skim the ten pages around it, and look for the moment that forces a change.

Act Two, Plot Point 11: The Midpoint Shock

It's time for your story to do a backflip. The Midpoint Shock is the second pivotal plot point (the first was the Inciting Incident), marking a major change at roughly the 50 percent mark. In *The Sticky Note Plot,* David Macinnis Gill lists three types of midpoints: a physical turn, an emotional turn, and a catastrophic turn. In the physical turn, something physical has changed about the character or world. An emotional turn happens when the protagonist sees themselves or another character in a new way. The catastrophic turn is a disaster like a tsunami.[1]

Ideas and Examples

1. Discovering the "dead" person is not dead (*Gone Girl* by Gillian Flynn)
2. Breaking up (*The Notebook* by Nicholas Sparks)
3. Experiencing an ally's betrayal (*Red Queen* by Victoria Aveyard)
4. Running from an attack (*Jurassic Park* by Michael Crichton)
5. Discovering an alien (*Project Hail Mary* by Andy Weir)

Day 53: 6 Key Elements of a Scene

Today we're going to take a pause to give you a chance to plan this next pivotal scene in detail.

Plan Your Book: Plan the midpoint in detail.

Step 1: Answer the following questions for your scene.

1. **Purpose:** What is the purpose of this scene? What are you trying to reveal? How does the scene move the story forward?
2. **Setting:** Where will you start? Time? Danger? Multisensory details?
3. **Characters:** Who's in the scene? Description? What just happened to them? How are they feeling and why?
4. **Goal:** What does the protagonist want to do right now? What do others want? Does anyone have a conflicting goal?
5. **Actions:** What physical actions do the characters take to pursue their goal?
6. **Conflict:** What is the internal conflict, fear, insecurity, or worry? What is the external problem or obstacle?

Step 2: Start your scene with a foreshadowing hook and setting description. Show the protagonist's thoughts about their goal.

Day 54: Twists and Reveals

It's always a good idea to add some hints before the big reveal, even before this point. If you haven't planted anything, you may want to plant one or two hints before this scene, but don't do it now. Add a comment in your manuscript to plant hints earlier, when you work on your next draft. Onward!

As you start this key scene, you can hook the reader by hinting at the upcoming twist. The reader may already have a suspicion about who's keeping a secret, who might betray the protagonist, or who has a secret identity, but the protagonist is in the dark.

Four Common Midpoint Twists or Turns

1. A character has a hidden or secret identity.

    Hints: The questionable character is not reachable, they avoid being in photos, they know something they shouldn't.

    Obvious Reveal: They slip up their name, someone recognizes them, a different ID shows up.

2. A character is a traitor or a cheater.

    Hints: Someone always seems to have been present when a plan got leaked, there are physical signs of their betrayal (boyfriend has lipstick on his collar), something feels false or rehearsed about their behavior.

    Obvious Reveal: They have knowledge only the traitor would have, they have a burner phone or an object from the enemy or the other woman/man.

3. A character is hiding something physical like a body or a magical object.

    Hints: The person's eyes flick to a hiding spot, they get nervous when someone walks near a particular area, the dog barks at a wall or another unusual place.

    Obvious Reveal: Something like black light or a sound reveals where it's hidden, something is out of place like a mismatched tile or brick, there's fresh paint or epoxy glue to hold a board in place.

4. A character is falling in love with the protagonist.

    Hints: The love interest offers small sacrifices like the last piece of sushi or use of the charger when their own battery is nearly dead, they talk of the future, their pet likes the protagonist, they randomly show up to help them paint or move.

    Obvious Reveal: The love interest confesses or someone else blurts it out.

Write Your Book: Hint at the coming reveal.

Act Two, Plot Point 11: The Midpoint Shock

Step 1: Before you start writing, imagine you're the protagonist. You're in a gripping setting with either emotional or physical danger. Go through the senses. What do you see, smell, and hear? What are you touching? How do you feel emotionally? Now use this sensory exploration to write a description of this midpoint scene from your character's perspective.

Step 2: Add a hint, foreshadowing the coming reveal of the midpoint. The protagonist may misinterpret it. Focus on their perceptions and thoughts, and add a confusing observation.

Day 55: Who Knows What?

The twists and reveals will land differently, depending on the timing and who learns the truth first. Information is power. Think about who knows what, who *thinks* they know the truth, who is lying, and who will be present when the protagonist learns the truth.

Information and Knowledge

1. What does the protagonist know?

   The whole point of a reveal is that the protagonist doesn't know something that other characters know, or they have only partial information. A detective may have part of the puzzle, but he hasn't put it all together. In a romance, often a misunderstanding will keep the two main characters apart; they each believe the other doesn't want them due to a missed message or a misinterpreted action—they have just part of the truth.
2. What does the reader know?

   Often the reader has figured something out before the protagonist has. We've seen the warning signs or the potential for betrayal.

3. What do other characters know?

   They'll have part of the truth, they'll know nothing, or they'll know it all but won't be able to share it. For example, maybe a sister knows her brother is cheating on her sister-in-law, but she can't tell her.

   ***Gone Girl* by Gillian Flynn:** Nick suspects Amy framed him but doesn't know exactly what happened or if she did it alone. The police know nothing and suspect Nick. Amy knows everything.

Write Your Book: Show who knows.

Act Two, Plot Point 11: The Midpoint Shock

Step 1: Go through each character—what do they know and how? What are they hiding?

Step 2: As you continue writing this scene, show your protagonist's thoughts and analysis of what they know. Maybe they ask questions in the dialogue as their suspicions grow, or perhaps they notice something they didn't notice before. Through this dialogue or eavesdropping, show what other characters know.

Day 56: External and Internal Stakes

A reveal works best when it shows what the protagonist and their allies stand to lose. When you increase the costs of the betrayal, attack, or lost romance, you raise the stakes. Maybe the reveal starts a ticking clock or shines a light on increased danger. Maybe it alters their life so much that they realize their life might not ever return to what it was before.

External stakes are what happens in the world if the character fails: Aliens take over, the monster eats the other kids in the school, the rival gang takes over the neighborhood.

Internal stakes are what's at stake for the protagonist. If they fail, their misbelief wins. They prove that people are not trustworthy or they're unlovable or greed is the answer.

Stakes aren't just for thrillers or fantasy, and they don't always mean someone's going to die. In a romance or a contemporary story, the external stakes might not be so great; maybe their job doesn't allow inter-office dating, so they risk losing their job (not the end of the world, but obviously not positive). The internal stakes may be more important; perhaps they have to be vulnerable to fall in love, but vulnerability is scary. This is what will touch the reader's heart.

Ways to Raise the Stakes

1. **Increase the reward:** Winning the football game means getting the girl.
2. **Add a ticking clock:** If they don't find the terrorists, the bomb explodes in three hours.
3. **Increase the demands:** Hostage-takers want more money.
4. **Threaten loved ones:** The serial killer knows where the detective's family lives.
5. **Add new consequences:** If they don't catch the murderer and someone dies, they'll also be fired . . . and lose health insurance for their sick kid.
6. **Give them an impossible choice:** Their mom or three kids?
7. **Increase the moral risk:** They must lie, steal, or kill to achieve the goal to save hundreds.

Write Your Book: Show the high stakes, either internal or external.

Act Two, Plot Point 11: The Midpoint Shock

Step 1: Today you'll complete the Midpoint Shock plot point, throwing your character into a whole new reality. When the external or internal stakes rise, what will the protagonist do? What decision will they make based on those increased stakes?

Step 2: Continue your scene, adding the external and/or internal stakes along with the big reveal or twist. Show the dilemma and decision. End the scene with a cliffhanger that shows the consequence or result of the decision.

Busy Writer Recap and Reward: Days 53–56

Act Two, Plot Point 11: The Midpoint Shock

You're flying along in this draft! In the last four days, you wrote the Midpoint Shock and worked on adding twists and turns to the story. You're past halfway. Congratulations! My reward suggestion for this week is to float in water anywhere. Just float. A bathtub. The lake. An ocean. If you don't like water, then get thee near fire! Roast marshmallows over a campfire, a fireplace, or your gas stove. One more suggestion: Buy yourself a hardcover book. You know that one you want to read, but you're waiting for the paperback? Don't wait. Buy it and get inspired.

Nurture Your Creativity

Go for a Brainstorming Walk, Run, or Swim

Go for a brainstorming walk, run, or swim to think about your next scene. Don't listen to music or a podcast, or anything else to distract your mind. Instead, just walk, run, or swim until your scene is fully alive within you and then sit and write—don't shower or draft an email or look at your phone. Just pour it out! A Stanford University experiment showed that 81 percent of participants generated more ideas when they were walking than they did when they were sitting—and fascinatingly, this study found that the heightened creativity continues after the walk stops. This is probably why writing immediately after exercise results in a state of imaginative flow, making the scene come alive on the page.

ACT THREE

Act Three generally takes us from the midpoint to the All-Is-Lost Moment. The big thing for Act Three is you've got to make things *worse* for your character. However, we still want hope: Aim for alternating Yes/No scenes—we still need small positive moments to keep us moving forward. In one scene, they overcome the obstacle, but in the next scene, they don't. The general feeling is life is going downhill. A chapter may have a couple of scenes, or it may just have one. If you come up with a better idea at any point for the earlier chapters, just make yourself a note in the margin and pretend that you've already made the change.

Act Three Scenes:

Plot Point 12: Reaction to the Midpoint (55–57%)

Plot Point 13: The Fuse (57–60%)

Plot Point 14: Flawed Plan (60–65%)

Plot Point 15: Subplot Complications (65–70%)

Plot Point 16: A Near Win (70–75%)

Plot Point 17: The Big Mistake (75–80%)

Plot Point 18: The All-Is-Lost Moment (80–83%)

Busy Writer Road Map Days 57–60: Reactions

In this section, we're diving into reactions to figure out how everyone responds to the midpoint. People rarely perform well immediately after a shock. Stress activates the lizard brain, and we dive into our most basic survival instincts: fight, flight, freeze, or fawn. Go ahead, think of your own traumatic events—How did it feel in your body? How did your brain react? In the next four days, you'll show their initial response and how they decide to move forward.

Act Three, Plot Point 12: Reaction to the Midpoint

After the shock of the midpoint, the protagonist doesn't usually make good choices or plans. Why? They haven't overcome their flaw or misbelief. If they did, they'd achieve their goal, and the book would be over. Sometimes the midpoint can bring good news, so this will obviously affect their reaction and plans.

Ideas and Examples

1. Pursuing a new goal (*The Girl on the Train* by Paula Hawkins)
2. Adopting the enemy's tactics (*Ender's Game* by Orson Scott Card)
3. Agreeing to work with an enemy (*Six of Crows* by Leigh Bardugo)
4. Breaking down emotionally (*The Kite Runner* by Khaled Hosseini)
5. Hiding whatever they've learned (*Gone Girl* by Gillian Flynn)

Day 57: Internal and External Reactions

My five-year-old daughter disappeared one sunny afternoon in Park Slope, Brooklyn, where we lived. We were walking to Pino's Pizza. She was a little speed demon on her scooter, and she raced ahead toward the intersection and flew around the corner. I didn't like her to be out of my view, and I wanted to run after her, but I told myself to mellow out, she'd be fine. When we rounded the corner, she was gone.

We couldn't find her in the pizza shop. She wasn't on the sidewalk or in nearby stores. I panicked. I screamed her name. My older daughter ran to check the bathroom in the pizza shop. No sign of her. My entire world shifted. My ears buzzed. I thought she'd been kidnapped, and I dropped to my knees like you see in the movies—I'm not kidding, very dramatic. I had bruises on my knees for the next week. It's embarrassing when I think of it, but this is what my body did.

It wouldn't be embarrassing if she really were kidnapped, of course. But since she wasn't, it was just me, overreacting. There I was, collapsed on the ground, panting, when I heard her sweet voice. "Mommy?" It turned out she was in the bathroom all along, behind the door.

Internal Physical Reaction

We all have an internal physical reaction to shock. The body responds to that surge of adrenaline. It's usually involuntary: shaking, gasping, throwing up, fainting, stumbling, collapsing, freezing, hugging ourselves. Shock shifts your perceptions. Your breathing changes. The reptilian brain is activated, and the body responds. You see everything different: Go through the senses. What are your character's perceptions?

Fahrenheit 451 by Ray Bradbury

Montag finds out that Clarisse, the girl who was curious and so full of life, has died. His wife says:

> "She's dead. Let's talk about someone alive, for goodness' sake." Montag did not look back at his wife as he went trembling along the hall . . .[1]

External Physical Reaction

Your protagonist and the other characters will also react physically by moving their bodies and talking. I mention physical action because, surprisingly, writers often miss this step. It's easy to get too in their heads about the shock and forget the need for movement. The external impulse is determined by a mix of their core impulse, the level of threat, their strengths and flaws. This external response will often lead into or start the next scene.

Then She Was Gone by Lisa Jewell

Laurel hasn't moved a muscle since SJ's pronouncement.[2]

Write Your Book: Show the characters' internal/external reactions.

Act Three, Plot Point 12: Reaction to the Midpoint

Step 1: Think of how your protagonist experiences shock, physically. Next, you'll write the sequel—the immediate reaction to the Midpoint Shock scene. We need the protagonist's thoughts about whatever has happened. If it's bad, and it usually is, show their worry about the increased threat or stakes. Let them catastrophize. This will add internal stakes for your protagonist. Describe their internal physical response, maybe with a metaphor or simile.

Step 2: Next, show their external physical response. They'll take action. Other characters may react in the opposite way, creating conflict. This may be the start of the next scene. If it is, remember setting opposites. This can be effective here to show the contrast between the setting of the midpoint and the setting of the next scene. Perhaps they were on a bright, noisy battlefield and now they're in a dark, quiet prison.

Day 58: Changing Patterns of Thought

After the initial internal and external response, your character will react to the shock of the midpoint with changed thought patterns. In stressful times, thoughts are not orderly; they are like a thousand small pieces of paper swirling in a tornado.

Since the midpoint is usually a bad shock, the protagonist will either disassociate or experience a rush of panicky thoughts. They may jump to fast conclusions or make a new plan immediately. They may be in denial—nope, that did not just happen. They could catastrophize and think of the very worst possible outcome, or dive into blame or self-blame. Even if the midpoint is good, like falling in love, their mind will process their world and experiences differently.

Below are three common types of thought shifts with examples from *The Outsiders:* "if" ruminations, "maybe" sentences with ellipses, and negative statements.

The Outsiders by S. E. Hinton

1. **A series of "if" ruminations:**

If Johnny got caught, they'd give him the electric chair, and if they caught me, I'd be sent to a reformatory.[3]

2. **A list of "maybe" sentences and use of ellipses:**

Maybe Johnny had been gone a whole week, and I had just slept. Maybe he had already been worked over by the fuzz and was waiting . . . Maybe Dally had been killed . . .[4]

3. **A series of negative statements:**

Don't think of them, I thought. (Don't remember how Johnny was your buddy, don't remember that he didn't want to die. Don't think of Dally breaking up in the hospital . . .)[5]

Write Your Book: Show the protagonist's changing patterns of thought.

Act Three, Plot Point 12: Reaction to the Midpoint

Step 1: Imagine the protagonist's feelings coursing through your body and listen to the protagonist's changing patterns of thought. Do they have one long thought, a bunch of fragments, a series of questions, or negative statements? Do their thoughts generally turn to blame, catastrophizing, rationalizing?

Step 2: Write the protagonist's initial disjointed rush of thoughts. When their brain clears, make the sentences longer. At this point, they may focus in on a specific object or sensory details, replanting themselves. Then show their physical actions in pursuit of their scene goal.

Day 59: Secondary Reactions

The midpoint is a moment of pivotal change, and it will trigger the protagonist's fatal flaw and misbelief, depending on how they see it. In her novel *Seduction of the Minotaur*, Anaïs Nin wrote:

> We do not see things as they are, we see them as we are.[6]

How will your character interpret what's just happened? What emotions will result?

Interpretation

In any shock, after the initial physical thoughts and reactions, we interpret what's just happened. Everyone reacts differently, so think about how your cast of characters will see what's happened.

A character's reactions and interpretations depend on a range of factors, including their trauma and resulting misbelief. If a woman experienced a breakup and had no misbelief around romance, she might think, *That's not the right person for me, clearly.* But if she has a misbelief that men aren't trustworthy, she may think: *He was just using me!* Or, *I bet he was cheating.* If she felt unloved in childhood, she may think: *I am unlovable.* Our brains tell us a lot of lies. What lie does your protagonist believe in this moment?

It Ends with Us by Colleen Hoover

After the wedding, Ryle physically hurts Lily at the midpoint, and the relationship turns abusive. Lily doesn't leave because her misbelief is that love can fix or stop abusive behavior.

Secondary Emotions

Emotions are complex and confusing: Let's dive into that complexity now. We often have a few feelings all at once. If a character is betrayed at the midpoint, they're going to feel a mix of emotions.

Gone Girl by Gillian Flynn

Nick discovers that his wife has framed him, but his first emotion isn't rage.

> Marrow-deep embarrassment, the kind that becomes part of your DNA, that changes you. After all these years, Amy could still play me.[7]

Secondary Behaviors

Your characters will respond to the shock now with a secondary wave of behavior, engaging in old defense mechanisms, coping behaviors, symbolic actions, or new habits.

This might bring their core flaw to the surface. They'll become aware of the fact that they fear criticism and have developed perfectionist tendencies to avoid it. Maybe they see that they don't trust anyone, and this has caused them to isolate themselves. But despite their awareness of this flaw and how it's played a part in the shock of the midpoint, they still need to grow more to overcome it. The pressure of the third act will help them get to that point.

Examples of Secondary Behaviors

Defense mechanisms (unconscious behavior): denial, dissociation, repression, projection, rationalization, reverting to childish behavior, humor (as a way of masking vulnerability)

Coping behaviors (conscious behavior): drinking, overwork, exercise, scrolling, sexual behaviors, cleaning, eating for comfort

Symbolic actions: tearing up photos, pawning the wedding ring, stuffing a medal into a drawer

New habits: taking a new route home from school, not visiting the old lady neighbor, quitting their favorite sport, not eating breakfast

Write Your Book: Show your character's secondary emotions and behaviors.

Act Three, Plot Point 12: Reaction to the Midpoint

Step 1: Now we see the protagonist's reaction to what just happened. You'll show their secondary emotions and behaviors in response to the midpoint. What is their typical defense mechanism? What are their coping behaviors? What can they do now to show how they feel?

Step 2: You've shown the multisensory description and hooked the reader. Now continue this scene. Show the protagonist interpreting what happened based on their misbelief. Show whatever secondary emotion they're feeling and a coping mechanism they use to avoid the pain. In general, stay aware of the feeling under the feeling, because suppressing this feeling may be guiding a lot of their actions at this point.

Day 60: Desire Line Shifts

The twist or turn of the Midpoint Shock usually shakes up the protagonist's desire line: In light of the new information, emotions, and realizations, what do they want now in terms of the big picture? The original goal may have changed: We'll use this scene to show *how*.

The deeper need usually remains unchanged, only now they may come to understand this need. This Midpoint Shock may serve to shift their priorities or their goal.

Some plots are two-goal plots—in these stories, the changed goal happens after the midpoint. If a tough sixty-year-old woman is climbing Mount Everest with the love of her life and her partner falls, she'll no longer want to get to the top; she'll want to save her partner's life.

The Tobacco Wives by Adele Myers

Once Maddie learns about the danger tobacco poses to women's health, she wants to find out more.

> I wanted to know more about MOMints and Mr. Winston, anything that might help me make sense of the letter from Dr. Hale. More than wanted—I *needed* to know.[8]

Write Your Book: Show the protagonist's current goal.

Act Three, Plot Point 12: Reaction to the Midpoint

Step 1: Ask yourself how the protagonist's goal has changed, shifted, or intensified. How about any of the other characters?

Step 2: As you write your scene, show their thoughts about the big-picture goal. Maybe they'll discuss it with someone. Show the new stakes or cost of achieving this goal—or of not achieving it.

Busy Writer Recap and Reward: Days 57–60

Act Three, Plot Point 12: Reaction to the Midpoint

You're over halfway! You might notice your energy is lagging a bit here; that's totally normal. People tend to experience a dip halfway through any big project. The good news is that your book should feel fresh with this big shift. Reward yourself with an experience! Do something new, something you've never done before—maybe it felt too expensive or it's something "other" people do. Treat yourself to that one thing you wouldn't normally give to yourself.

Nurture Your Creativity

Sit and Observe

This might be the most basic nurturing activity in the guide. Many people fail to do this in the middle of a busy life, including myself, yet it's essential for our own inner peace and our writing life. In a story, it's often the small observations that make the story feel real and create a reader–character connection, but to get those moments, we also need some quiet moments in life to sit, observe the world around us . . . and appreciate it.

Sometimes we're so busy we forget to be present. We forget to grab our favorite blanket and appreciate the coziness. We forget to listen to that sweet song our five-year-old is singing about how she's just singing. We forget to savor the perfect flakiness of a chocolate croissant. Instead, we turn on the TV or mindlessly scroll. We escape once more. Often, the very best thing we can do for ourselves is nothing. Try it now. Just "be." Observe. Savor something in your surroundings. Let a sense of calm fill your body.

David Levithan ***(Two Boys Kissing)***

on Being Unafraid

"My main piece of advice would be don't worry about being published—just write a really good book, but also don't be afraid to write a bad book. Give yourself permission to fail and don't be afraid."[9]

Busy Writer Road Map Days 61–64: Advanced Tension Devices

Throughout your novel, you'll use tension devices to make readers turn the pages. In this plot point, where we encounter the Fuse, we increase the stakes and add a ticking clock. The character will feel the pressure and make some bad choices. If we love your character, we will cringe and read with growing anticipation and worry about what will happen next.

Act Three, Plot Point 13: The Fuse

In this plot point, the stakes are rising, and usually there's a ticking clock—they must complete the task by a certain time. The antagonist (who may have had a midpoint victory) feels more powerful and appears to be winning. Meanwhile, the protagonist makes bad choices.

Ideas and Examples

1. Losing resources like food, water, warmth (*The Road* by Cormac McCarthy)
2. Racing against a looming deadline (*1984* by George Orwell)
3. Running out of food or oxygen (*The Martian* by Andy Weir)
4. Feeling pressure from an upcoming election (*Red, White & Royal Blue* by Casey McQuiston)
5. Fighting an escalating battle (*Red Rising* by Pierce Brown)

Day 61: Tension Through Character Development

Today, lead your reader through the Fuse plot point with character-driven tension devices. My encouragement is to finish an entire scene today, using *all* these devices. This challenge is "play." Aim for a trial-and-error mindset, not perfection.

1. **Hook the reader.** Open with something that alarms your protagonist: the creepy neighbor sneaking across the courtyard

with a bundle, a wolf's howl, any annoying sound, like a family member chomping on potato chips. They react.

2. **Include the sense of touch.** If you can show the sense of touch, you'll transport the reader into the protagonist's body, and they'll feel like it's happening to them.
3. **Foreshadow.** Use subtle, character-driven techniques to foreshadow disaster.

   Disregarded observations: The protagonist notices something's off, but disregards it.

   Flaws or mistakes: They do something we know will go badly, based on what we now know about them. (They're drinking at the office party but don't handle alcohol well.)
4. **Plant scene questions.** Sprinkle mysteries and red flags that the reader might catch, based on what they know about the characters. (Like your best friend's sketchy boyfriend? You can see it; they can't.) Show something mysterious or troubling so the reader starts guessing.
5. **Put decisions on the page.** Portray the character's thought process and we'll wince as they choose the *wrong* path, just as you wince when your friend texts their ex at two in the morning.

Write Your Book: Use tension devices to reveal character.

Act Three, Plot Point 13: The Fuse

Step 1: Pick a suspenseful setting to heighten the sense of unease. You might not add the Fuse yet, but you're building up to it in this scene. Imagine yourself in the protagonist's body so you add the sense of touch, transporting the reader.

Step 2: Write a hook that targets your main character's fear. Describe using all of the senses, especially touch and sound. Add foreshadowing by showing someone doing something suspicious. Plant a detail to make the reader wonder. Answer the questions in their mind. Then plan another detail.

Step 3: Show the protagonist's scene goal and decision-making process in their mind. The protagonist takes actions toward the goal and hits an obstacle that is particularly tough for the protagonist. Show them making a mistake, based on their flaw. This leads to the scene disaster. Next, don't forget the sequel or reaction.

Day 62: The Objective Correlative + a Deadline

Your twenty-four-year-old protagonist is taking the LSAT and a woman is tapping her pencil. He's already feeling heat from Dad about law school and now wants to snap that woman's pencil in half.

A couple is in a fight, but then a pipe bursts. They must move fast to save their new floors.

A dad misjudges a long hike and the heat; his kid is hot, hungry, and grouchy. Dad needs his kid to eat a peanut butter sandwich, and they need to get back before the afternoon sun hits. The kid says he hates peanut butter, and the tension rises.

In each of these examples, an object, action, or the weather carries the emotion of the scene. That's the objective correlative. Add a deadline or time pressure and tension rises.

Examples of the Objective Correlative with a Deadline

***Red Rising* by Pierce Brown**

Deadline: It's time for a big battle; everyone's nervous.

Object: Their gravBoots malfunction, amplifying the fear.

***The Martian* by Andy Weir**

Deadline: The rescue window is closing.

Object: The protagonist's dying potatoes mirror the fading hope.

Write Your Book: Use an object to amplify the tension.

Act Three, Plot Point 13: The Fuse

Step 1: Usually, this plot point takes up a few scenes. If you haven't finished the last scene, you could add stakes to it. Otherwise, start the next scene. Maybe switch to an opposite setting. What scene goal is your protagonist pursuing now? Can you increase the stakes for this goal? What is the obstacle? If you haven't added a ticking clock or clear deadline, could you do it now?

Step 2: Use the objective correlative (an object, weather, or repeated action) to amplify the fear or anger in the scene. End the scene showing the clock ticking down—metaphorically . . . or maybe you actually have a ticking clock!

Day 63: Decision-Making with Stakes

All day long, we face small and big decisions, from choosing between a turkey sandwich or pesto pasta for lunch, to telling your best friend she's too drunk to drive. Your lunch order might be relatively low-stakes, but taking your friend's keys away has higher stakes and requires on-the-page decisions. For any important decision they're making, let the protagonist explore the pros and cons in their thoughts or talk about their options with the other characters. This means we need to see it on the page. Give the reader a chance to think: *What would I do?* Or let them discuss it. Now they are cocreating the story, becoming an active participant. When this happens, they won't be putting your book down anytime soon.

Unfortunately, a common mistake I see in writers' work is that the characters simply act without thinking or making choices. This tells me that the writer is not participating in the narrative but rather watching the movie playing in their head. If you're simply showing us a movie, I'd rather watch an actual movie.

Books have an advantage over movies; they can transport the reader into the scene by showing the protagonist's thoughts, internal body sensations, as well as the senses of touch, smell, and taste. Readers want to be in the protagonist's body and mind. Transport your readers so they're making the decision along with your protagonist.

The Lord of the Rings by J. R. R. Tolkien

The group decides to cross a dangerous mountain pass to avoid detection, but then a snowstorm rolls in. They need to either go back or head to the dangerous Mines of Moria. This decision happens in conversation, and it has both internal and external stakes.

> Frodo looked troubled.
>
> "I wish I was back there," he said. "But how can I return without shame—unless there is indeed no other way, and we are already defeated?"
>
> "You are right, Frodo," said Gandalf, "to go back is to admit defeat, and face worse defeat to come."[1]

They choose the Mines of Moria.

Write Your Book: Your protagonist faces a tough choice.

Act Three, Plot Point 13: The Fuse

Step 1: What choice will they face? Think about a past decision your protagonist now regrets. Does this mistake affect the decision they make in this scene?

Step 2: As you write, show disagreements and body language that reveal everyone isn't on the same page. Dive into the protagonist's thoughts and let them process the pros and cons, and finally show them making the choice, for better or for worse.

Day 64: Stacking Obstacles

In Act Three, the obstacles get more intense. You can stack them, combining different types of obstacles, to put the pressure on. A teen has to rescue her sister from the killer in an hour at a warehouse on the edge of the city. She doesn't have a car, so she jumps on a bike and makes it to the highway, where a semi pushes her off the road. She tumbles into the ditch. Her arm breaks. The bike is toast. The sky cracks with lightning.

This is fun, people—cue evil laughter—make those characters suffer. *Mwahahaha!*

Types of Obstacles

Time Pressure: clock, deadline, increasing danger, incoming storm
Physical Challenges: trapped, injured, hungry, thirsty, exhausted
Emotional Challenges: romantic tension, rejection, criticism
Rules: laws, rules, moral code
Environment: unfriendly planet, hurricane, war zone, storm, aliens

Write Your Book: Stack at least three of the obstacles.

Act Three, Plot Point 13: The Fuse

Step 1: This is going to be a lot of fun to write today. Since it's likely to be an action scene, use shorter sentences and strong action verbs.

Step 2: Stack the obstacles and target the character's fear or flaw. Keep the stakes high enough that they won't give up.

Busy Writer Recap and Reward: Days 61–64

Act Three, Plot Point 13: The Fuse

Are you feeling tense? *Good!* That means you're embodying your character. Writing the third act can be tough. Using opposite scenes (success-failure, or a setting difference) can also be a great way to keep the audience (and yourself) engaged. If you get stuck at all, remember to keep going with your 15 Magic Minutes. If you're feeling particularly passionate about a future scene, write out of order—anything to keep going! Treat time: Go see an action movie or go speed-car racing. Look at the action and notice how it increases stakes and time pressure.

Nurture Your Creativity

Go to a Play (Even a Bad One)

Right now, I encourage you to book tickets to a play for this coming week or weekend. You can go to a high school performance if you don't have much money, or you can volunteer as an usher at any playhouse. Listen to the dialogue. Analyze what lands, what pulls you in, and what, if anything, doesn't feel true to the character.

Madeleine L'Engle *(A Wrinkle in Time)*

on Inspiration

"If the artist works only when he feels like it, he's not apt to build up much of a body of work. Inspiration far more often comes during the work than before it, because the largest part of the job of the artist is to listen to the work, and to go where it tells him to go. Ultimately, when you are writing, you stop thinking and write what you hear."[2]

Busy Writer Road Map Days 65–68: Advanced Dialogue

We're going to focus on advanced dialogue skills in the next four days, building on the dialogue skills we developed in Act Two. We'll work on tight dialogue with subtext, which will help your characters come alive on the page regardless of whether you're writing a lighthearted romance or a serial-killer thriller.

Act Three, Plot Point 14: Flawed Plan

At this point in the plot, the main character makes a key decision under pressure or out of fear, and it turns out to be the wrong one. Why? Stress hormones, such as cortisol and adrenaline, shift our thoughtful, longer-term reasoning to lizard-brain (or, reptilian) thinking. Basically, your protagonist isn't thinking straight. This bad plan will raise the stakes and conflict, creating a pressure cooker for their growth.

Ideas and Examples

1. Choosing a more dangerous path (*The Lord of the Rings* by J. R. R. Tolkien)
2. Breaking a rule (*Harry Potter and the Sorcerer's Stone* by J. K. Rowling)
3. Using a dangerous power (*The Name of the Wind* by Patrick Rothfuss)
4. Rejecting a mentor's advice (*Jane Eyre* by Charlotte Brontë)
5. Chasing the wrong lead (*The Da Vinci Code* by Dan Brown)

Day 65: Tight Dialogue—Start Late, Get Out Early

Most fast-paced books cut the greetings, the small talk, and the good-bye. Make the first line of dialogue pop. Something shocking. After, you can always summarize whatever information is needed to bring the reader up to speed.

Time and Tide by Edna O'Brien

"Do you believe her?" she said. Once said, it cannot be unsaid. That is the thing with words. You cannot wash them and wipe them the way you wipe dishes, which was what she was doing, merely to cancel out the brutality of what she had just said. Four words. Four treacheries. He said nothing, his anger taking a great inner lurch, and then he walked out of the kitchen, leaving the tap running.[1]

The opening line in this scene makes us curious and her lover's strong (wordless) reaction makes us even more curious. Sometimes silence speaks louder than words—we'll get to this in our next section:

Write Your Book: Start in the middle of the dialogue, at a shocking point.

Act Three, Plot Point 14: Flawed Plan

Step 1: Jump into the middle of a conversation in which the characters discuss what will reveal itself to be a flawed or incomplete plan, making your first line of dialogue in this scene pop.

Step 2: Make sure you describe the setting and any other important sensory details, either in the setup or mid-dialogue. Show the body language reactions of the characters.

Day 66: Subtext—What's Unsaid

Subtext is everything under the surface—whatever characters don't say. People rarely say what they mean, and this adds tension because the reader can sense the hidden secrets, desires, and lies. This is why on-the-nose dialogue bores the reader and feels unrealistic. Ernest Hemingway's Iceberg Theory applies to dialogue, too—most of it is under the surface. You'll show what they're hiding through body language or the dialogue itself.

1. What conflicting goals or desires do other characters have?

   All of your characters will have goals, and some of their goals may conflict with the protagonist's goal, but they often don't discuss their conflicting desires.

Dear Martin by Nic Stone

Justyce comes home from his boarding school and sees his mom.

> "Watchu doin' here, boy? It's a school night," was the first thing she said (without looking up from the book).
>
> "Can't I drop in to see my dear ol' mom when I'm missing her?"
>
> "Who you callin' old?"
>
> That made me laugh.
>
> "You gonna tell me what's really going on?" She closed the book and put it to the side then.
>
> "Come on over here and sit down."
>
> In all honesty, I didn't want to. Sit down is Mama-code for "spit it out."[2]

2. What feelings could characters be hiding?

   We hide difficult feelings, especially shame, depression, and sadness. Avoid on-the-nose dialogue in which a person shares exactly how they're feeling or exactly what they're thinking.

   Weak: "I'm angry that you're late for dinner."

   Strong: "I heated your dinner up twice."

Memoirs of a Geisha by Arthur Golden

The older sister is scrubbing a pot—notice the use of the objective correlative, in which the use of an object shows the hidden feelings. What hard feelings might she be avoiding by focusing on cleaning?

"Go outside and heat the bath," she told me, and brushed her unruly hair from her eyes with one of her wet hands.

"I don't want a bath," I said. "Satsu, Mommy is going to die—"

"This pot is cracked. Look!"

"It isn't cracked," I said. "That line has always been there."[3]

3. What lies or secrets are characters hiding?

   Characters hide their secrets for a reason, so once you come up with their lies or secrets, consider why they lied or why they aren't sharing this secret. Usually, it's to protect themselves or someone else, avoiding embarrassment, shame, or punishment.

   What clues can you give the reader? For example, they could deflect and answer a different question, give too many details, change the subject, fidget, joke, or check their phone to avoid scrutiny.

Write Your Book: Give the characters contrasting goals for subtext.

Act Three, Plot Point 14: Flawed Plan

Step 1: A common issue when writing dialogue is that the writer forgets to plant us in the scene, so it's like listening to a TV show when you can't see the screen—it's hard to figure out what's happening. Picture the setting and characters before writing. Think about the *other* characters before writing: Decide what they're hiding and what hints you'll give the reader.

Step 2: Now write the conversation. Use body language to show the subtext underneath what other characters are saying: a touch, a look, or the way they move an object.

Day 67: Power Plays in Dialogue

"Come home before midnight or don't come home at all."

You know that moment when someone says something and it shifts the entire power dynamic in the room? That's what we're working on today. In any scene, you have people with power and people without power, and that can shift at any moment; it often shifts through dialogue. We already looked at how the antagonist might assert their power through body language; make sure you're also using nonverbal communication along with the dialogue.

Consider the following power dynamic elements in dialogue.

Location: How does the location give any character more power than others? Who decided on this location for this discussion?

Physical power: Who controls the physical space? Who sets the meeting? Who makes the final decision on the plan? Who has the army, weapons, or physical strength to maintain control?

Control of information: What information do characters share or withhold?

Control of money, food, resources: Who controls the elements necessary for survival?

Body language: Does someone touch other people's personal items? Do they expand their stance or contract into themselves?

Refusal: What do they say they can't or won't do? What lines do they draw in their dialogue?

Concessions: What do they agree to do?

Result of the dialogue: Who gained power and who lost it?

A Game of Thrones by George R. R. Martin

You may have watched the TV series, but I recommend the books; they're gripping and well written, with rich characterization and dialogue, and every scene is about power: who has it, who wants it, and what they're willing to do to get it.

Power Dynamics and the Flawed Plan: The king has died, and the Hand of the King, Ned Stark, is in possession of the late king's letter asking him to be the Lord Protector of the Realm and act as regent, ruling in the king's stead until his son comes of age. Ned Stark believes he has the power, but he is proven wrong.

Location: The Throne Room—the king's son has not yet been sworn in, but he sits on the iron throne. Possession is nine-tenths of the law. Also in the room are the Kingsguard, loyal to the Lannisters, and the City Watch guards, who Ned Stark believes are loyal to him.

Control of Information: Ned Stark believes he controls the power since he has the knowledge, but the former king's son has beckoned Ned to the throne room, showing he has the real power.

Reframing of Power Dialogue:

Ned produced Robert's letter. "Lord Varys, be so kind as to show this to my lady of Lannister." The eunuch carried the letter to Cersei. The queen glanced at the words. "Lord Protector of the Realm," she read. "Is this meant to be your shield, my lord?" She ripped the letter in half, ripped the halves into quarters, and let the pieces flutter to the floor.

"Those were the king's words," Ser Barristan said, shocked.

"We have a new king now," Cersei Lannister said. "Lord Eddard, when last we spoke, you gave me some counsel. Allow me to return the courtesy. Bend the knee, my lord. Bend the knee and swear fealty to my son, and we shall allow you to step down as Hand and live the rest of your days in the grey waste you call home."[4]

In this scene, note the body language of power; Cersei tears up his letter. Having demonstrated her power, she tells him to bend the knee. Ned Stark refuses. He does not bend the knee and the two sides fight. At the end of the scene, Littlefinger holds a blade up to Ned Stark's neck and tells him he should never have trusted him. This disaster marks the end of the scene—remember scene-sequel? In the next scene with Ned Stark, we see the sequel—he is in prison and we hear his reaction in his thoughts of regret and rage.

Write Your Book: Portray the power dynamic in the dialogue.

Act Three, Plot Point 14: Flawed Plan

Step 1: Describe the setting and characters. Through dialogue and body language, show who's controlling the physical force, information, and resources.

Step 2: In the dialogue, show a shift in power. Someone refuses; someone concedes. Can you add a mistake, dilemma, or disaster by the end of the scene?

Day 68: Reveals in Dialogue

Reveals are like touching a lamp and getting an electric shock. Your best friend from childhood is actually your sister or your suburban homemaker mom is actually a CIA spy, or your grandpa faked his death and he's now living in Idaho as a rancher with his cowboy lover.

In *The Emotional Craft of Fiction*, Donald Maass writes, "Getting real is what happens when a scene's subtext bursts through. Any sudden shift in tone, unexpected openness, challenge, show of force, sudden softening, begging for compassion, or other call to genuineness and honesty can become electrifying and emotional. We don't show our true colors lightly. Telling the truth of things is risky."[5]

Write Your Book: Reveal something new in the dialogue.

Act Three, Plot Point 14: Flawed Plan

Step 1: First, decide on what you could reveal right now, then imagine any signs you could give the reader, i.e., hints that something is coming, like a character's incongruent behavior. Try to make it something juicy that will change the story or a key relationship once it's out.

Step 2: Start writing. Give the sign, then build your scene. Again, show the scene goal and add an obstacle. Then blindside your protagonist or, if your protagonist is doing the reveal, show the other character's shock. You can reveal the information in a variety of ways: Your protagonist can overhear people talking, a person could tell them a secret or reveal information by accident (or vice versa), or, in a burst of uncontainable emotion, your protagonist may talk for a sustained period, as a type of monologue with the reveal hidden within it.

Busy Writer Recap and Reward: Days 65–68

Act Three, Plot Point 14—Flawed Plan

Do your wild creativity dance! You're two-thirds of the way through this guide. That's a huge accomplishment. This week, you wrote about a faulty plan the character made and you worked on advanced dialogue skills, focusing on subtext, reveals, and planning in dialogue. What reward will you give yourself? I'm writing this in the hair salon—yes, you can write anywhere—and my hairdresser just told me that people often come in and tell her they had a bad day so they're getting a blowout. Personally, this had not occurred to me as a potential cure for a bad day. For your reward, treat yourself to a pick-me-up, something to care for your physical appearance. Maybe it's a haircut or a pedicure. (Yes, men get haircuts and pedicures too.)

Nurture Your Creativity

Do Something Brand-New

Shake up your life a little to inspire your writing. Book a flight to some exotic place for the weekend or get on a city bus to a strange area. Wear bright red lipstick or put a temporary purple streak in your hair or grow a mustache. Jump on the trampoline with your kid (expert tip for the ladies—pee first). Swim across a river. Give your partner a passionate kiss before work. Drive in the car for eighty-nine random minutes and then take eighty-nine pictures. Do something you've never done before. Feel the fear and do it anyway. It will shake up both your life and your writing in surprising ways.

Busy Writer Road Map Days 69–72: Character Development

In Act Three, increased pressure will push the protagonist to grow. We'll be developing the characters further through the subplot, which interferes with the protagonist's goal. Your job is to design the perfect obstacles that will force your protagonist and allies to make hard choices and mistakes—often this will be in the subplot.

Act Three, Plot Point 15: Subplot Complications

The subplot might be a secondary problem (a sick parent), a secondary goal (win the soccer match), an obligation (sister's wedding), or another character's problem (the best friend arrested).

Ideas and Examples

1. Struggling with the effect of past abuse (*The War That Saved My Life* by Kimberly Brubaker Bradley)
2. Losing a romantic interest (*The Assassin's Apprentice* by Robin Hobb)
3. Helping a sick family member (*Little Women* by Louisa May Alcott)
4. Being haunted by guilt (*Beloved* by Toni Morrison)
5. Helping an ally pursue their side goal (*Six of Crows* by Leigh Bardugo)

Day 69: Coping Mechanisms

Oscar Wilde wrote, "The only thing that one really knows about human nature is that it changes."[1] We don't always change for the better. At this point, characters often take a few steps backward. Coping mechanisms that once helped keep them safe now impede their growth.

Our character's core self is shimmering underneath their protective shield—and that shield may be causing more harm than good. For instance, maybe they're proud they can take a punch, no problem; it barely fazes them after a violent childhood. What is the harmful effect? This tough exterior might make them less trusting.

Maybe a teenager is good at helping calm down an agitated person with a mental health issue. What in life has given them this ability? Did they have a drug-addicted brother who had frequent nervous breakdowns, and it was their job to calm him down? Maybe now they always have to be the person who overfunctions for others and ignores their own needs. What are the negative impacts of these tough life lessons? What shields did they erect?

Think about your own coping mechanisms. In the personal, you find the universal.

Examples of Coping Mechanisms

Avoidance: television, doomscrolling, procrastination, oversleeping
Emotional dysregulation: eating, road rage, self-injury, perfectionism
Imagination: catastrophizing, revenge fantasies, daydreaming
Addiction: gambling, overexercise, workaholism, substance abuse

Take a second to consider what other characters have been up to while your protagonist has been stomping around making mistakes and learning lessons. What are their coping mechanisms? How could their behavior or habits interfere with the protagonist's main goal?

In order for a story to feel realistic, we also need to have a sense that there's a world going on outside of the frame of view. Are we still keeping track of the secondary characters' motivations? What are their physical and emotional needs going into this scene? Your side characters are essential to the plot. The complications they cause not only create external conflict, but they can also create internal conflict through torn identities or allegiances. Show how their problems make the protagonist's problems worse.

Write Your Book: Show your characters' coping mechanisms.

Act Three, Plot Point 15: Subplot Complications

Step 1: Choose the Subplot Complication—think about the subplots you've already planted involving other characters. If you haven't brainstormed this scene, do that now, at least mentally: setting, characters, scene goal, action, and obstacle. Think about the coping mechanisms your main character might use to deal with the conflict. Show how other characters' goals might conflict with your protagonist's scene goal.

Step 2: Start with the protagonist's thoughts about this Subplot Complication and describe any other characters involved.

Step 3: Show the protagonist's coping mechanism working at first, but then maybe it turns on them. Show the cost of this ineffective way of dealing with their emotions.

Day 70: Vulnerability

In *Walking on Water: Reflections on Faith and Art,* author Madeleine L'Engle writes: "When we were children, we used to think that when we were grown up we would no longer be vulnerable. But to grow up is to accept vulnerability."[2] The ability to be vulnerable is an essential part of the writing process.

Shame researcher Brené Brown has explored the power of vulnerability in releasing shame, as well as the harmful effects of not allowing yourself to be vulnerable. Her vulnerability prayer is this: "Give me the courage to show up and let myself be seen."[3] I've repeated this to myself many times while writing this guide. You guys, the struggle is real for us as writers and people, and it's the same for your characters.

Can your protagonist be vulnerable right now? Choose whether your protagonist cracks the door open and reveals their truth to someone they love or whether they slam it shut. Relationships have patterns of leaning in or leaning away. Love may be at the heart of your story, but even if it's not, it often plays a role in the subplot. Does your protagonist allow themselves to love or be loved?

Six of Crows by Leigh Bardugo

Kaz tells Inej he wants her, which is vulnerable for him, but she wants more. He never touches her with his bare hands due to a past trauma, and she doesn't know why—in fact, she knows very little about him because he can't be vulnerable.

> "How will you have me?" she repeated. "Fully clothed, gloves on, your head turned away so our lips can never touch?"[4]

This is his chance to tell her why he can't touch her with his bare hands, but he stays silent.

The Fault in Our Stars by John Green

After Augustus tells Hazel Grace that his cancer has returned, she sees him trying not to cry.

> You tell yourself that if they see you cry, it will hurt them, and you will be nothing but A Sadness in their lives, and you must not become a mere sadness, so you will not cry, and you say all of this to yourself while looking up at the ceiling, and then you swallow even though your throat does not want to close and you look at the person who loves you and smile.[5]

Write Your Book: Show their vulnerability or lack of vulnerability.

Act Three, Plot Point 15: Subplot Complications

Step 1: Make sure you know the answers to these questions about vulnerability: What is your protagonist's deeper need? Why hasn't this need been satisfied yet? What is their emotional armor? If they don't act on their truth, what is the personal cost?

Step 2: As you write the Subplot Complication plot point, show the protagonist's deeper need and longing. Make the reader desperate for them to lean into the person who makes them feel safe. Dive into their thoughts about becoming vulnerable. Let them think about what they would do to *not* reveal their secret longing.

Day 71: A Triggered Flashback

A triggered flashback is something in the immediate environment of the scene that brings the memory to the front of your character's mind. This flashback could involve other characters, or at least affect their relationships. Let it come about naturally, based on a sensory experience.

Triggers are specific and use all of the senses: ice in a glass, the smell of Old Spice, a specific country music song, a bloodred moon, crickets, cardboard, dogs barking, a belt falling on the ground, the sound of a match, a very soft touch on an arm, a blue plastic tarp.

Ghost by Jason Reynolds

Ghost is helping a shopkeeper clean up the stockroom, which is where he hid from his father when he was younger and his father shot at him and his mom. He gets triggered when the door locks and he can't get out—he describes a sensation like he's drowning.

Write Your Book: Write a flashback or tell a memory using dialogue.

Act Three, Plot Point 15: Subplot Complications

Step 1: Pick a sensory trigger—a sound, light, a smell, fabric. Then write the flashback with vivid imagery. Use action verbs. Put us in a scene.

Step 2: This triggered flashback should affect what the protagonist does next. Maybe it will make them realize they have to talk to someone. Or the trauma will interfere with their goal.

Day 72: The Feeling Under the Feeling

Ask yourself what the dominant feeling your character is experiencing at this point in your draft is. Now ask yourself what is underneath that feeling.

This is where you find the honesty.

Let's say a couple gets in an argument. They were going to go to a wedding together, but the flights are expensive, so the husband says he'll just go alone—after all, it's his friend. The wife starts yelling at him, "Oh, no, you're not going to that wedding without me! I told you to book those tickets weeks ago." She appears angry on the outside, but inside, she feels betrayed, and then, maybe under that feeling, sad, and maybe under that feeling, unappreciated and resentful. The feeling under the feeling is where it gets interesting.

Remember when we talked about surface-level wants versus deeper needs? It's possible that this feeling under the feeling is being driven not by whatever surface desire they're pursuing right now, but by a deeper need trying to make itself heard.

Write Your Book: Explore the feeling under the feeling.

Act Three, Plot Point 15: Subplot Complications

Step 1: Explore the character arc.

1. **Feelings:** How does the protagonist feel? What is their feeling under that more obvious feeling?
2. **Actions:** What do they do differently now?
3. **Appearance:** How do they dress differently? How are they taking care of their physical body?
4. **Observations:** How do they see people differently? The weather? What metaphors will they choose? What do they notice in terms of size of people, animals, plants, buildings? How big or small do they feel in comparison?

Step 2: If you're mid-scene, check to see if you have setting details and a time reference, especially if your character's goal has a deadline. If you're starting the scene, add these elements, and in the description, show rather than tell how they feel. The way they describe the setting and other characters will portray that feeling, as well as the feeling under the feeling. Show their scene goal, and then let the Subplot Complication interfere. Show two observable behaviors to reveal the feeling under the feeling for the other characters.

Busy Writer Recap and Reward: Days 69–72

Act Three, Plot Point 15: Subplot Complications

Remember to nurture your creativity. Go back to any of the exercises that have worked for you. This week, you worked through Subplot Complications. You may have some of your own interfering with your big goal of writing a novel. Remember, it's just 15 Magic Minutes a day to keep your head in the game. You're doing great. Now it's reward time. How are you going to treat yourself? Reward suggestions: Get bubbles and blow them out the window and see the joy you bring the world (or walk down the street with the bubbles). If gelato is available anywhere near where you live, get some gelato. Raspberry and stracciatella are my go-tos.

Nurture Your Creativity

Allow Vulnerability and Amplify Your Creativity

Let's just do the Brené Brown vulnerability prayer together: "Give me the courage to show up and let myself be seen." Your writing is a way to express your imagination and let yourself be seen. Here are Brown's three suggestions for creativity:

1. **Get deliberate.** Schedule time for creativity. Has your schedule gone off track?

2. **Get inspired.** Surround yourself with a community of creative people. Have you joined an uplifting writers' group or community? Join the Busy Writers Workshop community online.
3. **Get going.** Brown suggests taking a class to nurture your creativity. You're using this guide, so that's a big step.

Markus Zusak *(The Book Thief)*

on Playing with Your Writing

"You try another word. You try another colour on the wall. You try all sorts of things to make it feel whole. I just put things in, take them out, put them in a different order, switch it, and continue to try until I read it and it reads right."[6]

Busy Writer Road Map Days 73–76: The Muddy Middle

You may feel like you're in the swamp and your shoes are soaked in mud, and every step is a little harder to take. A midpoint energy dip is totally normal for any longer project, not just a novel. In the next four days, let's play a little to take your mind off the big picture for a few days.

Act Three, Plot Point 16: A Near Win

Your protagonist can taste success in this plot point—it feels so close. We raise hope so that we can break it, like the mean stepdad who brings home cake, only to eat it all by himself. The "disaster" in the scene comes at the end, revealing that they did not win, leading us to their bad reaction, the Big Mistake, and the All-Is-Lost Moment.

Ideas and Examples

1. Defeating the "villain," but he's a decoy (*The Princess Bride* by William Goldman)
2. Falling in love, but it doesn't solve the deeper problem (*Me Before You* by Jojo Moyes)
3. Escaping, but getting recaptured (*The Handmaid's Tale* by Margaret Atwood)
4. Winning a battle and then being betrayed (*Red Rising* by Pierce Brown)
5. Believing they've solved the mystery, but they haven't (*The Da Vinci Code* by Dan Brown)

Day 73: Research Sprints

Specifics are going to make the Near Win hurt even more by making it feel real. One of the most common mistakes in Act Three (or between the action of the midpoint and the crescendo toward the climax) is the tendency to rush things and be less specific with the writing, which can make it boring for the reader *and* for you, decreasing your excitement to write. To get past this muddy middle to the three-quarter point, I have a way to add back the spark—research.

Your main character may also need new skills at this point in your book, such as how to hold a gun, fight with a sword, hack into the Fed, or rob a bank. Researching how to break the law is fun. Just don't get flagged by the FBI.

You also may need to research the place. For my novel *Trafficked,* I traveled to Chisinau, Moldova, taking the same route traffickers use, and nearly got trafficked myself. I took a bus through the border stop between Moldova and Romania, where customs agents take your passports and then you have to get off the bus. I waited for three hours in the middle of the night in a giant, dark warehouse with a bulletproof glass office in the center. I expected men in trench coats with machine guns. My legs ached. I was told I couldn't sit on the ground—for a woman, that would be improper, and might "freeze your ovaries."

At this point, a woman in a fur vest approached me. She told me the customs agents were waiting for the bus company to give them a bigger bribe to let us through. She then showed me brochures of her "boyfriend's" hotel and told me I should come with her. Fortunately, I had done some research. Traffickers often use women for the first approach.

Finally, to my relief, we got on the bus. At three in the morning, it arrived in Chisinau on a random street. The woman in the fur vest tried to convince me to come with her into a black luxury car with a dangerous-looking man who I'd seen on the bus. I'll never forget how he looked at me. Down the street, I saw a flickering motel light. I said, "No thanks," and fortunately, I ran. I used everything I experienced in my novel: All's well that ends well.

Notice how research is applied in the following examples.

Transportation: *I Know Why the Caged Bird Sings* by Maya Angelou

A mile away ole Kansas City Kate (the train much admired but too important to stop in Stamps) crashed through the middle of town, blew its *wooo-wee* warnings, and continued to an unknown glamorous destination without looking back.[1]

Animal facts: *Wicked* by Gregory Maguire

Bats passed, making a guttering, sputtering sound that ended in an extinguishing *swoop*.[2]

Buildings: *Crime and Punishment* by Fyodor Dostoevsky

Raskolnikov visits a pawnbroker's house on the canal. This is based on a real location at 104 Griboyedov Canal in St. Petersburg, close to where Dostoevsky lived.

The outside:

It was a three-storied, old, and green-colored house.[3]

The room's shape:

Sonya's room had something barnlike about it; it was of a very irregular rectangular shape, which gave it an ugly appearance.[4]

Clothing and behavior (historical): *Rules for Heiresses* by Amalie Howard

She'd looked lovely, too, dressed in a stunning rose-colored muslin day gown with white stripes and dainty ribbons.[5]

Write Your Book: Add researched details.

Act Three, Plot Point 16: A Near Win

Step 1: Do a Five-Minute Scavenger Hunt

1. **Pick one concrete element to research:** a place, a vehicle, a uniform, a tool, clothing, food, a skill, transit
2. **Research three sensory details for that element:** texture, smell, sound, touch, taste, color

Step 2: Hook the reader with a researched detail. Make us curious.

Add more specific details to the action. Show your protagonist's goal in thoughts or dialogue and add a tough obstacle. Make it look like they're about to be successful in their end goal (but they're not).

Day 74: Play in the Muddy Middle

How will playing in the muddy middle help with your Near Win scene? A sense of play creates the trial-and-error mindset so essential for success. Don't take it too seriously. If it doesn't work, you change it. No big deal. Also, the Near Win plot point usually has fast-paced action, which works well for gamifying the writing.

1. **Popcorn writing:** You write a bunch of random words on slips of paper, which you ball up so they look like paper popcorn. Add colors, smells, sounds, dictionary words, random words family members give you. Set a three-minute timer. Every three minutes, one of those words enters your book. Write fast.
2. **Prop game:** You choose a key "prop" for your scene: a trophy, potato chips, a knife, a dead cockroach, a glass jar of teeth. Truly, the weirder, the better. The object passes among three of your characters. The third person does something different. Two people freak out about the cockroach; the third pets it and calls it Robert, the name of her ex. A guard has a knife, one prisoner takes it, and, in fighting with the guard, tosses it to another prisoner, who then uses it to slice a magical opening into another world.
3. **Three mini surprises:** As you write, include three surprises, making each one bigger.

Write Your Book: Play the games while you write.

Act Three, Plot Point 16: A Near Win

Step 1: Choose one of the games above and continue writing the Near Win plot point, using the game for inspiration.

Step 2: Choose another one of the games and keep writing.

Day 75: Fix Weak Writing Habits

In the Near Win, line-level mistakes can slow the pacing. Here are two common weak writing habits you can fix easily today.

Weak Writing Habit #1: The protagonist is the subject of every sentence.

Fix: Show what others are doing and cut filter words: "see," "smell," "hear," "recognize," "notice," "decide," "feel," "listen," "know," "think."

Weak: I see a boy walking toward me.

Strong: A boy walks toward me.

Weak: He heard crows cawing above in the maple tree.

Strong: Crows cawed above in the maple tree.

Weak Habit #2: Overuse of Gerunds (*-ing* words)

Gerunds are fine in moderation, but they're often overused or misplaced.

Fix #1: Move *-ing* clauses to the end so they modify the right subject.

Weak: Josie headed to the farm. Galloping on her horse, Roberta called out to her.

(Who's on the horse?)

If Roberta is the one riding: Josie headed to the farm. Roberta called out to her, galloping on her horse.

If Josie is the one riding: Josie headed to the farm, galloping on her horse. Roberta called out to her.

Fix #2: Use simple verbs unless actions are simultaneous.

Simultaneous: I opened the door, laughing.

Sequential: I opened the door and laughed.

Fix #3: Don't stack dialogue tags with gerunds.

Weak:

"Can we order pizza?" Bobby asked for the tenth time, making his voice whinier.

"Bobby, stop," his mom said, shutting the door.

"Can I have pizza?" Bobby demanded again, figuring she'd give in eventually if he kept asking.

"We have no money. Come," she said, grabbing his hand, pulling him to the grocery store.

Stronger (Notice I didn't cut them all; I just stopped the stacking):

"Can we order pizza?" Bobby whined for the tenth time.

"Bobby, stop," his mom said, shutting the car door.

He figured she'd give in eventually if he kept asking. "Can I have a pizza?"

"We have no money. Come!" She grabbed his hand and pulled him toward the grocery store.

Write Your Book: Vary your subjects and decrease gerunds.

Act Three, Plot Point 16: A Near Win

Step 1: Focus on varying the subject and cutting filter words.

Step 2: Show what the protagonist notices without saying that he sees it. We'll already know this because it's his perspective. Let other people act. Don't allow more than two sentences in a row to feature the protagonist as the subject. Cut filter words ("see," "hear," "smell," "realize," "decide") for direct verbs unless you need the narrative distance or you have an omniscient POV and want to show a switch to another character's perception of what's going on.

Step 3: Change some *-ing* phrases to simple past/present actions unless actions are happening simultaneously. Use clear, sequential actions.

Day 76: The Reversal Game

As you end this scene and approach the devastation of the Near Win, let's gamify the writing again. Create opposites within the scene, jumping from a win to a loss. Use reversals within the scene. Add escalating mini failures, which will lead to the Big Mistake next.

Round 1: Choose Your Type of Reversal.

You can roll a die or pick one:

1. **Price:** If they win this, they lose that.
2. **Fake:** Win the thing, but it's not real.
3. **Decoy:** Catch the guy, but he's not the actual villain.
4. **Resources:** Gain one resource (guns), lose one (water).
5. **Location:** The space goes from safe to not safe in one respect—lights, flooding, air, gravity, monsters.
6. **Betrayal:** Trust the person, but they turn on you.

Round 2: Finish your scene with win-loss-win-loss.

Make the reader believe the protagonist might win by giving them a win and then reversing it with a loss, and so on. Write a nail-biter, like a basketball game with a tied score and twenty seconds left in the last quarter.

Move 1: Pursue the goal and achieve the first mini victory.

Examples: The protagonist breaks into the safe; they kiss the girl; the two detectives find the killer hiding in a passageway.

Move 2: Reversal—the Twist

Examples: The safe is empty; the girl is an impostor; a giant cockroach appears in front of the killer in the passageway.

Move 3: Pursue a new goal based on the Twist and achieve another mini victory.

Examples: They find a second safe and open it to reveal the treasure; they search for the real girl and find her; they overcome the cockroach and run down the passageway.

Move 4: Reversal—the Second Twist . . . *Disaster*

Examples: They pick up one of the treasures and their hand burns off; the real girl says that her foot is attached to a timing device—take her and the city blows up; they corner the killer and then one of the partners points the gun at the protagonist.

Write Your Book: Play Rounds 1 and 2 of the Reversal Game.

Act Three, Plot Point 16: A Near Win

Step 1: You're finishing this plot point today, so play Round 1 on the Reversal Game for 15 minutes. If you've already brainstormed a reversal for this scene, use that, but otherwise, add one of the suggestions above.

Step 2: Play Round 2 of the Reversal Game. Add an extra challenge to the scene—a ticking clock, a precarious walkway, a lock, a small space, twenty scorpions, an incessant high-pitched alarm, a character's biggest fear (it doesn't have to be the protagonist), the worst smell your protagonist could imagine.

Busy Writer Recap and Reward: Days 73–76

Act Three, Plot Point 16: A Near Win

Congratulations! You finished the Near Win plot point—your character almost got what they wanted, but not yet. You're close to the end of Act Three!

Rewards: Pile every pillow on the sofa and it's cozy nap time. Thirty minutes, at least. If anyone bugs you, point to the guide. You've earned it. If you have one of those eye-mask thingies, put that on too. Then treat yourself: tomato soup and grilled cheese sandwiches or ramen noodles or whatever counts as a cozy meal.

Nurture Your Creativity

Interview Someone and Tell Them You're a Novelist

Own your truth; you are a novelist whether you're published or not. You don't need external validation for that. Part of being a novelist is doing in-person research, and it's a lot of fun to talk to people and fill your story with facts. For his *City Spies* series, James Ponti said, "I interview experts and have spoken with actual spies, police officers, Egyptologists, diplomats, and many others, trying to get things right."[6] How do you find people to interview? If you're looking for an expert, ask friends. Check out Facebook, LinkedIn, or a website. Maybe there's a nonprofit organization related to a topic in your book; before traveling to Moldova to research *Trafficked,* I contacted anti-trafficking organizations and they became an invaluable resource.

Lisa Jewell (***Then She Was Gone***)

on Continuing to Write, No Matter What

"You can get stuck for days on end without a clue how to move to the next section—you know what you want to happen next but have no idea how to get there. It's a bit like being lost on a journey, really. But the thing to remember is that all this is perfectly normal, and even though it feels like you'll never finish, actually, YOU WILL, and that's the key. Finishing is the key. That's what most people who want to write a novel never do."[7]

Busy Writer Road Map Days 77–80: Scene-Sequel

In the next four days, we'll focus on the domino effect: A decision leads to an action, which leads to a result, which leads to a reaction, which leads to a disaster. Nothing *randomly* happens.

Act Three, Plot Point 17: The Big Mistake

After the Near Win, the protagonist will make a devastating mistake with a tragic outcome, such as the loss of someone they love. This choice leads to the All-Is-Lost Moment, including the emotional fallout and the actions that follow. Later, the protagonist will look back on this moment and wish they'd chosen differently. From that place, they will grow.

Ideas and Examples

1. Lying to protect oneself and deepening suspicion (*Gone Girl* by Gillian Flynn)
2. Missing the one chance at a rescue (*Hatchet* by Gary Paulsen)
3. Failing to assess danger first (*The Alchemist* by Paulo Coelho)
4. Withholding love due to fear of rejection (*Normal People* by Sally Rooney)
5. Trusting an enemy's offer (*Oathbringer* by Brandon Sanderson)

Day 77: Flaws and Foreshadowing

Today, you'll turn your protagonist's flaw into an obvious warning sign. Make the reader cringe and cover their eyes, thinking, *Oh, no, don't do that!!!!* We've all made gut-wrenching mistakes, and often there were signs in advance that things wouldn't work out due to our flaws. For example, take a scientist who refuses to admit doubt—if he ignores signs that the lab might blow up or dismisses his chief assistant's warning, suspense builds.

Normal People by Sally Rooney

Connell's flaw is low self-worth and a fear of vulnerability and rejection. He loves his close friend Marianne, who has a boyfriend.

Scene: They're at a dinner party, where Marianne's boyfriend behaves aggressively. Connell hesitates at first, since this is his core impulse. But finally he stands up for her, making the reader feel hopeful.

Mistake: Back at his house, she says nobody loves her. This is his big moment, but Connell *still* doesn't tell her he loves her. His flaw wins. She withdraws.

Sequel: Connell spirals into depression, and Marianne enters another abusive relationship, leading to the All-Is-Lost Moment for both of them.

Write Your Book: Show the protagonist's flaw and add foreshadowing.

Act Three, Plot Point 17: The Big Mistake

Step 1: Again, setting matters. What setting would perfectly amplify the protagonist's flaw or misbelief and foreshadow that mistake? In the previous example, the nighttime dinner party setting amplifies the tension because Connell comes from a poorer background than the others and he's drinking too much alcohol.

Step 2: Foreshadow what's about to happen or show that something is "off" so that the reader's worry grows. Show the protagonist's flaw. You've made us love them; now make us ache for them as we realize they're about to make the biggest mistake of their lives.

Day 78: Complications

Every scene has a goal and an obstacle that stands in the way. You then complicate the obstacle with a twist, an added threat, a ticking clock, or an emotional trigger. These higher-stakes obstacles push characters from logic to more instinctual reactions, driven by fear, insecurities, flaws, and misbeliefs. Under pressure, someone will make a mistake.

Golden Son by Pierce Brown (Red Rising series Book 2)

Flaw: Darrow is reckless and overconfident.

Scene Goal: He wants to ambush a bigger, better-equipped army.

Plan: Hide beneath the river and use gravBoots to rise out of the river.

Obstacle: The other army.

Complication 1: His team is underwater and can't see the enemy.

Complication 2: The communication systems begin to fail.

Mistake: Darrow underestimates his enemy. A lookout says a girl is playing in the mud by the river, but Darrow dismisses her, thinking she's just a girl. (Foreshadowing!)

Realization: Then, as they rise above the river, Darrow realizes:

> She should be hiding out with her family, not out in a besieged city. Something is wrong.[1]

Mistake: When his second-in-command tries to shoot her, Darrow stops him impulsively because she's a kid.

Complication 3: The girl activates a device and Darrow's army sinks to the bottom of the river when their gravBoots deactivate.

Complication 4 (time pressure): Underwater, Darrow frees himself and tries to save others, but the oxygen is running out in their suits.

Consequence: Most of his army dies.

All-Is-Lost Moment: Darrow confronts the cost of his recklessness.

Write Your Book: Add complications and amplify the conflict.

Act Three, Plot Point 17: The Big Mistake

Step 1: What is your protagonist's goal and plan to achieve this goal? What are ways you can add obstacles, escalate the conflict, and increase time pressure or the stakes? What is their flaw that might make it hard to achieve?

Step 2: Show the protagonist's thoughts about the goal and their plan (or the leader's plan, if it's not theirs). In dialogue, show the plan is imperfect, with real risks. Readers might notice a problem with this plan before the protagonist does. Then add the first obstacle.

Step 3: Add a green light, something that makes the protagonist think the plan will go fine, despite the signs. Next, amplify the obstacle with a new complication. Keep increasing the pressure.

Day 79: Falling Dominoes

I love the image of dominoes for this skill. Push one domino, and it triggers the next and so on. The speed picks up as more dominoes fall. This is really the core of the scene-sequel pattern.

One action leads to the next, building toward a disaster within the scene. That disaster is followed by the sequel: the reaction, the dilemma, the next decision, and the next scene goal.

We've already worked on how the protagonist's flaw foreshadows the mistake and leads to poor decision-making. Their flaw will be the first domino that falls. It leads them toward the first obstacle, which creates the next complication, and the next. Each beat triggers another domino, creating a crescendo of cause and effect, making the Big Mistake feel inevitable.

You don't need this plot point to be a fight, battle, or chase scene; you can create this domino effect in a romance too . . . You'd build up to a devastating argument, each person triggering the other's insecurities, ending in the classic All-Is-Lost breakup scene.

Types of Dominoes

Flaw Dominoes: A weakness causes the problem.

Action Dominoes: An action by the protagonist or another character causes the problem.

Emotional Dominoes: Impulsivity and emotional outbursts cause the problem.

Information Dominoes: New or incorrect information alters the decision and leads them into trouble.

Environmental Dominoes: Weather or external conditions disrupt plans and force them to take a new course of action.

Lord of the Flies by William Golding

In this classic, a group of boys survive a plane crash and struggle to survive on a deserted island. Order erodes until the All-Is-Lost Moment, when Ralph's belief in rules without force sets in motion the chain of events that lead to Piggy's death.

Flaw Domino: Ralph believes in order and underestimates the threat from Jack.

Environmental Domino: Ralph brings Piggy to Castle Rock, a dangerous cliff, where Jack is in charge.

Emotional Domino: Ralph tells Piggy to stay hidden and confronts Jack, demanding that he return Piggy's glasses and relight the fire, believing that logic will work.

Action Domino: Jack and Ralph fight.

Emotional Domino: Piggy stands and yells at them to listen to Ralph, exposing himself to danger.

Action Domino: One of Jack's allies, Roger, pushes a giant rock down toward them, killing Piggy and knocking him into the sea.

Write Your Book: Show each event causing the next, like falling dominoes.

Act Three, Plot Point 17: The Big Mistake

Step 1: Decide on the scene goal. Now tip the first domino with the protagonist's flaw. Show what they do when they're triggered or stressed. No coincidences. Early dominoes fall slower, and then the chain picks up speed.

Step 2: This is usually an action scene. Show us who does what. Use strong verbs. Shorten your sentences. End on a strong image, like the image of the girl on the riverbank in *Golden Son*.

Day 80: The Sequel—What Have I Done?

Think of the worst mistake you've ever made. How did it feel immediately afterward? Show your protagonist's reaction and the dilemma they're now facing. Your character will realize just how badly they've messed things up, and that they might not be able to fix it.

Think of moments when you felt sure that you'd lost the person you loved, hurt someone badly, or felt the entire world was against you. Your perception of your senses changes too: sight, sound, taste, touch, smell. Use your character's warped senses to pull the reader deeply into the scene and make them feel as though they *are* the main character, confronting this mistake.

After more suffering (the next plot point), they'll make a decision and pursue a new goal.

Lord of the Flies by William Golding

Ralph realizes Piggy is dead and he runs. He no longer argues. He must choose between joining the tribe or surviving on his own long enough to be rescued. He chooses surviving on his own.

Write Your Book: Show the character's realization of their mistake.

Act Three, Plot Point 17: The Big Mistake

Step 1: Show your character coming to the realization that they've messed up, and how that manifests in their awareness of their surroundings.

Step 2: Write the sequel, the immediate reaction to what just happened. Show their emotional response in their thoughts or dialogue. Then force a new choice. Show them making a decision to propel them to the next scene.

Busy Writer Recap and Reward: Days 77–80

Act Three, Plot Point 17: The Big Mistake

You're putting your characters through a tough time at this point, and it's painful and even triggering to hurt your characters, but you've got to do it to help them grow. Be tender with yourself, but keep writing. Reward time: Try goat yoga and/or eat a sundae with your favorite toppings. If goat yoga isn't an option, play goat videos on your phone while you stretch.

Nurture Your Creativity

Cold Showers

Cold showers sharpen your senses and offer a reset before your morning writing session to really get those creative neurons firing. Start every day with a *very* cold shower until you hit Act Four. If you don't like it, you'll speed through these four days, and if you do like it, you might find that it clears your mind and jump-starts your creativity. Studies link cold showers to better circulation, less inflammation, and higher dopamine and norepinephrine, improving your focus and mood. If nothing else, it's great research for the next time you plunge your character into icy water—you'll be able to describe it perfectly.

Busy Writer Road Map Days 81–84: The Depiction of Suffering

You're entering the suffering phase of your protagonist's journey in the All-Is-Lost Moment, a necessary plot point for their growth. In *The Art of Dramatic Writing,* Lajos Egri writes: "A writer is supposed to catch people in crises. Unfortunately, in a crisis, no one behaves normally."[1] In the next four days, your descriptions and use of language can help the emotional and physical suffering hit home for the reader.

Act Three, Plot Point 18: The All-Is-Lost Moment

The Big Mistake leads to the All-Is-Lost Moment, sometimes called the dark night of the soul or rock bottom. Because of this mistake, the protagonist suffers. They have no hope or clear way forward. It's a kind of ego death, where they're forced to confront who they are and what they need. The internal battle is what we're exploring here. The characters must suffer in order to grow and be able to do what's required in the climax. Maybe that will be an act of great heroism to save humanity or maybe they'll finally be vulnerable enough to go after the person they love.

Ideas and Examples

1. Discovering the gift is actually a curse (*The Giver* by Lois Lowry)
2. Facing a devastating breakup (*Pride and Prejudice* by Jane Austen)
3. Feeling guilty over a protector's self-sacrifice (*The Devotion of Suspect X* by Keigo Higashino)
4. Losing a home, friends, and money (*The Color Purple* by Alice Walker)
5. Losing mental stability (*The Bourne Identity* by Robert Ludlum)

Day 81: Setting and Time Pressure

For this next scene, consciously design your setting to amplify and intensify the protagonist's emotions and the physical suffering. The setting and time pressure depend on the nature of the All-Is-Lost Moment—for example, a romance like *Beach Read* will have a different setting and time pressure beat than you'd see in a dystopian sci-fi novel like *Golden Son*.

Beach Read by Emily Henry

Setting: a bookstore reading with low attendance

Setting pressure: January is already feeling insecure due to poor attendance, even though she says it's typical for any author (it is). On top of this, she has to face a moment of humiliation and heartbreak in front of people, all while appearing to be "okay."

Time pressure: This setting uses time pressure in a different way than we normally see it. January can't escape the situation. She must live in this humiliation and heartbreak for the duration of the event, essentially trapped.

Write Your Book: Describe your high-pressure setting.

Act Three, Plot Point 18: The All-Is-Lost Moment

Step 1: Describe anything that could make the setting pressure worse for the protagonist, depending on their trauma and sensory sensitivities. Go through all the senses; consider bad weather, crowds, high-pitched noise, suffering children, smells, mosquitoes, dangerous animals, pain, darkness, bright light.

Step 2: Return to your protagonist's fatal flaw, misbelief, or vulnerability. How can you highlight that in the setting? How can the ticking clock trigger their unique set of fears and insecurities?

Day 82: Physical Suffering Reflected in Language

The All-Is-Lost Moment has arrived, and it's now your job as the author to make your protagonist suffer, not just emotionally, but also physically. You can hurt your poor protagonist in all kinds of ways: broken bones, thirst, heat exhaustion, disease, fever, sleep deprivation, burns, starvation. I'm sure you can think of more ways to torture them. The physical side will reflect the emotional. Portray the physical suffering through the use of figurative language: similes, metaphors, repetition, and imagery.

STARVATION: REPETITION AND IMAGERY

Deathless by Catherynne M. Valente

> Together they pulled down the wallpaper to get at the paste, and then they boiled the wallpaper to make bread. They were all mouth and bone, and their eyes slipped gears whenever they tried to meet. They ate their bread with paisley and flowers on the crust, and smeared paste on it like butter. Bread had never been bread, and butter had never been butter. They could not remember such things.[1]

NAUSEA: SIMILE

Beach Read by Emily Henry

January, a writer, is doing a joint event at a bookstore with her boyfriend, Gus, who's also a writer. She spots him gazing at his ex in the crowd and realizes she's losing him. He answers a question, turns to her, and his face

> was like the master bedroom in Dad's house: impersonal, scrubbed clean. There was nothing for me in it. I really felt like I might vomit.[2]

Write Your Book: Show their physical suffering.

Act Three, Plot Point 18: The All-Is-Lost Moment

Step 1: Describe the protagonist's physical pain. Add in their thoughts about their suffering, any memories of past suffering or experiences with pain, if they think they're going to die, and maybe even who they think about if they think they're approaching their final moments.

Step 2: Add imagery (Day 49) or repetition (Day 50) to amplify their emotion.

Day 83: Emotional Suffering Reflected in Language

Your character is at the low point of their journey. They've just lost everything: allies, resources, and even hope. Often, they are alone. Emotional suffering includes sadness, anger, fear, depression, blame, regret, and sensory overload. As you write, feel whatever kind of emotional suffering they're experiencing—use fragments or a long run-on sentence, whatever the emotion pulls out of you, but the trick is to feel it first and imagine it clearly. Otherwise, your sentence structure and tone might not match the scene at hand. The imagery must match the emotion.

ANGER: METAPHOR, ONOMATOPOEIA

Fahrenheit 451 by Ray Bradbury

Firefighter Guy Montag quotes poetry at home, and his wife turns him in. His boss pushes him too far and Montag sets his boss on fire.

> And then he was a shrieking blaze, a jumping, sprawling gibbering mannikin, no longer human or known, all writhing flame on the lawn as Montag shot one continuous pulse of liquid fire on him. There was a hiss like a great mouthful of spittle banging a red-hot stove, a bubbling and frothing as if salt had been poured over a monstrous black snail to cause a terrible liquefaction and a boiling over of yellow foam.[3]

DESPERATION: FRAGMENTS, SHORT SENTENCES

Bridge to Terabithia by Katherine Paterson

> *Leslie—dead—girl—friend—rope—broke—fell—you—you—you.* The words exploded in his head like corn against the side of the popper. God-dead-you-Leslie-dead-you. He ran until he was stumbling but he kept on, afraid to stop. Knowing somehow that running was the only thing that could keep Leslie from being dead.[4]

DISASSOCIATION: SIMILE

To Kill a Mockingbird by Harper Lee

Scout realizes Tom, the wrongfully accused Black man, is going to be convicted.

> What happened after that had a dreamlike quality: in a dream I saw the jury return, moving like underwater swimmers, and Judge Taylor's voice came from far away . . .[5]

DESPAIR: METAPHORICAL VERB, SIMILE

Beach Read by Emily Henry

January is doing an author event at a bookstore and sees her boyfriend gazing at his ex with longing.

> I was gritting my teeth and trying to socially tap-dance while inside, tumbleweeds were blowing through my desolate heart.[6]

SELF-BLAME: METAPHOR

The Secret Lives of Bees by Sue Monk Kidd

Lily thinks she's bad because she accidentally killed her mom. She hears a voice with "blades for lips" that says:

> You are unlovable, Lily Owens.[7]

Write Your Book: Use literary language to reflect emotion.

Act Three, Plot Point 18: The All-Is-Lost Moment

Step 1: Go through the senses. Notice the lighting. Get lost in the singular feeling of that moment, and then explore the feeling under the feeling. Think of a metaphor to represent that feeling.

Step 2: Now let it pour out of you so that the rhythm flows naturally out of the emotion.

Day 84: Portraying the Stages of Grief

After a devastating tragedy, people move through a range of emotions, and not always in this order: denial, anger, bargaining, depression, guilt, acceptance. What stage of grief is your protagonist experiencing now?

Denial: They may insist that the tragedy didn't happen. In *Bridge to Terabithia* by Katherine Paterson and *The Thing About Jellyfish* by Ali Benjamin, both protagonists face a friend's death and respond with denial.
Anger: They lash out at the people they love. Sadness often fuels anger.
Bargaining: They plead with any higher power. If only their daughter wakes up from the coma, they'll never yell again, or "Take me, not her."
Depression: Remember the weight of depression. Their body will move differently.
Guilt: They feel they did something that caused what happened, or they ruminate on their actions that led to this moment.
Acceptance: They forgive or accept what's happened.

A Monster Calls by Patrick Ness

Conor's mom is dying of cancer. At first, Conor is in denial about his mother's sickness, and this moves to bargaining and, finally, depression:

Conor's grief was a physical thing, gripping him like a clamp, clenching him tight as a muscle. He could barely breathe from the sheer *effort* of it, and he sank to the ground again, wishing it would just take him, once and for all.[8]

Write Your Book: Show the stages of grief.

Act Three, Plot Point 18: The All-Is-Lost Moment

Step 1: At the beginning of the chapter, show the protagonist's initial emotional reaction, and then show how it changes. Can you use a metaphor or their interaction with an object to show rather than tell their stage of grief? Let the reader understand it through imagery.

Step 2: Show the protagonist's movements to demonstrate whether they are in denial, anger, bargaining, depression, guilt, or acceptance. Give the reader something to look at instead of just ruminations or their thoughts about the mistake that led to the suffering. Whatever they touch, caress, or throw reveals the emotion they might be feeling in that moment. This is your opportunity to show, not tell.

Busy Writer Recap and Reward: Days 81–84

Act Three, Plot Point 18: The All-Is-Lost Moment

You did it! You've finished Act Three. You're in the home stretch of your creative marathon! First, let's take a moment to really breathe that in. You're in the final quarter of your book! Congratulations. For real, this is a big deal. You don't have far to go. What's the reward going to be? Hot chocolate with marshmallows? A late-night adventure at a dance club? Release that stress. It's good vibes (mostly) from here on out.

Nurture Your Creativity

Write Somewhere New and Bring Index Cards

Go to a joyful place to write. I love coffee shops. Write in the car wash. Write on the train, bus, or subway. Write on a roof. Write in a tent. Write in a yummy food place or a shady corner of the park or at the end of a bar or on the beach. While you're at it, bring index cards. In *Bird by Bird: Some Instructions on Writing and Life,* Anne Lamott writes that she brings index cards everywhere. "I fold an index card lengthwise in half, stick it in my back pocket along with a pen, and head out, knowing that if I have an idea, or see something lovely or strange or for any reason worth remembering, I will be able to jot down a couple of words to remind me of it."[9] I've taken up the habit. I like the unlined ones. Don't forget the pen.

ACT FOUR

At the beginning of Act Four, in the Lightbulb Moment, your main character overcomes the flaw or misbelief holding them back. Only then will they be ready for the climax and the ending. The characters have the tools to meet the climax head-on and go after what they want or need. Then, in the end, they're in a new situation. They have what they need, if not what they want. Create the feeling you want readers to have at the end of your book. Feel *all* the emotions as you write it. Become the character in order to help the reader connect deeply. You've got this!

Plot Point 19: The Lightbulb Moment (83–85%)

Plot Point 20: The Climax (85–95%)

Plot Point 21: Aftermath (95–97%)

Plot Point 22: The Ending (97–100%)

Busy Writer Road Map Days 85–88: Character Growth

After the All-Is-Lost Moment, the protagonist finally recognizes their core misbelief for the lie it is and begins to change. In a positive change arc, the protagonist has a realization. I call this the Lightbulb Moment: I am lovable; people can be trusted; I can forgive myself. If your story has a negative change arc, the realization deepens their flaw. In a neutral arc, the protagonist doesn't change, but instead sparks a breakthrough in someone else.

Act Four, Plot Point 19: The Lightbulb Moment

The Lightbulb Moment represents a realization or epiphany, like a lightbulb turning on: the moment when the protagonist grows and becomes ready to act. They gather allies and/or supplies to prepare for the final battle, or run to catch a taxi to stop their love at the airport. In overcoming their flaw or misbelief, they gain the courage, compassion, forgiveness, or whatever they need to succeed.

Ideas and Examples

1. Realizing that strength comes from teamwork (*The Hunger Games* by Suzanne Collins)
2. Discovering that what one seeks is within (*The Alchemist* by Paulo Coelho)
3. Choosing to be vulnerable (*Normal People* by Sally Rooney)
4. Reclaiming self-worth (*The Color Purple* by Alice Walker)
5. Finding courage (*The Fellowship of the Ring* by J. R. R. Tolkien)

Day 85: The Light Switch

Until now, the protagonist's actions and interactions have been informed by a misbelief about themselves or the world. The All-Is-Lost Moment has broken them. But reaching your lowest point can often reveal a new perspective or allow you to move past your blocks because you believe you have nothing left to lose.

Something will spark a new realization and reveal the misbelief for the lie it is. The moment of realization can be quick, even just a paragraph, but we'll need to see the trigger: Show *why* they overcome the flaw or misbelief now, when they didn't earlier. The trigger might be a line of dialogue, a memory, a symbolic object, a song, a saying on the side of a building, or a connection in nature. Whatever turns on the switch makes them realize something and move past whatever has been holding them back.

At this point, the character isn't going to be perfect, but they evolve enough to meet the challenge of the climax. Let's look at a few examples of the wound, the misbelief, the flaw, the light switch, and the Lightbulb Moment in popular books we've covered.

A Man Called Ove by Fredrik Backman

Wound: Ove loses his wife after years of caring for her due to a train accident that left her disabled.

Misbelief: Without his wife, his life is worth nothing.

Flaw: He's a rigid rule follower to maintain a sense of control and avoid his grief.

Light Switch: His suicide attempts have been repeatedly interrupted by the neighbor, Parvaneh, but finally, she's in labor and this time it's an emergency. She's no longer interrupting his suicide plans; he's actually needed.

Lightbulb Moment: He has worth and value without his wife. The neighbors love him.

Write Your Book: Show the lead-up to the Lightbulb Moment.

Act Four, Plot Point 19: The Lightbulb Moment

Step 1: Often the light switch or trigger happens early in this scene, and it's then followed by the realization. Decide on the setting. Is the current setting the place where they'll make the realization, or do you need to start the scene in another place?

Step 2: Write the lead-up to the Lightbulb Moment. Show a concrete trigger. Something the reader can actually see, hear, touch, smell, or taste.

Day 86: Wisdom and Theme in Action

The Lightbulb Moment will reflect your theme; the new wisdom or truth should be directly related to the character's growth. They can't just say or think their realization—they should embody it right after the Lightbulb Moment. To do this, show the realization and then show them in action, pursuing a new goal and facing an obstacle, which is a test, maybe something they would've failed in the past but which they will now overcome. Instead of relying on the old misbelief, the new wisdom is applied in action.

Ideas to Show the Protagonist Applying Their Newfound Wisdom

1. They're tempted to fall back on an old behavior or addiction but make a new choice.
2. They apologize for a past behavior.
3. They create a new boundary with someone.
4. They're kind to someone, when they would have been rude in the past.
5. They don't give up, when they would've given up before.

Angela's Ashes by Frank McCourt

After Theresa, the girl he loves, dies, Frank suffers. The trigger for his Lightbulb Moment is some advice from Uncle Pa. He tells him not to take a test for the post office:

> You'll be dead in your head before you're thirty and dried in your ballocks the year before. Make up your own bloody mind and to hell with the safeshots and the begrudgers.[1]

Standing outside the post office, Frank remembers his uncle's words; he applies for a new job and quits the post office where his boss shames him and says he's acting too good for them. Then she makes a reference to him doing something shameful. He thinks of the girl he loved, how when she was dying, they had consensual sex.

In the sequel to this scene, we get his reaction.

> I don't think I'm too good for the post office or anything else. How could I with my hair sticking up, pimples dotting my face, my eyes red and oozing yellow, my teeth crumbling with the rot, no shoulders, no flesh on my arse after cycling thirteen thousand miles to deliver twenty thousand telegrams to every door in Limerick and regions beyond?[2]

He wonders how his boss knew about Theresa, and he goes to the bar to have his first pint. Finally, he goes to confession to get the feeling of shame out of him before his sixteenth birthday the next day.

Three new actions to show his new mindset after his realization: He's never quit a job, had a pint, or confessed to having sex with Theresa before.

Write Your Book: Show them choosing a new action.

Act Four, Plot Point 19: The Lightbulb Moment

Step 1: Decide on the goal and the action the protagonist will take, the obstacle they'll face, and the new small action that might show their transformation.

Step 2: Write this scene. Upon making a different choice from their usual choices, let them reflect on this new action and how it feels for them. Riff a little here, so that the realization becomes meaningful to them and the reader's hope surges as we see what that will mean for them going forward.

Day 87: Seeing the World with New Eyes

How does your character see the world now? How have their relationships transformed?

In *The Little Prince* by Antoine de Saint-Exupéry, the fox gives the prince the following advice:

> "It is only with one's heart that one can see clearly. What is essential is invisible to the eye."[3]

Let's look at *Americanah* by Chimamanda Ngozi Adichie, comparing how the protagonist sees the world when she's in the throes of the All-Is-Lost and how she sees the world after her Lightbulb Moment.

Americanah by Chimamanda Ngozi Adichie

This gorgeous, bestselling novel is about a Nigerian woman, Ifemelu, who moves to America, starts a successful blog, and then moves back to Lagos, where she has to decide whether to live her truth or perform success, working for a superficial magazine.

Misbelief: Ifemelu believes success will make her whole.
Flaw: She distances herself from others when relationships get hard.
All-Is-Lost Moment: Her younger cousin Dike attempts suicide. After he's better, she returns to Lagos, still in the throes of the All-Is-Lost.
Perception of Lagos Before the Lightbulb Moment:

> At first, Lagos assaulted her; the sun-dazed haste, the yellow buses full of squashed limbs, the sweating hawkers racing after cars, the advertisements on hulking billboards (others scrawled on walls—PLUMBER CALL 080177777) and the heaps of rubbish that rose on the roadsides like a taunt.[4]

Lightbulb Trigger: A moment at her fluff magazine makes her realize she's not living her truth. One of the girls in the office has typhoid, and even though she herself has had typhoid, she didn't notice anything was wrong. She asks to see the girl's medicine, because when she had typhoid, the medicine wasn't strong enough. The bottle has no label, and she says they should do an article on how medicines need labels. The editor tells her she doesn't need to be an activist.

Lightbulb Moment: She imagines her own blog, one that speaks the truth of Nigerian life, not just glossy, fake cover stories for the rich. She pictures the stories she'll tell and comes up with the name—a dream is born.

Action: That day, she starts a new blog.

New Perceptions: Here is how she describes Lagos to her cousin Dike:

> Lagos became a gentler version of itself, and the people in their bright church clothes looked, from far away, like flowers in the wind.[5]

Write Your Book: Show how they see the world through new eyes.

Act Four, Plot Point 19: The Lightbulb Moment

Step 1: Climb into the protagonist's body and feel their feelings in this moment after their realization. Then close your eyes and, in your imagination, see what they see, smell what they smell, feel what they feel, and think their thoughts.

Step 2: In today's writing, show how they see the world with new eyes, now that they've connected in a deeper way to their own core spirit.

Day 88: A New Plan Shaped by a New Belief

The Lightbulb Moment allows your character to see past whatever blocks were preventing them from succeeding in their main goal; they're now ready to take on the challenges of the climax, but often they need a new plan because the old plan matched the old belief. They may use different tools or resources or gather different people to help, making different choices than they would've made in the past.

This will look different in different genres.

In an epic fantasy, maybe they're preparing for a battle, and maybe previously they've overlooked a short, sweet warrior girl who they now assign to a key position, or maybe they realize force will not help them succeed, so instead they wear maids' outfits to enter the castle and capture the king, under disguise.

In a romance, maybe a woman will seek out the help of her boyfriend's best female friend, who she's seen as a rival until now. Or maybe she's been terrified of horses, but a horse is the only way to get there in time, so she overcomes her fear to ride across the grassy plain.

Write Your Book: Show the preparation leading up to the climax.

Act Four, Plot Point 19: The Lightbulb Moment

Step 1: Think about a huge breakthrough in your life—maybe it was giving birth or giving a huge presentation that was transformative for your career. What was the energy of that moment as you headed toward achieving that goal? Now embody your protagonist. How are they feeling in this moment and how are they experiencing this within their body? The lead-up is important to make this moment land. Think about how you can show (don't tell!) their changed behavior now. What different people, tools, or resources might they use for their plan? How will their plan change?

Step 2: Describe where they are and who's there, especially if this is a fresh scene. Show the details they notice with this new mindset. We also need to know their scene goal. Show them gathering what they need and explore their thoughts about what's coming, perhaps discussing the plan with another character. Here, we also need an obstacle—don't make anything too easy; you need to build the tension. However, this is likely to be a success scene.

Busy Writer Recap and Reward: Days 85–88

Act Four, Plot Point 19: The Lightbulb Moment

Eureka! Your protagonist has had their big realization or epiphany, and they've experienced that moment of growth that's so rewarding for the reader. Now we're jumping up and down cheering for them. And I'm jumping up and down, cheering for you. Don't slow your pace. Three more plot points and you're done. For the reward, I suggest dark chocolate or oysters. For something non-food-related, maybe just stand on the grass at midnight in your bare feet. Ground yourself.

Nurture Your Creativity

Boost Your Endorphins

Endorphins are one of the happy chemicals in our bodies. They're released when we do various activities. Try one of the following for a happiness boost.

1. Breathe in the scent of lavender essential oil.
2. Do a fast walk or hike for thirty minutes with friends.
3. Eat dark chocolate.
4. Go see some live music.
5. Eat very spicy food.

Amalie Howard *(The Beast of Beswick)*

on Romance and Knowing Your Genre

"My best advice is to read a lot of romance novels that are bestsellers with themes you enjoy. It will help develop your own style. Today's romance is layered and inclusive with various heat levels, tropes and themes, and heightens the importance of consent. Characters have agency. Most importantly, romance must always have a HEA (Happily Ever After) or HFN (Happy for Now) ending. It's romance canon for readers to have an emotionally satisfying conclusion."[6]

Busy Writer Road Map Days 89–92: Action & Reaction

In the next four days, you'll use actions and reactions to build the pacing and tension in the climactic scene. Your entire book has been building toward this moment, culminating in this pivotal scene, when all the narrative threads come together. You're close to the end.

Act Four, Plot Point 20: The Climax

The climax is the final showdown between the protagonist and the antagonist. Here, the protagonist demonstrates their growth, armed with their new belief. Sometimes the climax is loud, maybe a battle or fight, and sometimes it's quiet, maybe a declaration of love or simply a new decision.

Ideas and Examples

1. Fighting a final battle (*The Hunger Games* by Suzanne Collins)
2. Confronting a bully (*The Kite Runner* by Khaled Hosseini)
3. Escaping from captors (*Sold* by Patricia McCormick)
4. Accepting a marriage proposal (*Pride and Prejudice* by Jane Austen)
5. Standing up to a family member (*The Secret Life of Bees* by Sue Monk Kidd)

Day 89: Curiosity and Danger

Driving into the climax, you want to hook the reader, plant questions, and make the reader curious about what will happen. At this point, the reader should be worried that the protagonist could fail or maybe someone will die.

Dungeon Crawler Carl by Matt Dinniman

Aliens turn Earth into a televised video game. Carl and his hilarious diva cat, Princess Donut (yes, she talks), head into the final challenge. The climax makes us curious the whole way through, by planting details that make us wonder.

This scene starts off with Carl and Princess Donut heading into a tunnel, where they hear loud guitar music and cheering. They (and readers) wonder: *Who's playing and why are they cheering?*

The two of them keep walking and find a huge dog kennel that appears to be empty. They figure out the aliens are cheering on an animal fight. The next question: What animals are fighting?

They look in the cages and find injured dingoes, curled up, terrified. The question: Why are the dingoes terrified? The story drops breadcrumbs, drawing us closer to the danger, until we find out the answer: They're fighting a giant attack gerbil. And guess who it's attacking next?

Write Your Book: Make the reader curious about what will happen.

Act Four, Plot Point 20: The Climax

Step 1: How can you make the setting for the climax different from any that we've seen so far? Imagine the climax before you write. Close your eyes and enter the scene in your imagination. Do you notice anything mysterious? How can you build the danger?

Step 2: Start with a hook . . . a mysterious detail to snag your reader's interest. The reader will be wondering something. As soon as you answer the question of the hook, plant a new question, and so on. Keep sentences tight. Use fragments. Build toward that climax.

Day 90: Climactic Twists

In the climax, a twist will often make it tougher for your protagonist to achieve their goal. It shouldn't be random, though. Remember, you aren't just waving your author wand. There has to be a reason for this twist. Tie it to something you set in motion earlier, often in the subplot. If you set nothing in motion, again, no worries; just give yourself a note to set this up.

Ideas for Final Twists or Surprises Before the Climax

1. An ally betrays the protagonist
2. The antagonist is not the actual antagonist
3. The rules change for victory
4. Allies refuse to help
5. A storm rolls in

Write Your Book: Add a final twist before the climax.

Act Four, Plot Point 20: The Climax

Step 1: Choose the twist. You've already set this into motion in an earlier scene, and if you haven't, give yourself a little note in the margin to add it in later. Don't go back.

Step 2: Feel the character's emotional state in your own body. Then write. Show their goal, stack the obstacles. Show allies' reactions through the perspective of the protagonist as they encounter the twist. They will have grown as well, so try to show how they might react differently at this point, not just the protagonist.

Day 91: Multisensory Chaos

Have you ever been in a big car accident?

I was on the college rowing team at University of British Columbia when our van flipped while we were driving home from a regatta. Glass scattered and bags flew. The van slid on its side across to the other side of the highway. My knee dipped down once and was stabbed with a piece of glass. My face hovered above the asphalt. I'll never forget the long, high-pitched scrape to a stop. Miraculously, nobody was driving on the other side of the highway. We all survived, though one of my teammates in my coxed four did break her back, and my knee was toast. I had glass lodged in my knee for the next year. This was the end of my rowing career.

Next we'll be talking about the aftermath of the climax—remember, everything does not go smoothly, according to plan—often there is a downside. Again, stories mirror life.

While I wouldn't wish a car accident on anybody in real life, that's the kind of sensory chaos we want in this scene. Also remember that we need to know the result of the climax. Do not cut to black. If I just showed you the accident and then you didn't know if we all walked away, that would be disappointing. I watched a movie recently about a nuclear warhead coming toward the United States. We never find out if the warhead lands or what the fallout is and people online were furious. So keep that as a warning: People need the result of the climax.

1. **Use short sentences and/or fragments.**

Sold by Patricia McCormick

I inch toward the steps. But I am too afraid to go down.

The American calls out.

I try to answer, but nothing comes out of my mouth.

I hear more cursing and the scuffle of feet. He is leaving. My American is leaving.

Something inside me breaks open, and I run down the steps.[1]

2. **Use strong action verbs.**

Percy Jackson and the Olympians: The Lightning Thief by Rick Riordan

He snapped his fingers. The sand exploded at his feet and out charged a wild boar, even larger and uglier than the one whose head hung above the door of cabin seven at Camp Half-Blood. The beast pawed the sand, glaring at me with beady eyes as it lowered its razor-sharp tusks and waited for the command to kill.[2]

3. **Use all the senses.**

The Kite Runner by Khaled Hosseini

Mostly, I remember this: His brass knuckles flashing in the afternoon light; how cold they felt with the first few blows and how quickly they warmed with my blood. Getting thrown against the wall, a nail where a framed picture may have hung once jabbing at my back. Sohrab screaming.[3]

Notice the use of specificity, light, temperature, pain, sound.

4. **Give the wide view of what's happening and then zoom in on a detail.**

The Underground Railroad by Colson Whitehead

They fought and grappled in the violence of their fall. In the jumble of collisions, Cora's head knocked across the stone. Her leg was ripped one way, and her arm twisted under her at the bottom of the steps. Ridgeway took the brunt. Homer yelped at the sounds his employer made as he fell. The boy descended slowly, the lantern light shakily drawing the station from shadow. Cora untwined herself from Ridgeway and crawled toward the handcar, left leg in agony.[4]

5. **Show us the win . . . or the fail.**

   Show the pivotal result. Your protagonist will usually get what they need, but not always what they wanted. Remember the amplification of the obstacle. You've shown the obstacle; now amplify it with a complication at the end—this is often the surprise of the climax—the moment an ally is killed or something negative happens.

Write Your Book: Show the multisensory chaos.

Act Four, Plot Point 20: The Climax

Step 1: Close your eyes and see the metaphorical car accident. What is the particular chaos in your book? Go through the senses. What does the protagonist notice? How is their decision-making or thought process affected? How can you make us nervous about the outcome of the climax?

Step 2: As you write, show the chaos. Use strong verbs and fragments. Limit adverbs. Be specific. Cut all but the most essential words.

Day 92: Reactions to the Climax

Freeze. Flee. Fight. Fawn. What's the protagonist's reaction to the climax? Go back to their core impulse and consider whether it has changed in any way. How are they different?

Again, this is the sequel to the climax. The reaction.

Widen your camera lens out to show others in the scene. How do their core impulses come into play? Everyone will react to what's happened, not just the protagonist. What might your protagonist notice in this scene as they evaluate what has just happened and what choices they'll make next?

The Name of the Wind by Patrick Rothfuss

Kvothe's enemy Ambrose breaks his beloved lute, and Kvothe names the wind, throwing Ambrose off his feet, hurting his arm. This is the reaction of the crowd:

> **Bystanders:** People looked around, dazed, their hair tousled and clothes in disarray.[5]
>
> **Antagonist:** The look of wild, confused fear he gave me was a brief, sweet pleasure.[6]
>
> **Crowd:** People began to pour from the Eolian and the other buildings around the courtyard. Musicians looked around wildly, and everyone was talking at once.
>
> . . . was that?
>
> . . . notes are all over. Help me before they get . . .
>
> . . . did it. Him over there, with the red . . .
>
> . . . demon. A demon of wind and . . .[7]
>
> **Friends:** Wilem and Simmon hurried me away.[8]

Write Your Book: Show the characters' reactions to the climax.

Act Four, Plot Point 20: The Climax

Step 1: How will your protagonist and the other characters react to the peak moment of the climax? Think through how each character will respond based on who they are and what they want. What would your protagonist notice?

Step 2: Write the wide shot, showing all the characters' responses. If it's dialogue in a nameless crowd, it's effective to share random lines without dialogue tags or attribution. Also show what others do and how your protagonist sees them.

Busy Writer Recap and Reward: Days 89–92

Act Four, Plot Point 20: The Climax

You did it—look at how close you are to 100 percent! Now you just have two plot points left: the Aftermath and the Ending. Your ending is so close; it's the barbecue down the block, and you can smell the meat cooking. Keep going!

Reward time: Go for a bike ride with a little whimsy. I've seen this in Venice, California . . . hundreds of people decking out their bikes and going for a ride together. Decorate your bike with lights and flowers. If there's no way you're riding a silly, decorated bike, okay, I've got another one: ax throwing. *Aaargh!* Be tough. Feel the win. You've almost finished this creative marathon. You've got this.

Nurture Your Creativity

A Forgiveness Meditation

Forgiveness is a common theme in many novels and memoirs. Let's try it today. A lot of creatives carry hurt within them—it can be the thing that pushes us to create, but it can also hold us back in a place of hurt and rumination. **If you wish you could forgive someone, repeat this mantra for five minutes:** "I love you; I wish you well; I forgive you." Focus all your loving energy on each statement. May you heal as you finish this book. Release that pain.

Busy Writer Road Map Days 92–95: The Fallout

In the next four days you'll show the aftermath of the climax. Often, something terrible has happened to an ally or a mentor; there's a downside. Forgiveness and/or healing may be needed.

Act Four, Plot Point 21: Aftermath

Your protagonist has defeated the antagonist and achieved their goal, but now comes the fallout. This beat, sometimes called the falling action or the downside, shows the consequences of the climax. It won't be a perfect ending. Show the messy aftermath and let the protagonist take any final actions to clean up what they can.

Ideas and Examples

1. Inspiring a larger rebellion, but many have died (*The Hunger Games* by Suzanne Collins)
2. Grieving an ally and vowing to fight the system (*The Maze Runner* by James Dashner)
3. Mourning a loved one (*The Road* by Cormac McCarthy)
4. Reuniting with a lover, but they've lost time (*The Notebook* by Nicholas Sparks)
5. Accepting they've lost their innocence and view of their former life (*The Fellowship of the Ring* by J. R. R. Tolkien)

Day 93: External Fallout

The climax doesn't end with the protagonist doing a tidy victory lap. The world may be physically destroyed, someone may have died, or there may be a consequence for what's happened. This will complicate the victory. Even in a romance, you could have external fallout. The couple is together, but who have they hurt along the way? This is also true in life—everything has its price and stories reflect that truth.

Write Your Book: Show the external fallout.

Act Four, Plot Point 21: Aftermath

Step 1: Decide who's going to react to the victory and any casualties—parents, a spouse, the media, the police, society, the government.

Step 2: Show any physical disaster. Choose three concrete sensory details to highlight.

Step 3: Create an external consequence. Let the external forces poke at the protagonist's old wound so they nearly reach for the old habit or negative thought pattern, but they resist.

Step 4: End with an image that shows your protagonist's inner state.

Day 94: Internal Fallout

Now let's look at the internal trauma from the climax. The stuff of nightmares. The protagonist didn't die, but they're not going to be okay after confronting their worst-case scenario. This is a new trauma. People may have died, depending on your genre, but even in a romance, they've hurt each other and they're going to have to do some healing.

Angela's Ashes by Frank McCourt

After Frank McCourt has finally achieved his dream of heading off on the boat to America, he thinks of how this act to save himself has some negative consequences.

> I could have brought in enough money for Michael and Alphie to go to school with proper shoes and bellies well filled.[1]

Lord of the Flies by William Golding

His voice rose under the black smoke before the burning wreckage of the island; and infected by that emotion, the other little boys began to shake and sob too. And in the middle of them, with filthy body, matted hair, and unwiped nose, Ralph wept for the end of innocence, the darkness of man's heart, and the fall through the air of the true, wise friend called Piggy.[2]

Write Your Book: Show the internal fallout.

Act Four, Plot Point 21: Aftermath

Step 1: Choose a physical sign of the protagonist's struggle (messy hair, shaking hands, an unwiped nose), and a mental sign (weeping, numbness, guilt). Describe what they're experiencing internally.

Step 2: Put them near a friend, an enemy, or a temptation and show their changed response.

Day 95: Forgiveness and Making Amends

Forgiveness is a radical mindset shift and shows transformation in a novel. It's a common beat in the ending. Who does your protagonist need to forgive (it might be themselves)?

***The Secret Life of Bees* by Sue Monk Kidd:** Lily forgives her mom.
***Gone Girl* by Gillian Flynn:** Nick pretends to forgive and nearly believes it.

One night I flew in lobster like the old days, and she pretended to chase me with it, and I pretended to hide, and then we both *at the same time* made an *Annie Hall* joke, and it was so perfect, so the way it was supposed to be, that I had to leave the room for a second. My heart was beating in my ears.[3]

Write Your Book: Show your protagonist forgiving someone or themselves.

Act Four, Plot Point 21: Aftermath

Step 1: Decide who the protagonist needs to forgive or who will forgive them.

Step 2: Show the protagonist's thoughts of forgiveness before the action.

Step 3: Show the apology in dialogue or action. Show the repair in the relationship, any new boundary that needs to be set, and the resulting emotional release.

Day 96: Tying Up Loose Ends

Think of the threads you've been weaving through your book, including the subplots. Now let's see what needs to be resolved before the ending. Does the protagonist need to say goodbye to someone? Do they need to fix something that went wrong or make amends? Whatever remains unresolved, find a way to answer those questions for your reader.

At this point, there should be a sense of retrospective inevitability. Looking back, everything needs to make sense, as with the phrase "hindsight is 20/20." As a reader, you should think, *Oh, yeah, that thing and that thing, it all makes sense, it adds up.*

Some authors like to let the reader paint their own ending for side characters and how relationships will resolve. One of the reasons I love this type of ending is that the characters continue to live in our imagination. However, if there is a question that's central to the story, make sure you've given at least a hint of an answer.

Write Your Book: Tie up any loose ends.

Act Four, Plot Point 21: Aftermath

Step 1: List unanswered questions and decide what you want to resolve in the last chapter.

Step 2: Close the loop on any details you planted about any characters so we aren't wondering—what about that? Bring back any characters we need to see or give us information about them in the protagonist's dialogue with another character.

Busy Writer Recap and Reward: Days 93–96

Act Four, Plot Point 21: Aftermath

You have one final plot point to go! That's a huge deal. You're blowing my mind. Are you blowing your own mind? I hope so. KAPOW. One final plot point—most likely, that means just one final chapter. Finish your book now, imperfectly, knowing you can revise the ending later. Now for the reward: Get a massage. Swing by the bakery and get cream puffs or something you love. Y'all know how I feel about bakeries. Even just standing in one is a happy moment.

Nurture Your Creativity

A Loving-Kindness Meditation

Repeat the following phrases out loud or mentally.

To yourself: "May I be happy. May I be healthy. May I be safe. May I live with ease."

Then repeat the following to a loved one, a neutral person, and then someone you don't like or you struggle to forgive, picturing them each in your mind: "May you be happy. May you be healthy. May you be safe. May you live with ease."

James Patterson (*Along Came a Spider*)

on Endings

"I almost never do the ending that's in the outline. So much has changed. . . . I think part of the problem is that the outline is a bit more logical than emotional. By the time I get to that ending, my emotions are really churning, and I'm always feeling it needs more. It can't just be about logic. It has to be logic and emotion. You've got to feel something . . . whether it's a tragic ending and you go no, no, no, no, no . . . A happy ending, that can be terrific, if it's honest . . . It's got to flow out of the rest of the book. Set up things that are coming, okay? All through the book, you know something's coming, you'll need to set it up for it to really be effective."[4]

Busy Writer Road Map Days 97–100: A Satisfying Ending

Let's give the reader an ending that will linger with them long after they finish that final page. Don't rush. Use all the craft skills you've been working on throughout this guide. You'll be working on imagery in your ending, showing the character growth, and leaving the reader with some wisdom.

Act Four, Plot Point 22:

The Ending

End your novel with the kind of ending you love. What emotion do you want the reader to feel? Do you want to leave readers with a hint of doubt or with a smile, like in *The Hitchhiker's Guide to the Galaxy*? Maybe a final line of wisdom and a few tears?

Ideas and Examples

1. Receiving a threat from the leader (*The Hunger Games* by Suzanne Collins)
2. Gaining a new appreciation for life (*The Catcher in the Rye* by J. D. Salinger)
3. Leaving home for a new place (*Angela's Ashes* by Frank McCourt)
4. Seeking to atone for what was lost (*Ender's Game* by Orson Scott Card)
5. Creating a found family (*The Secret Life of Bees* by Sue Monk Kidd)

Day 97: Description in the Ending—Tidy or Ambiguous?

A powerful ending isn't always a perfectly wrapped present. Often, it's more like the presents I wrap: with newspaper, hair on the tape, and one weirdly crunched-up end. An imperfect present. Your characters have suffered. Life is better now, but there are some negative consequences.

Some endings are tidy. The reader knows what happens next. Loose threads are tied up. Language is precise and clear—you tell us what is happening and give thoughts about what will happen next. Leave us with a beautiful, peaceful image.

Or maybe you want to leave a little up in the air. Fantasy author China Miéville prefers the ambiguous ending:

> One of the reasons it's so powerful to stare at an old, found photograph is because of the uncertainty of what's just beyond the edges of the image, just out of sight. Of what's about to happen. You want to know, and/but the wanting is what gives it power.[1]

In the ambiguous ending, you'd leave something up in the air. Maybe, for some reason, the door won't lock, or the protagonist hears a strange sound.

Write Your Book: Describe the closing setting.

Act Four, Plot Point 22: The Ending

Step 1: Consider the following: If you're making your ending tidy, how will you reflect that in the language? How precise will your descriptions be in their perspective? If it's ambiguous, could you make the language ambiguous? The character will likely be confused if the reader is confused. How could you reflect that in one thing they see?

Step 2: Describe where the protagonist is in your closing scene. Use tidy or ambiguous language to describe that setting, reflecting the confusion or order in the protagonist's mind.

Day 98: Show (Don't Tell) Growth

Your main character's growth is the key element that makes a story satisfying in the end. They've overcome their misbelief and their flaw to some extent, and they'll now get what they need or what they've yearned for, if they have not already satisfied this. I love the following ending because I think the advice is applicable to anybody with a dream. What a wonderful way to leave a reader.

Lessons in Chemistry by Bonnie Garmus

Elizabeth Zott quits her popular cooking show to go for her dream of being a scientist, and she does in fact achieve this goal.

> Courage is the root of change—and change is what we're chemically designed to do. So, when you wake up tomorrow, make this pledge. No more holding yourself back. No more subscribing to others' opinions of what you can and cannot achieve. And no more allowing anyone to pigeonhole you into useless categories of sex, race, economic status, and religion. Do not allow your talents to lie dormant, ladies. Design your own future. When you go home today, ask yourself what *you* will change. And then get started.[2]

Write Your Book: Show the character growth in the closing lines and images.

Act Four, Plot Point 22: The Ending

Step 1: What is the best setting to reflect a change in how the protagonist sees their life now? Start with a description of the place. An observation. A new appreciation. A zoomed-in detail.

Step 2: Add a conversation with another character. They could talk about something simple, not what's just happened, but rather something safe, like gardening or making watermelon juice, but underneath is the knowledge of what they've gone through.

Day 99: The Circular Ending

How will you end this book? What image, object, or action do you want to leave in your reader's mind? What feeling do you want to evoke?

One powerful way to move the reader is through the objective correlative, which, again, is the use of an object or action that reflects the protagonist's emotion, and therefore resonates in a bigger way because you're showing and not telling.

The Midnight Library by Matt Haig

In the opening, a girl is playing chess in the library with the school librarian, and the book ends with her as an older, changed woman playing chess in a retirement home with the same school librarian.

The Kite Runner by Khaled Hosseini

This novel starts with kite running in Afghanistan and ends with flying kites in America. The characters are different. Now the main character is flying a kite with his friend's son instead of with his friend, but once again, there is a moment of connection, a glimmer of hope.

Fahrenheit 451 by Ray Bradbury

Guy Montag is once again in front of a fire, only this time it's a fire that doesn't destroy. Fire, here, is another clear example of the objective correlative, showing how fire can transform. It now represents his connection with other people who value intellectual freedom.

Write Your Book: Mirror the beginning.

Act Four, Plot Point 22: The Ending

Step 1: Use an object you brought up in the beginning and midpoint again, but now think of it as a distorted mirror with one element changed—the protagonist has changed, and hopefully healed.

Step 2: Try to add action to this ending: playing chess, running with a kid, or heating hands around a campfire. Make it a moving image, not a photograph.

Day 100: Theme on the Last Page

This is it, people! You're going to finish a complete draft of your book today. In this last page or two, touch your reader's heart. Readers want to close your book feeling changed in some way, deeply satisfied and reluctant to say goodbye. Add the character's thoughts or dialogue, which demonstrates growth, wisdom, and theme.

Song of Solomon by Toni Morrison

For now, he knew what Shalimar knew: If you surrendered to the air, you'd ride it.[3]

What I Saw and How I Lied by Judy Blundell

I would never be what someone else wanted me to be. I would never laugh at a joke I didn't think was funny. I would never tell another lie. I would be the truth teller, starting today. That would probably be tough.

But I was tougher.[4]

The Fault in Our Stars by John Green

You don't get to choose if you get hurt in this world, old man, but you do have some say in who hurts you. I like my choices. I hope she likes hers.[5]

Write Your Book: Write your final page and add some wisdom.

Act Four, Plot Point 22: The Ending

Step 1: Take a deep breath. Think of the final image you'll leave in the reader's mind. What is the last piece of wisdom your protagonist wants to leave the reader?

Step 2: Now write. You've got this, oh, wise, brilliant, creative soul.

Busy Writer Recap and Reward: Days 97–100

Act Four, Plot Point 22: The Ending

You finished your book! Balloons, confetti, daisies—imagine them showering down on you as you sprint through the finishing tape in your creative marathon. You're jumping up and down, and so you should: You're in the top tier of writers who ever finish their book—only about 3 percent! What's the reward for finishing an entire book? A trip to Hawaii or a really nice dinner out? It's up to you. . . . For right now, you're invited to the barbecue party for novelists who actually finish their books. It's a big party and everyone's invited.

Nurture Your Creativity

Keep Writing

The best thing you can ever do for your creativity is to keep writing. Even 15 Magic Minutes a day. Especially on the days when you don't want to. Creativity is the key to a joyful life.

Matt Bell

(*Refuse to Be Done: How to Write and Rewrite a Novel in Three Drafts*)

on How to Revise Your First Draft

First, Bell suggests revising the outline so that you've made a plan for the second draft, and then: "the most necessary and productive thing I do, the real way I transition from the mess of the first draft to the tighter, better-made second draft: I retype my second draft from scratch, rewriting as I go, moving the book I've already drafted toward the one described by the outline I've spent the last weeks or months crafting."[6]

Editing—What Is the Next Step?

1. Do a grammar/spelling check and change the font so that it will feel like a different book when you read it later.
2. Print out your book at home, or on lulu.com. This is my recommendation—a paperback version costs $4 to $5, so it's cheaper than using your home computer and ink. It'll look like a real bound book, and seeing your work in print, even if it's just an early draft, can help you see it with fresh eyes. Don't just edit it on a computer. Print it.
3. Give yourself a mental break before you read it again. If you're printing it out on your home computer, put your book in a drawer. Wait a month before reading it.
4. Read your work out loud. You'll catch the awkwardness, the slow parts, and any repetitions. The ear is a better editor than the eye at this stage. As you read, be kind to yourself! Don't line edit yet; this is the biggest mistake people make. You might have to cut whole sections so any line editing will be a waste of time. You're identifying big-picture issues for tension and character arc. Look at where it sags and then refer to the guide to see if you missed a plot point. Remember, big picture first—then line-edit!

Dear Novelist,

I'm so glad to have taken this journey with you. As I wrote this guide, I imagined you writing away, bravely baring your soul and showing up with rare authenticity on the page. You took a chance and chased after your dream, revealing your truth in this beautiful story. You've finished a draft and now you can take a deep breath and know you've finished a book, something many writers never manage to do.

Celebrate. Enjoy this moment and take a break.

If this is your second, third, or fourth draft, that's impressive too. A traditionally published novel typically requires five or more drafts. It requires perseverance and a dedication to craft. The great news is that by following this guide, you've cut your drafting time way down.

I hope you've loved this journey. I hope you keep writing, either future drafts of this book or a new one. I hope you've fallen in love with storytelling and that you've felt the joyful effect of a more creative life. I hope you feel more alive, aware, compassionate, and empathetic. Most of all, I hope you love yourself.

Your words matter, and so do you.

With great admiration,
Kim

Where Did I Get All This Information?

I've built on all that has come before. This is a heavily researched guide, and I've given credit along the way. I've put the information in order, step by step, to help you write a solid plot while scaffolding your skills. Throughout, I've shared advice from craft books and bestselling authors. I've analyzed bestselling novels and memoirs, and shared examples to illustrate every skill. I'd like to give credit to methods and craft guides that particularly inspired me. Some I quote directly; others simply informed my journey as a writer and teacher.

First, for creative joy: *The Artist's Way* by Julia Cameron, *On Writing* by Stephen King, and *Bird by Bird* by Anne Lamott. Morning Pages in *The Artist's Way* led me to write about my stories, and this is how I developed the concept of 15 Magic Minutes. *On Writing* is a fun frolic through an incredible writer's life, and King's storytelling throughout is inspiring and a clear mark of his genius. *Bird by Bird* gave me permission to tell the truth and know that my first draft doesn't have to be perfect.

My favorite general craft book is *Writing Fiction: A Guide to Narrative Craft* by Janet Burroway. It covers the major elements of fiction, and her insights have helped my own understanding of every area of the craft of writing. For dialogue and subtext, I love the class by Lajos Egri: *The Art of Dramatic Writing.*

In developing the Busy Writer Plot, I've taken inspiration from the fifteen beats in *Save the Cat!* by Blake Snyder and Jessica Brody's adaptation for novelists: *Save the Cat! Writes a Novel.* I also incorporated Joseph Campbell's *The Hero with a Thousand Faces,* and Christopher Vogler's adaptation: *The Writer's Journey.* Finally, I recommend literary agent Donald Maass's plotting book, *Writing the Breakout Novel*—it will help anyone write a page-turner. I'd also like to recommend David

Macinnis Gill's book *The Sticky Note Plot.* He was an advisor in my MFA program, and his sticky note plotting approach was transformative and inspired my sticky-note wall recommendation in this guide. I also loved *Techniques of the Selling Writer* by Dwight V. Swain for his explanation of scene and sequel.

I also want to credit Randy Ingermanson's Snowflake Method—one of the few progressive skills-building approaches to novel writing. He simplifies plot beautifully: one pivotal plot point in each act. He suggests writing a paragraph for each act and key plot point, and this is also what I suggest in this guide.

For character development, I love *The Emotional Craft of Fiction,* also by Donald Maass—it helps writers touch their readers' hearts through character, our ultimate goal. I also recommend *Story Genius* by Lisa Cron, who dives into finding the beating heart of a story through a character's misbelief and trauma. *Story Engineering* by Larry Brooks is excellent for a wide range of skills, but especially the "Six Core Competencies of Successful Writing," and I've woven these competencies throughout this guide.

For scene dynamics and theme, *Story* by Robert McKee explores opposites within and between scenes, as well as theme and counter-theme. Another book that covers opposites and yes-no plotting is *My Story Can Beat Up Your Story!* by Jeffrey Alan Schechter.

Alongside many craft books, I've also leaned on self-development and psychology books, both for character analysis and the writer mindset . . . to help you finish and accomplish your dream. (Joseph Campbell drew on Carl Jung's work, so I'm in good company.)

I also want to acknowledge the hundreds of authors and their novels and memoirs I've quoted throughout this guide. I recommend every one of them. I wish I could have quoted even more. A novel challenges us to transform, when both reading and writing them. Therein lies the difficulty and the beauty of this mighty endeavor.

Acknowledgments

First, I want to express my profound gratitude to my thousands of students all over the world. You've given me so much joy. Thank you for sharing your hearts with me through your writing. I'm honored to have had this privilege, and I'm regularly awed by the power of your words.

Thanks so much to my agent, Jolene Haley. You're not only an incredible agent; you're also a kind human. You've given me detailed notes on everything I write, including this guide. You believed in it from our first meeting, and you always show me that you believe in me. I can't tell you what a difference this has made in my life.

Thanks also to the team at Ten Speed Press, and to my brilliant editor, Thea Diklich-Newell. Thea, you've gone above and beyond as an editor, even drafting a novel with this guide to test it out. Who does that? Nobody! Your dedication and notes are perfection. You've made this guide so much better, and I'm forever grateful. I'm grateful for my copyeditor, Amy Brosey, especially your attention to detail. Thanks to Andrea Lau for the book design and to Betsy Stromberg for my gorgeous cover.

Thank you to Keren Taylor, founder of WriteGirl L.A., for the chance early in my career to become the first curriculum director of WriteGirl, creating fun, multisensory experiments with you and leading workshops for teen girls and women mentors. Together, we tried out hundreds of different experiments for poetry, journalism, songwriting, memoir, and fiction. Some worked, some didn't; all informed my novel writing program and the writing of this guide. (Readers, if you want to make a difference for an underserved population, I recommend donating to WriteGirl L.A.)

So much gratitude to writers and friends who read this guide and suggested changes: Emma Kress, Jodi Targon, Elif Cercel, Rachel Purcell,

Barbara Bottner, Lesley Hyatt, Rachael Smith, Carol Schlanger, Susan Merson, Susan Cuscuna, Arlene Schindler, Tim Wynne-Jones, Kimberly Hendrickson, Ava Rahmani, Tara Drage, and Kathleen Garrett.

Thanks to my advisers and teachers at Vermont College of Fine Arts, where I received my MFA and endless inspiration, which I hope I've passed on. In particular, I'd like to thank Amanda Jenkins, Kekla Magoon, Tim Wynne-Jones, Cynthia Leitich Smith, and Amy King.

Thanks to every writer whose books have lit my way on those dark nights, during my own All-Is-Lost Moments; to those writers who gave me an escape when I needed to forget the world around me and whose words helped me grow. I've shared some of your books here in this guide, but I wish I could share *all* the books.

I'm so thankful to my amazing big family—it truly takes a village of people to show you that you are loved and important, and that your words matter. I don't take my family for granted. I appreciate every one of you: my mom, my dad, Jenn, Tara, Kyle, Lizzy, Zander, Huxley, my uncles, aunts, and cousins. I'm also grateful to my husband's family: my father-in-law, Doug; my mother-in-law, Judy; and all of his aunts, uncles, and cousins. I love you all.

Most important, I'm grateful for my husband, Gavin, and our daughters, Madeline and Harper, for your love, encouragement, and endless support. I worked many long hours on this guide, while teaching thousands of students, editing their books, and writing my own novel. This meant very long days—I truly lived the "busy writer" life while teaching more than full-time, on top of writing and taking care of my family. Harper, in your senior year of high school, you helped so much, cooking amazing meals and baking delicious carrot cake, bringing me coffee and helping to clean. Madeline, even though you were at college, you gave me so much fabulous feedback and joined my company, working part-time, so I could have time to think about this guide. You're an incredible writer and editor—your notes made this guide so much better. Gavin, you're always my first reader for everything and my first shoulder to lean on. Gavin, Madeline, and Harper, I love you to the moon and back.

Notes

Prologue

1. O'Connor, Flannery. *Mystery and Manners: Occasional Prose*. Farrar, Straus and Giroux, 1969, p. 84.

Ten Top Tips to Finish Your Book

1. Silver, Veronica. "Breaking Free from ADHD Paralysis: 5 Effective Strategies." *Myndlift*, June 9, 2023, myndlift.com/post/breaking-free-from-adhd-paralysis-5-effective-strategies.
2. Anders, Charlie Jane. *Never Say You Can't Survive: How to Get Through Hard Times by Making Up Stories*. Tordotcom, 2021, loc. 48–59.
3. Yousef, Sahar. "How to Find Your Most Creative Time of Day, and Make It Count." *It's Nice That*, March 9, 2020, itsnicethat.com/news/sahar-yousef-most-creative-time-of-day-opinion-090320.
4. Clear, James. *Atomic Habits: An Easy & Proven Way to Build Good Habits & Break Bad Ones* Avery, 2018, ebook, p. 88.
5. Fogg, BJ. *Tiny Habits: The Small Changes That Change Everything*. Mariner Books, 2020, Kindle ed., loc. 74.
6. Lukidis, Lydia, and Tim Wynne-Jones. "Author Tim Wynne-Jones on Creating Thrilling YA." *Lydia Lukidis*, January 8, 2020, lydialukidis.wordpress.com/2020/01/08/author-tim-wynne-jones-on-creating-exiting-ya.

Busy Writer Road Map Days 1–4: Your Story Idea

1. Klein, Cheryl B. *The Magic Words: Writing Great Books for Children and Young Adults*. W. Norton & Company, 2016, p. 36.
2. Tagen-Dye, Carly. "Rebecca Yarros Says It's Been 'Comforting' to See Readers Relate to Chronic Illness Representation in *Empyrean* Series." People.com, March 21, 2025, people.com/rebecca-yarros-says-its-comforting-to-see-readers-relate-chronic-illness-representation-books-11700731.
3. Bundy, Andrew. "Author A.S. King Speaks with Brockway Students." *Courier Express*, December 1, 2021, thecourierexpress.com/news/author-a-s-king-speaks-with-brockway-students/article_bd04be9e-e323-5194-9446-1fb08e370921.html.
4. Ellison, Ralph. *Invisible Man*. Random House, 1952, p. 1.
5. Purcell, Kim. *Trafficked*. Penguin, 2012, p. 1.
6. Jenkins, A. M. *Damage*. HarperTeen, 2001, Kindle ed., p. 1.
7. Verghese, Abraham. *The Covenant of Water*. Grove Press, 2023, p. 3.
8. Zusak, Markus. *The Book Thief*. Knopf Books for Young Readers, 2005, p. 6.

Busy Writer Road Map Days 5–8: Characters and World

1. Vogler, Christopher, and David McKenna. *Memo from the Story Dept.: Strategies for Structure and Character.* Michael Wiese Productions, 2011, Kindle ed., loc. 70–74.
2. McFadden, Freida. *The Housemaid.* Grand Central Publishing, 2022, p. 1.
3. Lawhon, Ariel. *The Frozen River.* Doubleday, 2023, p. 3.
4. Black, Holly. *The Cruel Prince.* Little, Brown Books for Young Readers, 2018, p. 1.
5. Moss, Tyler. "The Writer's Digest Interview: Andy Weir, Author of 'The Martian' and 'Artemis.'" *Writer's Digest,* January 22, 2018. writersdigest.com/be-inspired/martian-author-andy-weir-artemis-scifi-research-process.
6. Bubble Bubble Books & Trouble. "A Q&A with Lisa McMann, Author of *Cryer's Cross.*" April 10, 2011, booksandtrouble.com/2011/03/26/a-qa-with-lisa-mcmann-author-of-cryers-cross.

Busy Writer Road Map Days 9–12: Your Story Architecture

1. Zied, Elisa, and Emma Kress. "Novelist Emma Kress on Dangerous Play and Writing." *Elisa Zied,* 2021, elisazied.com/writing/novelist-emma-kress-on-dangerous-play-and-writing.
2. Cron, Lisa. *Wired for Story: The Writer's Guide to Using Brain Science to Hook Readers from the Very First Sentence.* Ten Speed Press, 2012, p. 9.
3. Verghese, Abraham. "Abraham Verghese: To Plot or Not to Plot." *Literary Hub,* May 3, 2023, lithub.com/abraham-verghese-to-plot-or-not-to-plot.
4. Castle, Jennifer. Interview with Kim Purcell. August 15, 2025.
5. Gill, David Macinnis. *The Sticky Note Plot: A Step-By-Step Guide to Plotting Novels That Sell.* David Macinnis Gill, 2024, p. 80.

Act One, Plot Point 1: The Imperfect Life

1. Smart, Maya. "Meg Medina on Building the Courage to Write." 2013, mayasmart.com/meg-medina.
2. Poehler, Amy. *Yes Please.* Dey Street Books, 2014, p. xiv.
3. Maass, Donald. *Writing the Breakout Novel Workbook.* Writer's Digest Books, 2004, p. 7.
4. Riordan, Rick. "Advice for Writers: Rick Riordan." *Welcome to the Online World of Rick Riordan,* January 17, 2021, rickriordan.com/about/advice-for-writers.
5. Ng, Celeste. *Everything I Never Told You.* Penguin Press, 2014, p. 1.
6. Lowry, Lois. *The Giver.* Laurel-Leaf, 2002, p. 1.
7. Nelson, Jandy. *I'll Give You the Sun.* Dial Books for Young Readers, 2014, p. 1.
8. Connelly, Michael. *Desert Star.* Little, Brown and Company, 2022, p. 3.
9. Reid, Taylor Jenkins. *The Seven Husbands of Evelyn Hugo.* Atria Books, 2017, p. 3.
10. Pullman, Philip. *The Golden Compass.* Knopf Books for Young Readers, 1996, p. 3.
11. Rennison, Louise. *Angus, Thongs and Full-Frontal Snogging.* Storytide, 2006, Kindle ed., loc. 51.
12. Hoover, Colleen. *It Ends With Us.* Atria Books, 2016, p. 3.
13. Christopher, Lucy. *Stolen.* Alfred A. Knopf, 2010, pp. 6–7.
14. Sebold, Alice. *The Lovely Bones.* Little, Brown and Company, 2002, p. 7.
15. Cowley Heller, Miranda. *The Paper Palace.* Riverhead Books, 2021, p. 4.

16. Flynn, Gillian. *Gone Girl.* Crown, 2012, p. 15.
17. Lawson, Jenny. *Furiously Happy: A Funny Book About Horrible Things.* Flatiron Books, 2015, p. xiii.
18. Salinger, J. D. *The Catcher in the Rye.* Little, Brown, 1951, p. 1.
19. Haddon, Mark. *The Curious Incident of the Dog in the Night-Time.* Vintage Contemporaries, 2004, pp. 3–4.
20. Lardner, Ring. *Haircut and Other Stories.* Touchstone, 1991, p. 1.
21. James, Marlon. *A Brief History of Seven Killings.* Riverhead Books, 2014, p. 17.
22. Bowling, Dusti. *Insignificant Events in the Life of a Cactus.* Union Square Kids, 2017, p. 4.
23. Steinbeck, John. "John Steinbeck, the Art of Fiction No. 45 (Continued)." *Paris Review,* Fall 1975.
24. Steinbeck, John. *Of Mice and Men.* Penguin, 1993, pp. 8–9.
25. Backman, Fredrik. *A Man Called Ove.* Washington Square Books, 2015, p. 71.
26. Warrell, Laura. "Jacqueline Woodson's Windows." *The Writer,* October 21, 2018, writermag.com/improve-your-writing/writing-for-young-readers/jacqueline-woodsons-windows.

Act One, Plot Point 2: The Inciting Incident

1. Castle, Jennifer. *The Beginning of After.* HarperCollins, 2011, p. 1.
2. Stiefvater, Maggie. *The Scorpio Races.* Scholastic Press, 2011, p. 8.
3. Taylor, Laini. *Daughter of Smoke & Bone.* Little, Brown and Company, 2011, p. 1.
4. Bradbury, Ray. *Something Wicked This Way Comes.* Simon & Schuster, 1962, p. 5.
5. Gurliand, Ilia. "Reminiscences of A. P. Chekhov," *Teatr i Iskusstvo,* No. 28, July 11, 1904, p. 521.
6. Alam, Rumaan. *Leave the World Behind.* Ecco, 2020, p. 76.
7. Atwood, Margaret. *The Handmaid's Tale.* McClelland & Stewart, 1985, p. 22.
8. Garvin, Jeff. *Symptoms of Being Human.* Balzer + Bray, 2024, p. 4
9. Garvin, *Symptoms of Being,* p. 6.
10. Dahl, Roald. *Charlie and the Chocolate Factory.* Viking, 2022, Kindle ed., p. 45.
11. Reid, Taylor Jenkins. *The Seven Husbands of Evelyn Hugo.* Atria Books, 2017, p. 37.
12. Reid, *The Seven Husbands,* p. 57.
13. Reid, *The Seven Husbands,* p. 73.
14. Reid, *The Seven Husbands,* p. 84.
15. Reid, *The Seven Husbands,* p. 87.
16. Reid, *The Seven Husbands,* p. 147.

Act One, Plot Point 3: First Response

1. Collins, Suzanne. *The Hunger Games.* Scholastic Press, 2008, p. 21.
2. Collins, *The Hunger Games,* p. 22.
3. Atwood, Margaret. *Bringing Characters to Life Through Detail.* MasterClass, Inc., 2020, masterclass.com. 00:35–02:12.
4. Stewart, Trenton Lee. *The Mysterious Benedict Society and the Perilous Journey.* Little, Brown and Company, 2008, p. 5.
5. Tartt, Donna. *The Goldfinch.* Little, Brown and Company, 2013, p. 9.

6. Gantos, Jack. *Joey Pigza Loses Control*. Farrar, Straus and Giroux for Young Readers, 2000, p. 3.
7. Salinger, *The Catcher in the Rye*.
8. Kafka, Franz. *Metamorphosis*. Simon & Schuster, 2014, p. 5.
9. Steinbeck, John. *Steinbeck: A Life in Letters*. Edited by Elaine Steinbeck and Robert Wallsten, Penguin Books, 1979, p. 737.

Act One, Plot Point 4: The New Goal

1. Vonnegut, Kurt. "The Art of Fiction No. 64." *Paris Review*, no. 64, 1977, www.theparisreview.org/interviews/3605/the-art-of-fiction-no-64-kurt-vonnegut.
2. Jong, Erica. *Fear of Flying*. Holt, Rinehart and Winston, 1973, p. 16.
3. Shwab, V. E. "This Book Is Broken, and Other Things I Tell Myself While Writing." August 30, 2016, veschwab.wordpress.com.

Act Two, Plot Point 5: New World and Allies

1. Smith, Cynthia Leitich. *Indian Shoes*. Heartdrum, 2021, p. 1.
2. Rothfuss, Patrick. *The Name of the Wind*. DAW, 2007, p. 114.
3. Levithan, David. *Every Day*. Alfred A. Knopf for Young Readers, 2012, Kindle ed., p. 3.
4. Dashner, James. *The Maze Runner*. Delacorte Press, 2009, p. 1.
5. Gansworth, Eric. *If I Ever Get Out of Here*. Arthur A. Levine Books, 2013, Kindle ed., loc. 75–87.
6. Golding, William. *Lord of the Flies*. Penguin Books, 2016, Kindle ed., p. 7.
7. Rogerson, Margaret. *Sorcery of Thorns*. Margaret K. McElderry Books, 2020, p. 1.
8. Burroway, Janet. *Writing Fiction: A Guide to Narrative Craft*. University of Chicago Press, Chicago, 2019, p. 25.
9. Zinsser, William. *On Writing Well: The Essential Guide to Mastering Nonfiction Writing and Effective Communication*. HarperCollins, 2016, Kindle ed., p. 70.
10. Lahiri, Jhumpa. *The Namesake*. Houghton Mifflin Harcourt, 2003, p. 1.
11. Murakami, Haruki. *Kafka on the Shore*. Translated by Philip Gabriel. Vintage, 2005, Kindle ed., loc. 117.
12. Stewart, Trenton Lee. *The Mysterious Benedict Society*. Little, Brown Books for Young Readers, 2008, p. 15.
13. Riordan, Rick. *The Lightning Thief*. Disney-Hyperion, 2005, p. 2.
14. Russo, Meredith. *If I Was Your Girl*. Flatiron Books, 2018, p. 1.
15. Janowitz, Jessie. *The Doughnut Fix*. Kindle ed., Sourcebooks Young Readers, 2018, p. 3.
16. Gilbert, Elizabeth. *Eat, Pray, Love*. Riverhead Books, 2006, p. 63.
17. Whitehead, Colson. *The Underground Railroad*. Doubleday, 2016, p. 149.
18. Jackson, Shirley. *We Have Always Lived in the Castle*. Penguin Books, 2016, Kindle ed., p. 10.
19. Stone, Nic. *Dear Martin*. Crown Books for Young Readers, 2017, p. 3.
20. Beck, Martha. *Beyond Anxiety: Curiosity, Creativity, and Finding Your Life's Purpose*. The Open Field, 2025.
21. Tiers, Melissa. *The Anti-Anxiety Toolkit*. Melissa Tiers, 2015, p. 49.

Act Two, Plot Point 6: The Antagonist Threatens

1. Petit, Zachary. "Stephen King on Creating Believable Bad Guys." *Writer's Digest,* November 17, 2009, writersdigest.com/traditional-prompts/stephen-king-on-creating-believable-bad-guys.
2. Jewell, Lisa. *Then She Was Gone,* Atria Books, 2018, p. 230.
3. Paulsen, Gary. *Hatchet.* Simon & Schuster. 2006, p. 8.
4. Sanderson, Brandon. *The Way of Kings,* Tor, 2010, p. 38.
5. Sutherland, Tui T., *Wings of Fire: The Dragonet Prophecy.* Scholastic Press, 2012, Kindle ed., p. 26.
6. Jacobson, Melanie. "Romance Structure." Interview with Kim Purcell, September 1, 2025.
7. Anderson, Laurie Halse. *Speak.* Farrar, Straus and Giroux, 1999, p. 97.
8. Bottner, Barbara. *I Am Here Now.* Imprint, 2020, pp. 24–25.
9. Pullman, Philip. *The Golden Compass.* Alfred A. Knopf, 1996, p. 70.
10. Sedaris, David. *David Sedaris Teaches Storytelling and Humor.* MasterClass, Inc., 2020, www.masterclass.com, lesson "Observing the World." 3:57–4:30.
11. Maass, Donald. *Writing the Breakout Novel Workbook.* Writer's Digest Books, 2004, p. 35.
12. Zafarris, Jess. "YA Author Cassandra Clare Reveals the Practical Magic Behind Her Bestselling 'Shadowhunter' Series." *Writer's Digest,* December 21, 2018, writersdigest.com/writing-articles/ya-author-cassandra-clare-reveals-the-practical-magic-behind-her-bestselling-shadowhunter-series.

Act Two, Plot Point 7: Skills and Information

1. Hosseini, Khaled. *A Thousand Splendid Suns.* Riverhead Books, 2007, p.137.
2. Garber, Stephanie. *Caraval.* Flatiron Books, 2017, p. 240.
3. Obreht, Téa. *The Tiger's Wife.* Random House, 2011, p. 267.
4. Lowry, Lois. *The Giver.* Dell Laurel-Leaf, 1994, p. 88.
5. Rushdie, Salman. *Midnight's Children.* Penguin Books, 1991, Kindle ed., p. 63.
6. Leonard, Elmore. "Writers on Writing; Easy on the Adverbs, Exclamation Points and Especially Hooptedoodle." *New York Times,* July 16, 2001, nytimes.com/2001/07/16/arts/writers-writing-easy-adverbs-exclamation-points-especially-hooptedoodle.html.
7. Riordan, Rick. "Advice For Writers." Rick Riordan, 2016, rickriordan.com/about/advice-for-writers/.
8. King, Stephen. *On Writing: A Memoir of the Craft.* Charles Scribner's Sons, 2000, p. 124.
9. Burroway, Janet. *Writing Fiction: A Guide to Narrative Craft.* University of Chicago Press, 2019, p. 60.
10. Tahir, Sabaa. *All My Rage.* Razorbill, 2022, p. 22.
11. Garmus, Bonnie. *Lessons in Chemistry.* Doubleday, 2022, p. 34.
12. Sebold, Alice. *The Lovely Bones.* Little, Brown and Company, 2002, p. 84.

Act Two, Plot Point 8: Subplot Challenge

1. Jewell, Lisa. *Then She Was Gone.* Atria Books, 2018, p. 5.
2. McCourt, Frank. *Angela's Ashes.* Scribner, 1996, p. 1.

3. Cron, Lisa. *Story Genius: How to Use Brain Science to Go Beyond Outlining and Write a Riveting Novel.* Ten Speed Press, 2016, p. 4.
4. Kress, Emma, and Brendan Reichs. "In Which @brendan.reichs Gives Us His Secret Sauce." Instagram, 2021, instagram.com/kress.emma/p/CIJIiy-HEqS, 4:50–5:30.

Act Two, Plot Point 9: Escalating Obstacles

1. Dashner, James. *The Maze Runner.* Delacorte Press, 2009, p. 344.
2. Haig, Matt. *The Midnight Library.* Viking, 2020, pp. 27–28.
3. Mafi, Tahereh. *Shatter Me.* HarperCollins, 2011, p. 1.
4. Mafi, *Shatter Me,* p. 163.
5. Capote, Truman. *In Cold Blood.* Random House, 1965, p. 179.
6. Hornby, Nick. *High Fidelity.* Riverhead Books, 1996, p. 16.
7. Ng, Celeste. *Everything I Never Told You.* Penguin, 2014, p. 6.
8. King, A. S. *Dig.* Dutton, 2019, p. 2.
9. Backman, Fredrik. *A Man Called Ove.* Washington Square Books, 2015, p. 69.
10. Cameron, Lainey. "Episode 84: Adele Myers, Author of *The Tobacco Wives.*" *The Best of Women's Fiction.* bestofwomensfiction.com/episodes/adele-myers.

Act Two, Plot Point 10: False Hope

1. Wynne-Jones, Tim. *The Emperor of Any Place.* Candlewick Press, 2015, p. 198.
2. Gorman, Amanda. "The Writing Toolkit." *Amanda Gorman Teaches Writing and Performing Poetry,* MasterClass Inc., www.masterclass.com, 2022. 6:01–6:05.
3. Backman, Fredrik. *A Man Called Ove.* Washington Square Books, 2015, p. 106.
4. Sherman Alexie, *The Absolutely True Diary of a Part-Time Indian.* Little, Brown and Company, 2007, Kindle ed., p. 196.
5. Morrison, Toni. *The Bluest Eye.* Vintage International, 2007, p. 127.
6. Zusak, Markus. *The Book Thief.* Knopf Books For Young Readers, 2005, p. 111.
7. Brown, Mark. "Douglas Adams' Note to Self Reveals Author Found Writing Torture." *The Guardian,* March 22, 2021, theguardian.com/books/2021/mar/22/douglas-adams-note-to-self-reveals-author-found-writing-torture.

Act Two, Plot Point 11: The Midpoint Shock

1. Gill, David Macinnis. *The Sticky Note Plot.* David Macinnis Gill, 2024, p. 9.

Act Three, Plot Point 12: Reaction to the Midpoint

1. Bradbury, Ray. *Fahrenheit 451.* Simon & Schuster, 2012, p. 68.
2. Jewell, Lisa. *Then She Was Gone.* Atria Books, 2018, p. 160.
3. Hinton, S. E., *The Outsiders.* Viking Press, 1967, p. 65.
4. Hinton, *The Outsiders,* p. 70.
5. Hinton, *The Outsiders,* p. 159.
6. Nin, Anaïs. *Seduction of the Minotaur.* Sky Blue Press, 2010, Kindle ed., loc. 1984.
7. Flynn, Gillian. *Gone Girl.* Crown, 2012, p. 229.
8. Myers, Adele. The *Tobacco Wives.* HarperCollins, William Morrow, 2022, p. 187.
9. Levithan, David. "'Don't Be Afraid to Write a Bad Book': David Levithan on Every Day." *The Guardian,* October 7, 2013, theguardian.com/books/2013/oct/07/david-levithan-every-day-interview.

Act Three, Plot Point 13: The Fuse

1. Tolkien, J. R. R., *The Fellowship of the Ring: The Lord of the Rings,* William Morrow, 2012, p. 433.
2. L'Engle, Madeleine. *Walking on Water: Reflections on Faith & Art.* Convergent Books, 2016, p. 140.

Act Three, Plot Point 14: Flawed Plan

1. O'Brien, Edna. *Time and Tide.* Farrar, Straus and Giroux, 1992, p. 3.
2. Stone, Nic. *Dear Martin.* Crown, 2017, p. 34.
3. Golden, Arthur. *Memoirs of a Geisha.* Alfred A. Knopf, 1997, p. 17.
4. Martin, George R. R. *A Game of Thrones.* Bantam Books, 2003, p. 509.
5. Maass, Donald. *The Emotional Craft of Fiction: How to Write the Story Beneath the Surface.* Writer's Digest Books, 2016, p. 116.

Act Three, Plot Point 15: Subplot Complications

1. Wilde, Oscar. "The Soul of Man Under Socialism." *Fortnightly Review,* April 1891.
2. L'Engle, Madeleine. *Walking on Water: Reflections on Faith & Art.* Convergent Books, 2016, Kindle ed., p. 182.
3. Brown, Brené. *Daring Greatly: How the Courage to Be Vulnerable Transforms the Way We Live, Love, Parent, and Lead.* Avery, 2015, p. 42.
4. Bardugo, Leigh. *Six of Crows.* Henry Holt & Co., 2015, pp. 433–34.
5. Green, John. *The Fault in Our Stars.* Dutton Books, 2012, pp. 213–14.
6. Day, Simantini. " 'I Just Try to Write Somebody's Favourite Book': Markus Zusak, the Author of 'The Book Thief.' " News18, March 13, 2019, news18.com/news/buzz/i-just-try-to-write-somebodys-favourite-book-markus-zusa-the-author-of-the-book-thief-2065303.html.

Act Three, Plot Point 16: A Near Win

1. Angelou, Maya. *I Know Why the Caged Bird Sings.* Ballantine Books, 2015, p. 153.
2. Maguire, Gregory. *Wicked: The Life and Times of the Wicked Witch of the West.* Regan Books, 2004, p. 237.
3. Dostoevsky, Fyodor. *Crime and Punishment.* Richard Pevear and Larissa Volokhonsky, trans. Vintage Books, 2021, p. 314.
4. Dostoevsky, *Crime and Punishment,* p. 315.
5. Howard, Amalie. *Rules for Heiresses.* Sourcebooks Casablanca, 2021, p. 213.
6. Kalb, Deborah. "Q&A with James Ponti." *Book Q&As with Deborah Kalb.* August 28, 2024, deborahkalbbooks.blogspot.com/2024/08/q-with-james-ponti.html.
7. Jewell, Lisa. "Lisa Jewell's Top Tips for New Writers," 2016, penguin.co.uk/articles/2016/07/lisa-jewell-s-top-tips-for-new-writers.

Act Three, Plot Point 17: The Big Mistake

1. Brown, Pierce. *Golden Son.* Del Rey, 2015, Kindle ed., p. 342.

Busy Writer Road Map Days 81–84: The Depiction of Suffering

1. Egri, Lajos. *The Art of Dramatic Writing: Its Basis in the Creative Interpretation of Human Motives.* Rare Treasures Editions, 2025, Kindle ed., p. 417.

Act Three, Plot Point 18: The All-Is-Lost Moment

1. Valente, Catherynne M. *Deathless.* Tor, 2011, p. 282.
2. Henry, Emily. *Beach Read.* Berkeley Romance, 2020, p. 308.
3. Bradbury, Ray. *Fahrenheit 451.* Simon & Schuster, 2012, p. 113.
4. Paterson, Katherine. *Bridge to Terabithia.* HarperTrophy, 1993, pp. 157–58.
5. Lee, Harper. *To Kill A Mockingbird.* Harper Perennial, 2002, p. 248
6. Henry, Emily. *Beach Read.* Berkley Romance, 2020, p. 309.
7. Monk Kidd, Sue. *The Secret Life of Bees.* Viking, 2002, p. 242.
8. Ness, Patrick. *A Monster Calls.* Candlewick, 2011, p. 190.
9. Lamott, Anne. *Bird by Bird: Some Instructions on Writing and Life.* Anchor Books, 1995, p. 134.

Act Four, Plot Point 19: The Lightbulb Moment

1. McCourt, Frank. *Angela's Ashes.* Scribner, 1996, p. 335.
2. McCourt, *Angela's Ashes,* p. 338.
3. Saint-Exupéry, Antoine de. *The Little Prince.* General Press, 2018, Kindle ed., p. 83.
4. Adichie, Chimamanda Ngozi. *Americanah.* Vintage Books, 2014, p. 475.
5. Adichie, *Americanah,* p. 518.
6. Howard, Amalie, interview with Kim Purcell, December 2025.

Act Four, Plot Point 20: The Climax

1. McCormick, Patricia. *Sold.* Hyperion, 2006, p. 263.
2. Riordan, Rick. *Percy Jackson and the Olympians: The Lightning Thief.* Disney Hyperion Digital, 2009, Kindle ed., p. 324.
3. Hosseini, Khaled. *The Kite Runner.* Riverhead Books, 2003, p. 252.
4. Whitehead, Colson. *The Underground Railroad.* Doubleday, 2016, p. 302.
5. Rothfuss, Patrick. *The Name of the Wind.* DAW, 2007, p. 605.
6. Rothfuss, *The Name . . .*
7. Rothfuss, *The Name . . .*
8. Rothfuss, *The Name . . .*

Act Four, Plot Point 21: Aftermath

1. McCourt, Frank. *Angela's Ashes.* Scribner, 1996, p. 358.
2. Golding, William. *Lord of the Flies.* Penguin, 1954, p. 202.
3. Flynn, Gillian. *Gone Girl.* Crown, 2012, p. 404.
4. Patterson, James. "Ending the Book." *James Patterson Teaches Writing,* lesson 14, MasterClass Inc., masterclass.com, 2017. 1:59–3:45.

Act Four, Plot Point 22: The Ending

1. "Interview with China Miéville." Goodreads, January 5, 2016, goodreads.com/interviews/show/1092.
2. Garmus, Bonnie. *Lessons in Chemistry.* Doubleday, 2022, p. 360.
3. Morrison, Toni. *Song of Solomon.* Alfred A. Knopf, 1977, p. 337.
4. Blundell, Judy. *What I Saw and How I Lied.* Scholastic Press, 2008, p. 262.
5. Green, John. *The Fault in Our Stars.* Dutton Books, 2012, p. 310.
6. Bell, Matt. *Refuse to Be Done: How to Write and Rewrite a Novel in Three Drafts.* Soho Press, 2022, p. 89.

About the Author

Kim Purcell is a novelist, editor, writing teacher, and creativity coach with more than twenty-five years of experience teaching fiction to kids and adults. She's the author of two acclaimed novels, *Trafficked* and *This Is Not a Love Letter,* as well as many other unacclaimed and unpublished novels, each of which has taught her something essential about life, humanity, or herself. More novels are on the way. Her dream is to spread a love of writing fiction without the need for any end goal, such as publication, fame, or money, just as people paint or sing for the sheer pleasure of diving into one's imagination and the positive impact it can have on one's life and the world.

A passionate teacher of novel writing for kids, teens, and adults, she has built an international company called Purcell Publishing, which helps writers of all ages and all over the world discover their voices, complete their novels, and publish them. Purcell was the first curriculum director of WriteGirl, the nationally recognized writing and mentoring organization for teen girls. Then she started teaching the Busy Writer Workshop to help busy adults achieve their creative dreams. She went on to build a novel writing school for kids and teens worldwide called Kim Purcell's Story Studio on Outschool, where she's helped thousands of kids and teens write and publish novels. Drawing on her years as a novelist and educator, she's developed this daily guide to help busy writers just like her.

She was born in Victoria, British Columbia, and grew up in a small town in northern Canada called Prince George. She wrote her first novel when she was ten, despite being a delayed reader with ADHD. In her adult life, she's lived in more than twenty different homes in Vancouver, Guadalajara, Seoul, Los Angeles, and Brooklyn. Who knows where she will be when this guide comes out; perhaps she will be living next door to you.

For fun, she loves board games, particularly Catan, running on the beach, dancing (awkwardly and wildly), and swimming.

For more on Kim Purcell, her books, and her workshops:

kimpurcell.com
YouTube: authorkimpurcell
TikTok: authorkimpurcell
Instagram: authorkimpurcell